NYC STOP WORK ORDER
Partial Stop Work Order
Full Stop Work Order
MW00562894
THE FOUR HORSEMEN
EL FARO No. 8
SUPERMARKET
the four horsemen
brooklyn
www.fourhorsemenbk.com

HORSEMEN

NOTE
TO
SELF:
BE KIND.
BE KIND;
BE KIND.

THE FOUR HORSEMEN

FOOD + WINE FOR GOOD TIMES

NICK CURTOLA

WITH

GABE ULLA
+ JAMES MURPHY

NOTES ON WINE BY JUSTIN CHEARNO

ABRAMS, NEW YORK

CONTENTS

WINE NOTES BY JUSTIN CHEARNO:

PREFACE

BY JAMES MURPHY

The Four Horsemen is almost nine years old as of this writing. We are a tiny restaurant in Brooklyn, New York, with thirty-eight seats split between a little bar and a modest dining room. We have the same head chef as when we opened—actually, from well before we opened . . . more on that later—and the same four partners. We've had the same general manager for over eight years. We also still retain some of the very same staff, both in the kitchen and front of house, from our first friends-and-family seating. And many who leave for different cities or careers come back to work with us again. Of this we're probably most proud.

These days we have a Michelin star and a waiting list for tables, a James Beard Award for the best wine program in the United States, and a significant reputation both here and abroad. Excellent winemakers are happy to have cuvées on our list. Good purveyors trust us with their best ingredients. Here we are, writing and releasing a cookbook. It wasn't always like this. There were so many indicators along the way that this current state of the restaurant was so laughably implausible that, along with the recipes of Nick's amazing food, it feels worthwhile to try and tell some of the story of how our place came to be. Maybe it can serve as much as a cautionary tale as it might a potential inspiration.

As unglamorous as it may seem, it really is a story about caring, patience, attention, trust, and dumb luck. But mostly about caring. Caring about the forks and knives. The glasses. The butter. The food and wine, obviously, but also the toilet. The toilet paper. The bathroom floor. The menu paper. The wine books. The acoustics. The speakers. The soundtrack. The way the food is and is not explained. The water. The way the water is served. The way the garbage is managed. The way the guests are cared for. The way the staff are cared for. The floor. The walls. The air. Each other. Caring allowed us to survive and even benefit from some of our terrible decisions and mistakes, a pandemic, delays, failures. To work together well enough that we created a new thing that not one of us could have envisioned alone. To create a successful and happy restaurant without having any of the elements one usually assumes that requires.

Four completely naive and inexperienced partners found a largely unheralded chef and opened a restaurant in New York City. This reads like a death sentence. And we did almost everything wrong, glacially carving a full cellar out of the rocky earth below Williamsburg, Brooklyn, to store wine that maybe nobody would buy. We spent that full year of construction cooking and developing a menu, only to then undercut ourselves out of the gate by announcing the place as a "wine bar." We chose ancient flatware from my childhood that we all had to track down on the internet, sometimes one fork at a time, and then installed the same system as Noma and Le Bernardin for our free still and sparkling water because we thought it was the best. We were patient in the beginning when it was slow. We let things play out. I think our inexperience helped us there most: We had no real option but to trust in the people we had chosen to run the place. To give them support and time and authority and pushback to develop into the best versions of themselves. Being too ignorant to demand that they be

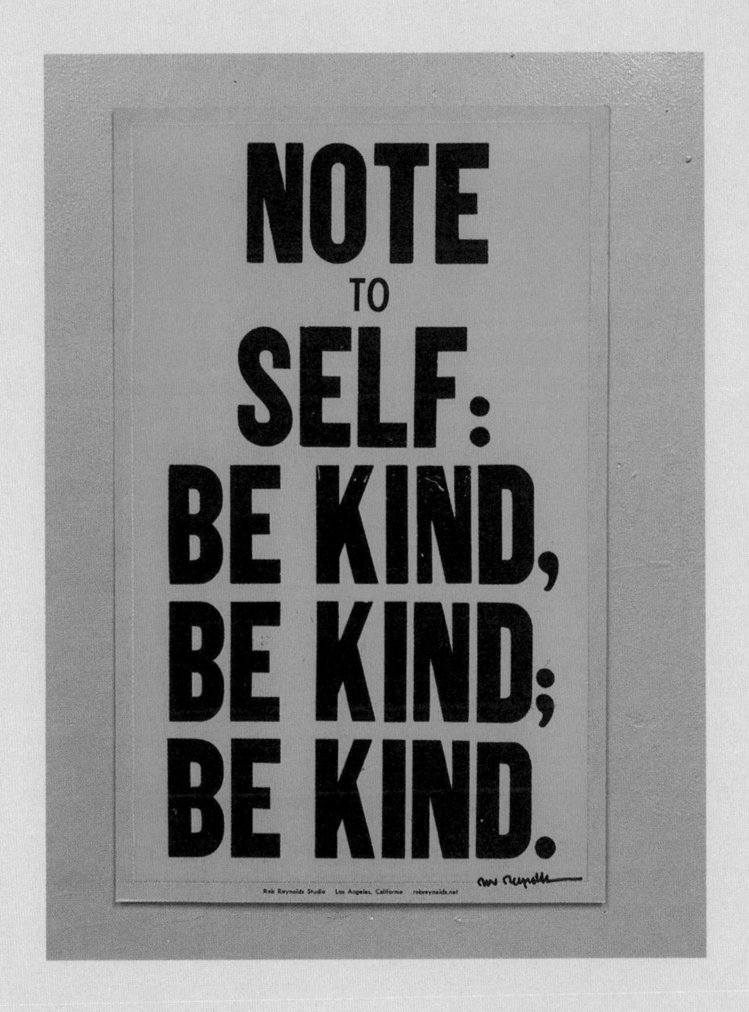

anyone else. We believed in our team, and in the detail and care we put into our sometimes ridiculous wants and ideas, so we were hopeful that it would work out. There are nine million people in this city. We figured we only needed thirty-eight.

At risk of sounding like I'm about to start crying or breaking out into a Broadway number, I love this place and these people. Christina, Justin, Randy, and I got our hands very dirty making this place, for sure, and sweated so many little things that I look back in wonder at how we even had the time or headspace for any of it, but we're like the parents of grown children now, and the restaurant is living in the world, doing its thing, with its unbelievable people that we're honored to know. I have enough operational distance from The Four Horsemen to allow myself to be proud of what it has become. Although, Justin is still in the maelstrom running the beverage program, so maybe he's like that crazy parent who moves with their kid to college or something. He kind of messes up my metaphor. It's OK. The moment is gone. I'm fine.

Ladies and gentlemen, without further ado, the story, style, wine, and food of The Four Horsemen.

INTRODUCTION BY JAMES MURPHY

HOW HARD CAN THIS BE?

In February of 2013, Christina and I went to a little place in Tokyo's Shibuya neighborhood called Ahiru Store. It looked to us like only three people worked there—a chef, a baker, and a sommelier—all of whom also seemed to be owners of the place. There was room for maybe sixteen people. A handful of seats at the tiny bar. The rest had to stand around a few upended wine casks plopped throughout the cramped space, using them as tables. A manageable variety of good natural wine was displayed on shelves in what amounted to the dining room, with basic descriptions on little cards and prices written directly on the bottles themselves in white paint pen. One small toilet. Good music. We were happy there—at peace. And so was everyone around us. "It's so small," we figured. "How hard can this be?"

Justin Chearno and I knew each other from punk rock university, our two middling bands playing the same dingy circuits around the US throughout the self-serious '90s, but had only really become friends at the very end of that decade when we worked in the studio together on his band Turing Machine's first album. In 2002, between rock tours, Justin landed this sweet job at Williamsburg's Uva Wines, in its miniscule original space in that weird mall, at first stocking the shelves, then selling the wine, then ordering the wine, then running the whole show and slowly leading us all away from our crap beers or pints of Maker's and ginger, out into the weird world of low-intervention wines and tiny, singular restaurants. He had just recently quit Uva after over ten years to go and work with friend and brilliant importer Zev Rovine, bringing some of the best wines to the city. When Christina and I returned from Japan, it was Justin we wanted to sit down with to talk about our experience at Ahiru Store. See what he thought. Nothing serious. Just maybe bounce some ideas around for fun. That can't be a problem. Just friends talking.

Later that summer, when a small space on Grand Street near where we had been living looked like it might become available, the three of us, woefully vulnerable to the idea of opening a restaurant, went to sit with the landlord.

Neighborhood Restaurant serving food until 11pm and pouring wine till 1am ~~daily~~ every day. We open at 5pm.

HE KIND OF JUST APPEARED ONE DAY

There are theories and debates about how our fourth horseman, Randy Moon, came to be a part of our world. My bandmate Nancy Whang often takes credit for introducing him around, but regardless of Randy Moon's actual provenance, as far as I'm concerned, he kind of just appeared one day. Randy Moon at a small table in a weird place no one knew about. Randy Moon rolling into an apartment dinner with some insane wine from an obscure Australian radicalist grower. Randy Moon sitting at the friends-and-family opening of the new spot by the former sous chef from this other legendary place. That we also happened to be at. On a different continent. Randy Moon even showing up, seemingly unannounced, at a food event Christina and I were throwing in SoHo with Kris Yenbamroong of LA's Night + Market.

Nancy Whang and Whitney Bedford kept telling me that I should meet Christina and James because they were opening a wine bar. At the time, I was basically living at the Ten Bells, trying to figure out how to break into wine. But I was interested in getting to know Christina and James more than anything else. We had so many mutual friends.

I met Christina first. It was at the Pines, Angelo Romano's old restaurant in Gowanus. Then I met James at his and Christina's engagement party in LA. I wanted to make a good impression, so I brought a case of wine. One of the bottles was Ulysse Collin's Le Magnum. None of us had tried it before, and we all loved it.

Back in New York a few weeks later, James emails me to set up a meeting. Justin would be there, too. By the time we get together, I had practiced this whole pitch, outlining what I could bring to the table. I show up to the meeting and, right away, James goes, "OK, here's the team: It's the four of us." —RANDY

In August of 2013, while on a trip out West, Christina and I got engaged and decided to celebrate by spontaneously having some people over to a friend's Los Angeles house we were borrowing. We'd been told about this excellent taco guy who, with just a phone call, backed his pickup into the driveway and proceeded to make enough tacos for a party of about seventy-five. I think there were eleven of us. Christina had already been in touch with Randy Moon, who showed up not with, like, a "thoughtful bottle." Randy Moon showed up with a crate full of beautiful rare wines and Champagnes, unceremoniously trundled them onto the counter, and said, "Hi." He wanted to try the wines. And wanted to share. Word was Randy had worked in early tech, exited that, and had now set himself to investigating the worlds of food and natural wine with a focused and detailed intensity. Had moved to Australia in pursuit of new experiences. Along with Randy and our tiny gaggle of other guests, Christina and I did our best to eat back the rising tide of food, and, with little more intel than what we had gleaned over the course of an impromptu taco party, asked ourselves: "Why not Randy Moon?"

AMATEURS AT WORK

September 25, 2013, was our first "all hands" meeting with Justin, Randy, Christina, and me, and the four of us started building an idea of what this thing could be, listing wants, looking for a name. I somehow got myself invited to this "Vin Vignerons Vinyles" event in Montreal (apparently to DJ, but I wasn't sure and forgot to bring my records). As a lark, I asked the promoters to put up the whole gang, and to call us "The Four Horsemen of the Oenocalypse." The name actually made it onto their poster alongside proper winemakers we liked to drink, like Catherine Breton and Thomas Pico. The "Oenocalypse" bit didn't stick, but we all liked The Four Horsemen. It sounded like a pub at the end of the world. So we had a name.

Though New York at that time had many places that we all loved, we all felt that there was room for something new and absurdly presumed that we four amateurs were just the right people to make it happen. We were each inspired by special little places around the world—radically different from one another but perfect in their own unique ways. Tokyo's Ahiru Store, yes, but also London's Brawn, Le Châteaubriand and Le Verre Volé in Paris, Ved Stranden 10 in Copenhagen, 10 William Street in Sydney . . . Restaurants where you thought you'd just have a glass of wine, and then another, and then a meal because, well, you're hungry now, texting friends to join you, making new friends, until you find yourself closing the place down. Places you "loved." We were into the relaxed but precise service styles of these spots and how they both matched and contradicted their cities—at once a good representation of a local culture as well as a respite from it. We wanted that in our hometown.

Thus formed, Team Horsemen spent the tail end of 2013 eating, drinking, negotiating a lease, and getting ahead of ourselves with big ideas about what we wanted in a restaurant. We wanted a place that provided the type of service where everyone knows exactly what to do, what side to serve from, how to clear correctly and discreetly but always casually, like it's a coincidence, so that every guest feels welcome and in good hands, whether it's someone's visiting mother who rarely eats out or a seasoned server from a three-star restaurant on a night off. We didn't want a restaurant that felt intimidatingly highbrow or formal but also weren't interested in some of the too-cool energy we were getting bored of in Brooklyn. It needed to be New York but also a bit of a relief from New York. *Here you will be taken care of.* "Care" kept coming up.

Justin really wanted a place where he felt normal drinking wines that blew his mind, the way we'd felt on our 2009 trip to Le Verre Volé and Racines in Paris. Where it didn't have to be a Big Deal to sit down and experience something elevated and transformative. He was always pushing for the place to be better and not fancier. Christina, who grew up in Denmark, made some demands about wood and bread. She really wanted something different from the dark reclaimed style that dominated Brooklyn at that time and had dreams of high-integrity joinery and cabinetry, beatiful yet functional Danish furniture, and lighter tones. It was also pretty horrifying to her that so many good NYC restaurants didn't make their own bread. Unthinkable in Copenhagen. We would have to make our own bread, and it needed to be right. Randy wanted to be a part of creating a restaurant that gave others the feeling he got at his favorite places back in Sydney—more fun than serious, a place for going deep with friends and only realizing later that you'd walked away with a new persepctive on wines. This had as much to do with having the right wines as the right people, food, energy in the room. Personally, I really wanted a dining room that sounded good. I could never hear music clearly in restaurants, and Christina was developing tinnitus from the shock of eating out in New York, so we needed a place where it wasn't all brutal hard surfaces, punishing ironic music, and screaming people. A place where someone had done the work required so that you could enjoy a song, have a comfortable conversation, and clearly hear your friend but maybe not the next table. For all of us, I think, it came down to bothering to care. About absolutely everything.

In February of 2014, lease handled and keys for our filthy new space in hand, the four of us calculated that we would probably be open and serving guests in maybe three months time, what with all the construction, etc. to deal with. Three months sounded ambitious but doable to me. With that deadline locked in, we obviously needed to immediately find a chef.*

* This may be a good time to point out that of the four people starting this venture, James had the most restaurant experience, and that experience was two months working as a busboy at a golf course clubhouse in semirural New Jersey in 1987. Sure, Justin had worked in some NYC bars and at least had a proper handle on wine, and Christina and Randy had eaten basically everywhere in the world you might care to eat, but nobody-seriously, not one person-had any idea what it meant to run a restaurant, let alone build one out.

Maybe this was James being optimistic (or maybe it's his alarmingly poor memory talking), but I don't recall thinking that we would be open in three months. That same optimism of his also seeped disastrously into our build-out budget and operating projections, and it also fueled many of his stubborn ideas for The Four Horsemen.

The list of James Ideas that got nixed before we even opened includes:

- Somehow sticking a private dining room in the back, when there is no "back."
- Bulding an illegal cheese affinage room.
- Bulding an illegal meat curing room.
- Setting up our own preprogrammed hospital-grade Miele laundry space (for doing all our dirty linens ourselves and avoid overpaying the "New York Linen Mafia." This included a trip to Miele in New Brunswick to try to also get them to modify a glasswasher for us . . .).
- He wanted me to make custom ceramic coffee cups. That was a reduced ask after being shot a glance when he started to make noises about turning all the plates by hand ourselves, too . . .
- And then, of course, he wanted to personally churn our house butter. Every day.

While all intriguing ideas, they're pretty funny to anyone who has ever set foot in our microscopic place.

Some James Ideas that did get pushed through but were sooner or later retired included:

- A full professional espresso setup in the back of our tiny bar.
- Pancake brunch (granted, the best pancakes you will ever eat).
- Only allowing full-length, James preapproved albums to be played during service, including all the obscure, droning, and super long songs that you would normally skip over (staff hated this one so much I think they would have staged a walkout had we not relaxed that particular policy).

For all the messes it's made, I do believe James's optimism and selective memory might have been one of the necessary sparks that got us going in the first place, kept us going when it seemed like a really terrible idea, and pushed us to be more uncompromising and ambitious, to care about everything, when more seasoned (read: sane) restaurateurs would have and should have relented. He just puts blinders on and plows forward. It's annoying and terrifying sometimes. As a recovering lawyer endowed with far less optimism, I would try to apply the brakes and ended up running point on things like getting the finances right, HR, legal, and reporting to our investors (who had somehow entrusted us with chunks of their personal savings). I dreaded the idea that we'd end up as one of those restaurants that shutter after only a couple of years. I was scared of letting down our investors and staff, and of being judged as dilettante part-time restaurateurs who wasted peoples' trust, time, and money. I definitely spent some energy informing James that this or that was a really terrible idea (even if it was also maybe a very good idea . . . ?). While I don't think you can build a New York City restaurant out of pure fear of failure, I do think you need at least a small measure of reality in order to build a successful and lasting one. —CHRISTINA

MAYBE THIS IS OUR GUY?

In February of 2014, while having lunch at Estela with our friend Anna Polonsky, Christina and I asked for her help finding some chef candidates, and instead of doing the honorable thing and trying to talk us out of it, Anna mentioned that she might know this chef, Nick Curtola. He was leaving popular Brooklyn spot Glady's because the owners were planning to change the food program from a full menu to, like, Caribbean sandwiches or something, and this guy wasn't having it. He sounded a little uncompromising. Maybe this is our guy?

Justin had already met Nick while bringing wine to Glady's and emailed us Nick's most recent pre-sandwich menu, adding that our potential candidate liked to drink a lot of the same wine we did. That was promising. Of course, Randy had also eaten Nick's food at Glady's. And at the previous place he'd worked called Franny's. And a place he'd worked at before Franny's called Yunnan Kitchen (and also at some pop-up dinners put on by Randy's Australian chef friend Thomas Lim where Nick had also cooked. I'm telling you all this so you get some idea of the magical enigma that is Randy). Christina emailed Nick the next morning, and we planned a sort of test dinner for that coming Sunday. It was all happening so fast, sure, but now that we had our space, we really needed to find out if he was a good fit posthaste, what with our imminent opening in May (maybe June? July?) 2014.

Just a week after our Estela lunch, into our apartment walked Nick. He was relatively quiet and serious. Less boisterous and imperious than what we'd come to expect in a "head chef." Less outgoing, even, than the cook friend he'd brought to help him out. He was reserved and restrained. Even so, he couldn't hide the look of dismay that ran across his face when he saw our shitty, Reagan-era NYC apartment gas range and lone, sad induction hob (bought just for the occasion). He put his stuff down on the counter and began preparing, made some caveats. He didn't have any experience with this stove, and this induction hob was, well, I don't know. Moving expertly around our crappy kitchen. Shrugging a little. Nick wasn't doing anything to try to sell himself, just head down, cooking. We didn't really know what to make of this guy yet, but here was our first taste of something really important about Nick. There was no bullshit. Always undersell. Always overdeliver.

At our makeshift plywood kitchen table, Nick served us his remarkable food (important to note: Nick cringes now at almost every dish he made us back then. They were all impressive, but just to provide some clarity about Nick . . .), watched us try everything. Relaxed. Smiled. We all sat together for the first time and began talking, over great wine and food, about restaurants we liked, and found that we had so many in common. We talked about what we thought was missing in New York. About the dumb ideas we had for our little place. Nick got into what he did and didn't like about tasting menus, hamburgers, seafood, open kitchens, aprons. He laughed. We grilled him on how restaurants actually worked, unabashedly showing our inexperience. Why did New York places all seem to do things the same way, and not like Cañete in Barcelona? Nick was actually heading back out to Europe the following week, and we all agreed to email him with some favorite spots that he hadn't been to yet. He and his friend packed up their knives and containers, said good night, and left us.

Almost more important than the delicious food we ate that evening was that rambling conversation about what made a restaurant special, what held one back, what moved us, and what Nick was into. It was validating that an actual professional shared some of our thoughts and hopes and ideas, found inspiration in many of the same places. The four of us were left feeling both very good about Nick and pretty sure that no matter how well we all seemed to hit it off, he'd be too rational to come work with a bunch of neophytes who clearly had no business opening a restaurant.

The following day, Nick wrote us a very warm email. He called us "like-minded professionals," which made us laugh out loud, and told us he was "very intrigued and excited" about our project. We scrambled to schedule some more test dinners together for when he returned from Europe, but it seemed, against all odds, that we maybe had landed a chef on our first attempt.

They cared. They were curious. Really into the details. Because they had never really worked in restaurants, they asked questions I wasn't used to hearing from owners. Why do restaurants look like this? Why do they do it like that? Is there another, better way?

That was another big factor in my decision: their optimism. They were actually trying to find a new way to operate. The New York restaurant scene is incredible, but you can get a lot of, "Nope, you can't do that here." I wanted to be in a different environment. Something closer to what I found in at a lot of those smaller places we all liked in Europe. And, frankly, maybe these people wouldn't just sit over my shoulder about numbers and dishes and stuff, like a more seasoned restaurant person might. I knew how to run a kitchen and really wanted that responsibility. Maybe there would be more room for my ideas here, and I could grow.

I was taking a risk, sure. I guess it just felt like the right one for that moment in my life. But they were taking a risk by hiring me, too. I was virtually unknown.

It also felt like all of us were genuinely interested in drinking some wine, spending time together, and learning from the process of opening a restaurant together. I'm glad that was the case because of how long that build-out wound up taking. There was, frankly, a lot of process to learn from. —NICK

THE WRATH OF CHANG

We had been telling people we were opening a "wine bar" because that seemed more doable. But a bit later, after we'd begun talking to Nick, we stupidly asked Dave Chang (of Momofuku infamy) if he knew anything about our potential chef, and he lost his shit. "Wait . . . what do you need a CHEF for!??! Are you doing FOOD?!?? You can't do food!!!! Do you know where the fucking grease trap is?? Do you even know WHAT a fucking grease trap IS?? Do you know what to do when human shit is pouring out of the clogged toilet in your bathroom and into your dining room?!?!? Because that is 100 percent definitely going to fucking happen!!!" There is a series of photos of him screaming at James in apoplectic horror, standing among the grease-caked detritus and ruin of the shuttered old Foodswings kitchen before we'd begun renovations. None of them fully capture his rage, nor James's flailing and unconvincing defenses. He was totally right, of course, but we remained idiotically undeterred. It was by then just too late to stop it. We had signed a lease, after all! We were talking to a real, actual human chef! If this chef would somehow agree to place his career in the hands of four completely inexperienced dummies, then all we needed was, like, the rest of a staff, a manager, equipment, a design, a million licenses, twenty-two fire extinguishers, suppliers, something called an ANSUL . . . You know: a restaurant.

THE YEAR OF COOKING AND THE THIRD THING

As it turns out, four utterly inexperienced dilettante restaurateurs proved to be profoundly wrong about how long it takes to build out and open a restaurant in New York City. It was, to put it mildly, not three months. It was longer. It was long enough that Christina and I managed to go from an unmarried couple to planning a wedding in Denmark, getting married, getting pregnant, and then having the kid. It was long enough that all of the wines we had been gathering to serve had new vintages. Our previous, optimistic opening date prediction of May or spring 2014, based on which we had hired our head chef, was at least partially correct. Just off by a year.

This could have been a disaster—and in many ways it absolutely was—but in that year of cooking, something like real osmosis happened. All of our disparate ideas and elements had a chance to coalesce. Things marinated. And began turning into something new.

Almost weekly, we all meet, drink wine, eat Nick's food, talk. Nick trying new recipes and concepts, high and low, going through different sous chefs along the way, all leaving eventually to go get real jobs. Because we still don't open. The four of us trot out ideas, good and bad, make comments, pleas, suggestions. After a few months, we grow to trust one another and to understand more about each individual's strengths, weaknesses, and tendencies. After a full year working like this, without guests? Or without the pressure of eyes on us? The food, the restaurant—it grows into something none of us are expecting. It doesn't wind up being the menu Nick has planned. And it's not what the four of us had envisioned, either—it's something better. A genuine collaboration that would be almost impossible to cultivate in the nerve-racking environment of an active restaurant. We developed the Third Thing.

THE YEAR OF MAKING

This year of construction also gave us a moment to drill down on all the design and functional details that we obsessed about. The burlap walls and sound-absorbing ceiling panels hidden behind the soft cedar slats, to make the room sound gentle like a studio. The plates and glasses and cutlery, tracked down, tested, lived with, dropped and whacked against counters, tables, and sinks. We inherited our colorful Opinel knives from Christina's and my wedding in Denmark, having scored them cheap directly from the factory through one of Justin's contacts in France. The original tables we made by hand with our friend Gorman, just using my track saw and a hand sander, IKEA butcher-block countertops, budget restaurant legs, rope, and some chalk paint. I made the little soap dispenser holder in the bathroom out of bar teak scraps, glue, and a clamp, and Justin and Randy became the Teak Patrol, regularly oiling every wood surface maniacally and nearly setting Christina's and my construction site of a home on fire with a bag of rags after one particularly late session. Randy, Christina, and I wrapped rope around poles while Justin and our dear friend Mike Vadino dragged a glasswasher into position in the bar to save some money with the plumber. Christina, nine months pregnant, painted our crappy Craigslist chairs (ten for $125 total!), then climbed to the top of our ladder in the dining room to check the height of the lamps. She also sent our Chinese construction crew into an existential spiral one day when she overheard them talking shit, and, after a year of secret linguistic spying, politely told them in Mandarin where they could stick it.* In October, we hired our first general manager, Katrina Birchmeier, whom Randy discovered while eating at her restaurant, Garagistes, in Tasmania, Australia (good Randy fact there), and she flew out to New York to start planning with us. We dug down in the basement and built wine shelves in our actual wine

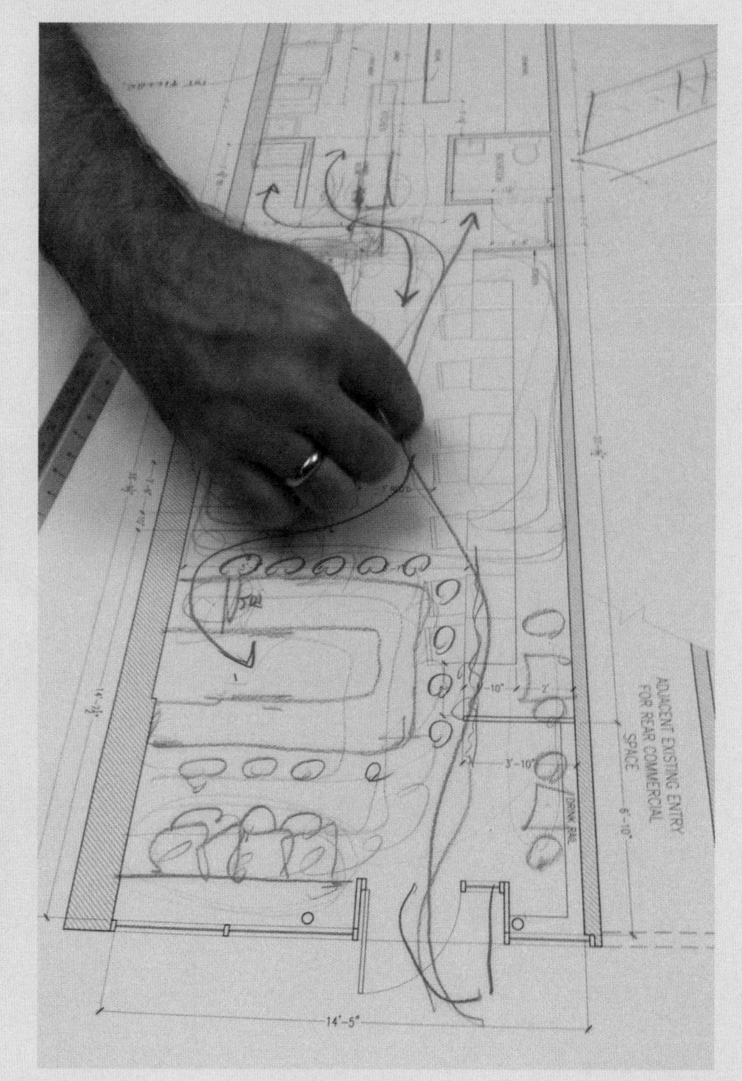

* There's a particular face that people make when they try to remember every messed up thing they've overconfidently said in front of the wrong person over a long period. Somewhere between "That's a tart lemon!" and "I just stepped on a nail!"

cellar, which doubled as the office (complete with a parka on a hook just outside the door so no one would freeze to death in there paying bills and printing menus), then loaded them with the unbelievable array of wines that Justin was bringing in.*

When it came time to design the restaurant's logo, I think we all wanted to find somebody who'd treat it like a commission and not a "brand identity." I mentioned to my wife, Stacy, that we were thinking this logo should be along the lines of Picasso's *Don Quixote* sketch, and she immediately said that it sounded like a job for Mike Paré. I knew Mike a bit. In the early 2000s, he had an art studio in the legendary Monster Island building on Kent Avenue, which is where we'd often go to parties and see DIY gigs. He actually used to host a pirate radio show only blocks from where we'd eventually build our restaurant.

The logo, which he absolutely nailed, was only the beginning: Mike would go on to create an entire visual language for The Four Horsemen. He designed the menu, the choking signs; there's an entire custom font based on the letters in his drawings. He did Randy's wedding invitations. He paints a new Four Horsemen poster every year. And, by now, his illustrations have been printed on probably eight thousand tote bags. I guess what I'm trying to say is that Mike means a lot to us. —JUSTIN

* Digging out that cellar was insane. The original basement beams holding up the floor of the previous tenant (vegan fast-food joint Foodswings–think seitan buffalo wings) were rough trunks of trees with little bits of lumber wedged under them for added height, all sitting on a cracked rat slab. Terrifying. We had to dig down to make it all standing height, pour a real floor. There were so many giant boulders! Who knew Brooklyn had so many giant boulders hiding under its skirts?

FOUR HORSEMEN

For our menus and wine books, we had cheap handmade paper shipped regularly from a lady in Goa that Christina and I had met while at a friend's wedding there, and we used that until I think she stopped manufacturing it, or the office got tired of massive bundles of weird handmade paper that all had to be cut into usable sizes. Christina made all those early wine books by hand with that paper, covers of oiled blue cardstock, a hole punch, an embosser, self-inking stamps, and a box of Chicago screws.* Finally, in June of 2015, a full eighteen months after we brought Nick on, we opened the doors of The Four Horsemen for the first time. And made another critical mistake.

MISTAKE NO. 2: CALL IT A WINE BAR

I feel like I can take a lot of the hit for this one. Nick, to his credit, never loved referring to the place as a "wine bar." It seemed to undermine what he was doing in the kitchen. I had some convoluted idea about . . . surprising people? Like, "We'll just call it a wine bar, and then BOOM! It's this great restaurant, too! And you didn't even see it coming!" I don't entirely know why anyone went along with it—we had put so much work into the food and service at this point—but they all did. And unfortunately, so did many of the guests.

So the consensus early on seemed to be that you'd visit us for a drink and a snack before going out to a real dinner somewhere else nearby. Or maybe drop by on the way home from your meal to have a glass of wine. To be honest, I think we were a little insecure. The owners had no experience, and I was a complete unknown. We were almost scared to call The Four Horsemen a restaurant.

At least with "wine bar," we figured we could undersell and overdeliver. I think this was the beginning of that idea becoming our mantra. Undersell, overdeliver. Pretty easy to achieve at first considering no one really expected anything from us. —NICK

Honestly, there weren't a lot of wine bars like us in New York at that time, and we partially figured that might be more of the unique, defining selling point for the place, versus being "another restaurant." So wine bar it was.

There was also a vague fear that we'd get too much press, and risk being some sort of Next Big Thing, overrun by ding-dongs all trying to be at the new hot spot, every one of whom would bail once the shine wore off. We didn't want it rammed with people who might repel locals or drive away anyone who might take us seriously down the line. And we got our wish.

It wasn't rammed.

* They didn't start with oiled covers. But almost immediately, the original blue paper would get some oil on it and not look as nice, so Christina got the brilliant idea to just pre-oil the covers with mineral oil. People constantly stole them, which was flattering and sweet, but also kind of a nightmare since they took forever to put together, especially when sleep-deprived with a new baby at home.

WINE
WINE

We got a bit busier with time but remained largely under the radar. Maybe we had shot ourselves in the collective foot.

But we took the time to get into every detail of that menu, and it got tighter and tighter. We dialed in our service. No weird drop lines at the table like, “The chef recommends you start with this and work your way toward . . .” blah blah blah. No uniforms. No special glasses for people drinking expensive bottles. Keep working. Get better.

Maybe it doesn’t seem like the greatest plan on paper, but it definitely gave us some much-needed time and space to figure things out—and to experience a slow burn and create word of mouth, especially among our peers in the industry. Pretty soon, our dining room was filling up mostly with chefs, servers, cooks, and locals. And we had actual regulars. That genuine trust and rapport made us feel like we had license to push. We got more and more serious. —NICK

The "Wine Bar" thing may have saved us by giving us that time and space to grow. I don't think we knew how big of a deal it is to have good, local regulars that come in all the time and hang out. To have cooks, chefs, servers, wine importers as guests as well. At least I didn't fully understand that in the beginning. When you have a good relationship to the people in the community around you, they remind you of what you're there to do: to be someone's place. In turn, they don't bail on you so easily. When you turn the corner and start to succeed, they cheer you on instead of resenting you for being "too busy now." If you'd been too cool and all that shit from day one, these very people who make the absolute best regulars, who are the soul of your business, wouldn't set foot in your restaurant. "Fuck that place." But make a spot for them at the bar, appreciate them genuinely, always remember them—they'll stick with you through pandemics, Michelin stars, waitlists. The good and the bad. Because they feel genuine ownership about their place. The same way we felt such fierce ownership of the many places that were ours.

AMANDA'S PLACE

Jules Dressner told me that you guys were opening a wine bar and he was all, "Oh, you don't know about The Four Horsemen?" I thought, That sounds so fun. And I want to work there.

I think I asked Jules: Do they have a GM? And he said, "Yeah, it's this woman they brought in from Australia," blah blah blah. And I was like, Ugh. I want that job.

I met Katrina when I was working at Marlow. She would come in all the time and was always really nice to me. I wrote to her and asked if I could bartend or work there, but she said it was fully staffed.

I was so excited about it opening because I figured: That's what I want, a place to go and just drink beautiful wine and it not be at a restaurant necessarily. I really thought it was going to be a wine bar. And then I went in for the first time. I remember, it was pretty stark in there—really bright. And I remember the dining room was empty, because it was all reservations, which no one did in Brooklyn at that time. And the music was too quiet. There was so much to love already, but I just wanted to get my hands on that room. —AMANDA

When, after only a few months, Katrina told us she needed to head back to her native Australia, we were thrust into trying to find a new manager (which anyone who works in restaurants will tell you is the hardest position to fill). Amanda McMillan came recommended to us via, like, four different people. From the moment she came in, she begged us to let the place breathe, relax, sing. She came with little to no fine dining experience—she just wanted everyone to have, like, the *best time*. She was expansive, welcoming, warm. She wanted to fill the room. Always make it feel alive. More flowers, more candles, lower light, louder music. At first, the entire rest of the team almost collectively gasped and recoiled, like that old lady in the Twisted Sister video. *We're serious here. This is a serious restaurant!* Our original plan to also be a relaxed place got somewhat lost in the fog of restaurant opening anxiety. I fought her (and happily lost) on using candles because I had been told that the tables were absolutely too small. But Amanda pressed on, almost foolhardily, uphill, undeterred. She threw staff parties with karaoke party busses. Made sure there were going-away gatherings for anyone who moved on from the team. If you come to The Four Horsemen now, have your night, and the place *feels amazing* to you, that's Amanda. Sure, we all wanted this—we had specifically talked about it—but she made it. Sometimes against everyone's wishes. And she brought out the best in everyone as a result.

It was so important to suddenly get a new voice into The Horsemen during that opening year—Amanda was the first "outsider" to break into this protective coterie, to make changes. The only one who had first experienced the restaurant as a guest, who could see its singular success and failures. Its potential. And who wasn't exhausted from a year and a half of building the place.

THE ODD COUPLE

We joke a lot about Nick's tendency to at first say no way. It's impossible. The way he did when we begged him to start serving lunch in the early days of the restaurant. *Can't do it. Kitchen's too small. Gotta prep for dinner at the same time in the same space. Ridiculous to even suggest it.* Then, when he finally does it, the guy creates a completely different set menu every week, new recipes each time, ranging anywhere from greatest hits from the first St. John cookbook to red-sauce classics and Northern Thai. Absolutely insane.

With Amanda? Everything was possible the moment it was proposed. She loves to say yes. All the time. *We can totally do that!* And she would somehow make whatever it was happen.

On the surface, they seemed like complete opposites, but they were more similar in critical ways than you might imagine: Nick would say no to things often because he couldn't bring himself to half-ass anything. He knew precisely what saying yes meant. Feared it. It was going to be brutal. He and his team would have to do whatever it took to make some new additional thing good enough to meet his standards. And he wouldn't commit until he knew it was possible. Amanda, on the other hand, *hated* to say no: to our crazy ideas, to diners looking for impromptu seats, to people trying to wrangle a reservation on a fully booked night. Letting people down seems to pain her deeply, so she says yes and then, I have to imagine, maybe lies in bed at night thinking, *Why on earth did I add that to my already insane workload?* Their differences are obvious, but what makes them similar is that they both absolutely refuse to fail.

For both of them to really succeed, they needed one another. Nick needed Amanda to say yes, push him out of his comfort zone. Needed her focus on the overall guest experience and vibe to kick out any unnecessary, lingering crutches of seriousness on which the "fine dining experience" can lean. And Amanda needed Nick—to make critical demands on the service and space, to ensure that nothing was undermining the excellence of the meals he and his remarkable cooks were putting out. If it was going to be a party, it needed to be a party built on solid foundations he could stand behind.

Somehow, the restaurant would have to be both a night out and a proper restaurant. The best meal your in-laws have ever had, and your drinking-to-drown-your-sorrows night. Your tenth anniversary. A glass of wine and a surprise revelation of a salad for a tired chef needing a quiet meal alone prepared by someone, anyone, else on their one night off. The perfect first date. A riot. A Wednesday. For anybody.

THE

THE LONG HELLO

When Nick and Amanda really found their symmetry, The Four Horsemen began its transformation into the place it is now. Candles on the table, menu going through dish after dish, introduced, phased out (I still miss that shrimp tajarin), replaced with something better. The place was getting stronger and more focused. It was also getting busier. But slowly.

When traveling in Europe, we all found that The Horsemen had a reputation there. More and more chefs, cooks, servers, visiting Parisians and Londoners began to show up with their suitcases to have a meal. But somehow it still seemed like crickets in our own town. There was very little press or acknowledgment from the food establishment of New York, and after a time, the team just accepted that we were probably never going to get anything like a real *Times* review. It was comical to even consider a James Beard Award, let alone a Michelin star. Sometime in 2017 or 2018, feeling outside the restaurant scene, feeling outside the restaurant scene, idling out there in Brooklyn, no impressive owner group, no big chef, no Instagram followers or clever posts, no hotshot sommelier, storied manager—just our gang, working furiously—we had a big meeting and decided that we had no choice but to embrace it. To act as if The Four Horsemen already had a Michelin star that we absolutely refused to lose. Everything became about keeping up standards. Being the best version of this restaurant we could be.

On October 14, 2019, the Michelin Guide released its list of Bib Gourmands for NYC, and I lost it. Nothing. I was gutted for Nick, for the entire team. I sent an angry email to everyone about it, moaning and whining about how unfair it all felt. It felt more clear to me than ever that the restaurant was alone in the woods. When, a week later, they announced the stars, and we were completely blindsided. I hadn't even considered that a star was a possibility. Before a *NYT* review, or anything, really, The Four Horsemen, our little thirty-eight-seat place in Williamsburg, got a Michelin star. We were all ecstatic—so happy for Nick most of all. Our friend Nick was now a Michelin-star chef! However much he clearly, to us, deserved it, it still felt completely insane. It was so immensely gratifying that Nick, a guy who never pushed himself forward into the limelight, who just kept his head down, working and trying to get better and better, a chef's chef, really, was recognized for the truly exceptional food he and his kitchen were putting out night after night.

Two years later, when Justin went to gather the James Beard Award for Outstanding Wine Program, we were stunned again. I think about how sore I had always been, grumbling about him not getting enough respect. There's a great picture of him walking up that aisle with Billy, looking a little nervous and out of place, almost shaking with excitement. I could still see the same punk rock Justin that I had known for all those years in there, wearing his nice suit, both in and out of his element. Bending the element to make room for him. For us. He's worked so hard for so long, made so many lasting and real friendships with winemakers, importers, sommeliers. Being himself. Still fighting for the place to be better and not fancier. The same guy I rolled around on barroom floors with twenty years before, getting his due.

I really believe in Justin. I really believe in Nick. In Amanda. I think we all believe in one another at The Horsemen. Stand up for one another, like a family. There are so many stories, too personal for this space, of this team showing up in profound ways when one of their own was in need. I wish I could write them in this intro, but people's lives are their own private things, and I won't betray them here. I mean, this is supposed to be a cookbook, after all. But honestly, during that pandemic nightmare, watching Amanda, Nick, and Ben putting boxes of food, supplies, toilet paper together, and then driving those boxes all over an apocalyptic New York to hand-deliver them to stranded cooks, servers, dishwashers, not knowing what was going to happen. I think the care and love and fierce, defensive determination everyone shows reminds me a lot of siblings. Siblings are all different—they argue, roll their eyes at one another from time to time, give each other shit. But if anyone or anything messes with any one of them, it's on. I'm eternally grateful, as a small part of this restaurant, to be able to witness this care.

As I'm finishing writing this, Christina and I are returning from Singapore, where we went to see Nick at The Four Horsemen pop-up event at Le Bon Funk. It was great. He was there with Ben and Dylan, the three of them walking around in a jet-lagged fog, eating, rallying themselves to spend hours trying to re-create their food on the other side of the planet. We went both nights we were in town, and after our second dinner Nick told Christina about him turning down the lights as low as he could get away with. Changing the playlist. Stuff he never concerned himself too much with back in New York, really. "For Amanda," he told her, "because she isn't here."

IN CONCLUSION

In the beginning of this endless introduction essay, Christina and I asked ourselves the question: "How hard can this be?" The answer, of course, is *infinitely hard*. If any of us had known just how hard, I think we may have backed away in horror, our hands in the air. It certainly would have been the smart thing to do. But then we wouldn't have had all of the incredibly rewarding experiences that this restaurant has brought us. For me, by far the most important gift this place has given me is the people. Being a part of something that so many remarkable, gifted, and intelligent people give so much of themselves to has been humbling and beautiful. I think we all feel this way. And I got to learn so much about so many different things. Like soundproofing and air conditioning. Hood extraction and fire supression. Plumbing, too.

To be honest, Chang was right to yell at us back in 2014, standing there in that decimated kitchen. We had no idea what we were getting ourselves into. Maybe it wasn't just outrage . . . Maybe it was a form of kindness—trying to save his friends from their own foolishness. We didn't know what a grease trap was: It was absolutely true. And I personally would have no idea what to do if the toilet backed up into the dining room. But I think I found a hack. I don't know why everyone doesn't do it this way. It's so incredibly obvious when you step back and think about it.

You just put a floor drain under the toilet bowl.

295
PARADISE

"WHO IS THIS GUY?"

BY NICK CURTOLA

I grew up in a town actually called Pleasanton, California, just outside San Francisco. My mom was an excellent cook who had filled our house with an extensive collection of cookbooks and back issues of *Bon Appétit*, *Gourmet*, *Saveur*... She taught cooking classes out of my local high school home economics room, and in 2000, having barely graduated high school (school and I don't really get along) and with little else going on, I decided to try to help her out a few days a week doing prep work and mise en place.

Cooking made me feel better than sitting in a classroom, and it wasn't long before I started wondering if a job in food might be something I could get myself into. I signed up at the nearest and most reputable-seeming cooking school: the now defunct CCA (California Culinary Academy) in San Francisco. They made promises of six-figure positions waiting for its graduates just a few years after completing their program—a claim that eventually got them sued by a bunch of disgruntled alumni who had found themselves in the real world of restaurants and food. Professional cooking is really fucking hard and pays quite poorly, even at the highest levels. I don't think you can get into it for the money. Not if you want to be happy.

True to form, the academic classroom piece of the CCA wasn't my strong suit. I did, however, find out I was a quicker study hands on. I loved seeing and touching produce, tasting sauces, and smelling stockpots simmering away. I loved holding a knife, thinking of it as an extension of my hand. And I liked that the information I encountered this way really stuck with me as memories.

I also quickly discovered that I knew pretty much nothing about food. On the first day of my "basics" course, the instructor told me to gather parsley, sage, and rosemary. I had no idea what two of the three looked like. In addition to helping my mom out, I had watched a few cooking shows when I was little, like *Yan Can Cook*, *The Galloping Gourmet*, and Julia Child's *The French Chef*. I loved the chefs' energies and how fun they made cooking seem, but I didn't retain any real information. Now, through the act of actually cooking, everything began to stick.

I ended up graduating—again, by the skin of my teeth, but I felt good. I was at least excited about something.

I started cooking in Oakland at Bay Wolf, an institution run by Michael Wild and Larry Goldman. It opened just a few years after Chez Panisse, with a similar menu and ethos. Located in an old Craftsman-style home, they served dishes like Caesar salad with hand-torn croutons, duck liver pâté with green peppercorns, and a summer vegetable tian with Laura Chenel's chèvre. In the kitchen, I ineptly butchered all those items and many more. I was terrible. Luckily, I was also unpaid. So instead of being fired, they just stuck me in the back and had me pick herbs, make vinaigrettes, peel potatoes. I burned my arms constantly. Whenever I reached into one of their huge ovens to remove something, like custards from a water bath, I'd hear the singe of my skin on the racks. Smell the scent of arm hair on fire.

I was twenty-one and in awe of the cooks working there. They were older, maybe in their late twenties and early thirties, and seemed so focused and capable. They could power through a grinding, busy service with ease and still find the calm to execute small, fine details late in their shifts. All I could do was get in their way, make their lives more difficult. They all seemed so intimidating, and knew so much about food. They spoke an almost secret language of references that I desperately wanted to understand. I wanted to become one of them, so I started reading on my days off.

Anthony Bourdain had just released *A Cook's Tour*. Like a lot of cooks at that time, I was super into his writing. When he released his *Les Halles Cookbook* a few years later, my mom went to a reading he did at my local bookshop and had him sign my copy (I couldn't make it because, well, cook's hours). He drew a skull with a chef's knife in its teeth. I thought it was the most badass thing I'd ever seen. In 2010, I made the pilgrimage to Asador Etxebarri way up in the Basque Country hills outside San Sebastián because I had seen it featured on Bourdain's show. Etxebarri is now among the world's most popular bucket-list culinary destinations. Before Bourdain, it was largely unknown.

Making your way to Etxebarri isn't easy. In 2010, it meant asking the small hotel's front desk to print out your MapQuest directions, then coordinating them with paper road maps from the Spanish travel center before setting out on the winding two-hour drive. Maybe longer, what with all the wrong turns we made. That Etxebarri experience remains one of the top three meals of my life. It was a wake-up call and changed the way I thought about being a cook from then on. It was at that meal that I really started to understand the pure, clean flavors of ingredients in their peak season. Cooking over coals and burning various types

"WHO IS THIS GUY?"

of wood for particular flavors and effects became fascinating to me. Etxebarri's chef, Victor Arguinzoniz, was quietly executing some of the simplest, yet most beautiful cuisine in the world.

I also got really into Richard Olney's detailed descriptions of foods from around the world in his *Good Cook's Encyclopedia*, going so far as to seek out different volumes in antiques shops while on treks around the United States. Those books are now so old that I remember reading his recommendation for placing hot dishes on an asbestos pad to protect your countertops. Even for back then, I think they might have been dated in style and appearance, but so much of the stuff in there is timeless. I really liked his romantic but unpretentious way of writing, and *Simple French Food*, Olney's seminal work on French cuisine, is just pure genius. After twelve-hour shifts in the Bay Wolf kitchen, I would hop on the train, open my copy, and be instantly transported to hilltop towns in Provence, where tables were filled end to end with platters of roasted whole fish, stews heavy with garlic, and chilled green beans with loads of shallots doused in effervescent red wine vinegar. It was magical.

I had every Chez Panisse book and used menus saved from the precious meals there as bookmarks. I read *The Physiology of Taste* by Jean-Anthelme Brillat-Savarin and visited his gravesite on a trip to Paris in the early 2000s. I scoured vintage bookstores for old copies of works by Elizabeth David. After devouring the River Cafe cookbooks, I tried to visualize that legendary dining room in London, imagining what it would be like to work with chefs Rose and Ruth. If you come into The Four Horsemen, you can see, right above the pass to the kitchen, a small shelf stuffed with cookbooks. They've always been such a big part of how and why I became a cook.

During my apprenticeship, a new kind of cuisine was attracting the attention of all my cooking peers. This style was a world apart from regional market–driven cooking. A Catalan chef by the name of Ferran Adrià and his restaurant, elBulli, perched on a seaside cliff in Roses, Spain, was, by the sound of things, doing for cooking what Picasso and his pals had done for painting. Like every other ambitious young cook, I wanted to be part of his and his brother Albert's small army of stagiaires. So, in 2004, I found a number and faxed (yes, faxed) a CV and cover letter to Ferran, asking to work a season at elBulli.

I never heard back. It was sobering. It felt like Europe was out of reach. Trying to shake off my first, small defeat, I worked at a mom-and-pop putting out solid food, nothing too creative. I did some catering at a local winery in the East Bay, cooked tapas in Berkeley, and held down a few stations at another humble place in Danville.

I sound like a grumpy old man saying this, but I think young cooks now are lucky to have access to so much information about restaurants and chefs online. You can find a phone number or an email address for just about any place in the world in a few seconds—or just DM the chef you want to work for; I get messages all the time. That contact may be harder to parlay into a position, for sure, but after my fax vanished into the Spanish ether, I really felt like I had hit an informational dead end. How could I get my foot in the door at a restaurant abroad? If not with Ferran Adrià in Spain, then how about Pascal Barbot or Alain Passard in France? I wasn't asking for so much! I just wanted to work at any of the most lauded restaurants in the world! Or at least try to cook somehow, somewhere in Europe.

In 2006, on a night off from cooking, I joined my parents for a special dinner at one of their favorite places: chef Suzette Gresham's Acquerello in San Francisco. That evening, she had brought in Fulvio Siccardi from Italy to present his Northern Italian classics—preparations like vitello tonnato, agnolotti dal plin, carne cruda, sformato di cardi, gnocchi with fonduta. It was incredible. At the end of the meal, I walked up to him and asked flat out if I could come work for him and his wife at Conti Roero, their Michelin-starred restaurant in Monticello d'Alba. To my surprise, he said yes.

In keeping with tradition, I was remarkably underqualified for the position. In Italy, I had expected to cook with tomatoes, seafood, light herbs, and plenty of olive oil. Instead, we used butter, cheese, wild game, truffles, mushrooms, and other hallmarks of hearty mountain food. The preparations were incredibly detailed, yet still seemed simple. This was the most challenging time in my cooking career, as I was completely out of my depth and scrambling to keep up with the work in that kitchen. Six days and eighty hours a week. By the end of my time at Conti Roero, I had lost thirty pounds and gained lessons in cooking that would change my life. And I had made it to Europe.

Taking the opportunity to travel a bit around Liguria, Lombardy, and Valle d'Aosta, I realized that the cuisines of each were profoundly different, despite what looked like their close proximities on the map. This type of regional specificity isn't unique to Italy, of course. You can see this in almost every other country. But it was a revelation to me, and I was impressed by the focus on high-quality seasonal ingredients and a solid technique above everything else.

RUSS

When I returned to the Bay Area in 2007, I brought a lot of this thinking back with me. I wanted to make simple, well-executed food. Intense fussiness, particularly the now pejoratively dubbed "tweezer food" I had once dreamed of studying, became far less appealing to me (maybe it was some sour grapes after my lone, imploring fax went unanswered, Ferran!).

My timing was pretty lucky as I found the ideal job as part of the opening team of Camino in Oakland. Russell Moore, the chef, had worked at Chez Panisse for years and was branching out on his own. Virtually all the cooking at Camino was done using wood-burning sources of heat; a massive hearth and a wood-burning oven were the heart of the restaurant. Primal, timeless—and, ironically, ahead of its time, considering the wave of restaurants of this style that would follow.

Russ had great respect for sourcing. His understanding of each and every vegetable that came in through the door was inspiring. Russ also taught me a great deal about leadership. During an era in which machismo and swashbuckling were the norm, and many forms of harassment were commonplace—a given, really—in kitchens, Russ was entirely different. He opened my eyes to the weaknesses of the screaming chef, and the strength of respectful calm. I consider myself very lucky to have had this lesson relatively early in my cooking career.

In 2010, after almost three amazing years at Camino and nearly three decades in California, I needed a change. I felt like I needed to test myself, to see if I could cut it with the best cooks in the world in one of the greatest restaurant cities. I decided to pack my bags and head to New York. I wish I could say that I was been full of confidence on that move away from my home state. I was more than nervous. Maybe it's part of being young and wanting to do something with your life, but I felt like everything was a stake, and I had no idea how it would go.

HERE IS NEW YORK

I hopped around and did trials at about a dozen restaurants. They all had one thing in common: At some point in the experience, another cook would tell me that I needed to eat at Franny's, a Neapolitan pizzeria on Flatbush Avenue in Park Slope, Brooklyn. Franny's was, in fact, much more than a pizzeria. At this hole-in-the-wall in the heart of Brooklyn, two chefs who had trained at places like Per Se and Alain Ducasse were using those skills and produce from some of the region's best farms to make food in the tradition of Alice Waters and Judy Rodgers, two of my heroes. For a West Coast kid, it was a perfect fit.

I worked every station at Franny's. The pasta cooks oversaw six boiling baskets of noodles, which they finished on a blazing-hot French flattop. It was New York summer, and I was sweating in a completely new way, filling my shoes, salt lines making map coastlines on all my shirts after every service. But those pastas were some of the most delicious I'd ever made: maccheroni with sausages, loaded with fennel and caciocavallo cheese; chewy bucatini cacio e pepe; paccheri, roasted swordfish, and summer peppers. While on garde-manger, I put out crostini slathered with ramp butter, draped in housemade pancetta; pea shoots tossed in Meyer lemon juice and covered with salty ricotta salata cheese; sections of golden citrus laced with fermented peppers and swimming in Sicilian olive oil. Then, of course, there was the pizza. My favorite was a provolone pie topped with charred onions that had been prepared in the wood-burning oven. Crowned with juicy, briny olives, it was otherworldly.

I was comfortable there. So much so that one day I woke up and realized it had been two years since my move to New York. I took some time off to travel, get reinspired—Copenhagen, Amsterdam, Paris, and Rome. I did some required eating at lauded destinations like Relæ and Arpège, but I also ate at equally inspiring, lesser-known restaurants. In Umbria, I ate lamb sausages prepared over an ancient grill by a nonna with forearms as thick as my legs. In Rome, I drank house wine and ate fried salt cod on paper tablecloths. In Amsterdam, I slurped down herring with friends after a long night of Heinekens (which do, actually, taste way better in Amsterdam). I also ate at some smaller, remarkable places with adventurous young chefs, food, service, all of which were so different than the places I'd known in New York and California. Somewhere between the local haunt and the wait up all night to get a reservation in three months places. These were very interesting to me.

A CHANCE MEETING, AND A TERRIBLE IDEA

When I got back to New York, I did odd jobs. I helped friends open restaurants, cooked in pop-ups—spun my wheels a bit. It was frustrating. I didn't just want to wind up with the same type of job as I had when I left town. I wanted to build something of my own, assemble a team, try out some of the things I'd learned on my travels. But I couldn't see any clear path to get from where I was to where I wanted to be.

My wife, Sara, got a tip from an industry friend: Some folks she knew were looking to hire a head chef for this restaurant they were opening in Brooklyn, and she had put my name forward. This was promising, as her friend Anna Polonsky was pretty tuned in, and she vouched for the new owners.

Of course, there's always a catch. These people weren't restaurateurs. They didn't even work in the industry. One of them was a known musician, which made me kind of nervous. I wanted the next thing I did to be real. I didn't want to open some PR flash in the pan that petered out when a bunch amateurs lost interest in their new toy. But I was also curious.

RECIPE LIST

A BOWL OF...

SEAFOOD

MEAT

CONTINUED

DESSERT

YOUR ESSENTIALS: CONDIMENTS, DRESSINGS, PICKLES + MORE

NOTES ABOUT THE RECIPES

unless otherwise noted:

All olive oil is high-quality extra-virgin.

We use two types of salt at the restaurant: kosher salt and Maldon sea salt. As a general rule, kosher is for seasoning most things, including stocks, dressings, meats, and fish before cooking. Maldon is used for finishing.

All cream is heavy whipping cream.

All onions are medium Spanish onions.

All eggs are large.

Sugar is granulated.

Black pepper is always freshly ground from a pepper mill.

All herbs are fresh. All herbs are washed according to the guidelines on page 48.

All parsley is the flat-leaf Italian variety.

All fish in this book is sashimi grade, even if it's cooked.

All beef, chicken, pork, and large eggs are from sustainable sources whose farms practice ethical treatment of animals. They're all pasture raised and antibiotic and hormone free.

All mentions of "Parm" refer to Parmigiano-Reggiano cheese, not parmesan.

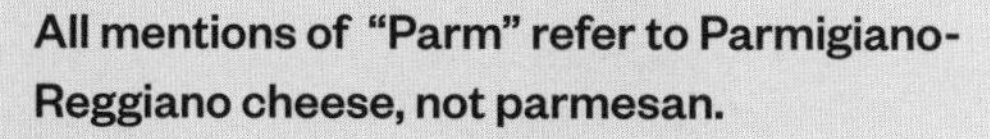

"Taste and adjust" is used a lot in this book. It generally means to taste the recipe at the point to which you've prepared it and decide if the flavors are to your liking, then, if the dish isn't quite right for you, adjusting the seasoning as needed. I'm mostly referring to salt and acid here.

I highly encourage you to use the metric measurements provided in this book, as they are more precise and consistent with what we use at the restaurant. Imperial measures, especially by volume, are less exact, so there may be some slight variations in the equivalents provided for the same ingredient from recipe to recipe. This is especially true for small amounts of food or very light foods such as salt, spices, and herbs.

Home ovens are generally less precise and powerful than commercial equipment. I encourage you to spend a few dollars on an oven thermometer and see how yours lines up, since even a 10- to 15-degree (Fahrenheit) difference can mess up a recipe. Also, the cooking times in this book reflect the conditions at The Four Horsemen and in my home kitchen, so think of them more as guidelines than gospel. As always, use your common sense and understanding of your own appliances when judging whether something is "done" or not.

When deep-frying, as noted on page 70, never leave the stove unattended. Be careful when lowering foods, especially those with a high moisture content, into hot oil. Never just drop anything into hot oil, unless you like weird oil-burn scars on your forearms.

INGREDIENTS TO KEEP CLOSE BY

Throughout this book, I go into deep dives on what I believe are absolute essentials—olive oil (page 142), vinegar (page 136), salt (page 108), black pepper (page 91), and garlic (page 176). Here I'll briefly lay out some of the other critical basics.

unsalted butter

I always keep a nice block of demi-sel (lightly salted) cultured butter at home for toast and whatnot, but for cooking, stick with the unsalted. This makes it easier to control the amount of salt in a finished dish. I typically go for Kerrygold, but that might have something to do with my wife being Irish.

whole spices

Using whole spices will make you throw out a lot of your pre-ground stuff. A simple pounding with the mortar and pestle or a quick turn of a spice grinder, and you've got a fresh rub for grilled chicken or roasted carrots. Whole spices are essential to building flavor. In addition to black peppercorns, coriander, cumin, and fennel make a great foundation. Do your best to keep them as fresh as possible. When you buy new ones, maybe use a little piece of tape to label each container with its purchase date. Once you've hit the one-year mark or there's dust on the cap, just get rid of them. They won't kill you, but they will have lost their best flavor.

cheeses

My home fridge is generally stocked with some Parmigiano-Reggiano for pastas and salads; a nice salty sheep's-milk cheese or two, like Manchego and pecorino di fossa; some crowd-pleasing aged Gouda; a soft Brie-style cheese; and maybe some feta that I can use for a quick marinade. Heading into the weekend, getting a ball or two of burrata isn't a bad idea, especially to accompany grilled asparagus in the summertime or roasted mushrooms in the fall. Right there you have snacks, salads, and antipasti covered.

chiles

I have a serious affinity for balanced heat. If you do as well, look for a few different types of chiles: dried New Mexicos are nice and neutral, with chocolaty notes, while dried chiles de árbol pack a punch. Calabrian chiles are another spicy variety; at the restaurant, we buy them in pickled form, preserved in oil, and they bring a vibrant, moderate heat to plenty of dishes in this book. Yuzu kosho is a chile-based condiment from Japan that balances salty umami with pungent citrus. Fresh chiles like jalapeño, Thai (bird's-eye), and serrano are all great for an instant dose of spiciness.

citrus

Often when we're getting ready to add a new dish to the menu and we know it's not quite there yet, a small amount of lemon will get it where it needs to be. That brightness and fresh, electrifying acidity shouldn't be underestimated. Lemon pairs well with a remarkably wide range of foods: a squeeze to finish a buttery bottarga-rich pasta, a few drops on a delicate seafood crudo, a simple wedge to accompany a bowl of crispy fried squid. In addition to lemons, I also like to have oranges, limes, and yuzu on hand whenever they're available. You can try to add citrus when something isn't focused enough. And use the zest as well. There are so many essential oils in there—you can see them mist into the air when you bend the peel of an orange. At The Horsemen, we try to use the entire fruit; with this one item you can push a dish in so many different directions.

fish sauce

At the restaurant, I stock four types of fish sauce. Maybe it's a bit overkill, but for me, very few single ingredients add the kind of complexity to so many dishes that fish sauce brings. It's ridiculously delicious and builds flavor in a dish so easily that using it can feel a bit like you're cheating. Modern fish sauce, primarily made from fermented anchovies, can be traced back to the garums of ancient Rome, so that's pretty cool, too.

Fish sauce is a dominant flavor in the cuisines of Southeast Asia, where it shines against loads of herbs and ingredients like lemongrass, ginger, lime, and fresh chiles. It's thankfully much easier to find in stores today than it was only a few years ago. If I had to pick one brand, I'd go with Three Crabs from Thailand; it's the fish sauce on my shelf at home. You get roundness, richness, and a most pleasant salinity. Colatura di alici is another great option, if you can find it. It's made in Italy and is a little subtler than other varieties.

fresh herbs

I kind of fell in love with fresh herbs during my time at Camino many years ago. Anise hyssop, lovage, sorrel, fig leaves, chervil, savory: I'd never even heard of some of those until I worked there. I also found a renewed respect for the classics—mint, cilantro, parsley, basil, chives, tarragon. I can't imagine cooking without them now.

It's funny to train new cooks at the restaurant, because they often don't believe me when I tell them to add more herbs—

then more, and more, and more. Handfuls, really. When we use them in a dish, it's with purpose; they're one of the stars. Somewhere along the way, it feels like herbs got relegated to bit parts: playing the garnish or "adding a bit of color" to a plate. But they're one of the most compelling and powerful tools in cooking. Especially when making simple, light, fresh food.

I recommend cleaning your herbs just as you get them home, so they'll be ready to use when you need them. Let them sit in plenty of cold water (no ice!) for about 5 minutes, agitating gently now and then to remove sand and grit. Carefully scoop them out with your fingertips and transfer them to a salad spinner. Make sure not to crowd them. Give them a light spin or two, ditch the water in the spinner bowl, then spin again. Lay the herbs out onto a sheet tray lined with a tea towel and allow to dry for about 10 minutes. Transfer them to paper towels, roll them up carefully, and store the whole lot in a zip-top bag in the fridge, where they can last for a week or more. Put them in one of those little drawers, or "crispers,", if your fridge has one.

And, depending on what kind of fridge you have, you may be able to control the humidity of its crisper to better preserve produce. General rule of thumb: High humidity is the optimal environment for ingredients prone to wilting, like herbs, greens, and thin-skinned vegetables. Low humidity is best for ingredients prone to rotting, like apples and pitted fruits.

really nice anchovies

I never disliked anchovies. I was one of the weird kids who wanted them on their pizza. Over the past couple of decades, more Americans have come around to their briny, complex power, and we're the better for it. When I say "nice" anchovies, I'm talking specifically about hand-filleted fish that have been packed in sea salt and then preserved in olive oil. The best examples, in my opinion, come from the Bay of Biscay in Northern Spain, and in particular from the Cantabrian Sea. They'll run you anywhere from $10 to $40 per tin (or jar) but are worth it; I always have a couple of tins in my pantry. Anchovies make a delicious low-labor snack, paired with olives and salty cheese, and they're also great on sandwiches and in pastas and salads. And pizza. They're still brilliant on pizza. Look for the Don Bocarte and Ortiz brands, as they're made the correct way.

canned tomatoes

A few cans of San Marzano tomatoes can save you when you're scrambling. They provide a solid base for a bunch of really good impromptu meals (like a puttanesca: Just fry some onions, anchovies, garlic, and olives, and quickly cook with those San Marzanos and their juices). Soups, eggplant parm, chili, and lasagna all benefit from the bright flavor of tinned tomatoes. The true Italian ones from Campania are phenomenal, and are crucial to Vera Pizza Napoletana, but Bianco DiNapoli out of California is a great organic brand.

canola oil

Besides olive oil, the only other oil I keep around is organic canola oil. I use it mostly for searing and deep-frying, due to its higher smoke point.

THE TOOLS

As cooks working in professional kitchens, we have a lot of tools at our disposal. At home, my setup is simpler. Here's my best shot at a list of most used things, from basics to some more complex and pricier "next level" tools that, if you invest in them, will last you years.

1. A sturdy **silicone spatula**. I recommend GIR: Get It Right brand. Theirs never break or crack.
2. A 6-inch (15 cm) **spider**. A spider is a skimming basket attached to a wooden or metal handle. They're cheap and incredibly useful, but home cooks rarely have them. Thank me later.
3. A solid pair of **metal tongs**. Sizing tongs can get a bit Goldilocks—too long, and they're tough to control; too short, and you burn yourself trying to grab hot food. Get something sturdy and about 8 inches (20 cm) long, or whatever length feels just right for your arm. I like the ones with the locking mechanisms, so they're not always splayed open in your drawer. Avoid silicone-tipped tongs; they're often too slippery for gripping food.
4. A **fish spatula**. A slotted fish spatula with a wooden handle serves a somewhat specific purpose, sure, but you'll reach for it more often than you'd think.
5. A good **balloon whisk**. I like an ergonomic handle with stiff metal tines. Again, avoid the silicone-tipped models—just go classic. Ten to twelve inches (25 to 30 cm) long should be fine. The short ones look cute, but they don't really do the job, unless they're for a toddler to "help" with.
6. A small fine-mesh **strainer** with a lip. I use one of these almost daily for straining small amounts of pasta and vegetables. The little lip makes it easy to rest it on a bowl or pot.
7. A nice pair of **kitchen scissors**. I prefer Joyce Chen brand. They are razor sharp and come in a load of different colors, if you like that sort of thing.
8. Plastic and metal **bench scrapers**. Get one of each. They're ideal for scooping up items and transferring them from cutting boards to bowls. They're also effective for cutting pasta shapes like gnocchi, or even cleaning a counter or workstation: Scrub the surface with a wet, soapy sponge, then use the bench scraper to pull the water toward the edge of the counter and into a trash receptacle.

on knives

Please don't bother buying a shiny, ten-piece knife set in a wooden block for $1,000. Just buy three good knives that fit well in your hand. Get a paring/petty knife, a chef's knife, and a serrated bread knife.

Korin has a beautiful store here in New York City (and, like everything now, online) with affordable knives from a host of different reputable brands. Our more junior cooks lean toward Korin's own Suisin line. Bernal Cutlery in San Francisco and Japanese Knife Imports in Los Angeles are also great resources.

In general, I'm a staunch advocate of Japanese steel knives; the blades are made from quality steel and shaped and honed by artisans who take serious pride in their work. I also prefer the more ergonomic and less common Eastern handle to the more familiar Western style you'll find on most German and American knives. The flat sides of the Eastern style make it easier to control for me, while a Western handle tends to feel a bit more slippery and bulky and can roll in your grip.

If it's possible, go handle a few knives in person. It's important to buy knives that are comfortable to hold, in a length that doesn't feel awkward to manage. Whatever knives you get, keep them sharp. Find a decent kitchenware shop that can do this for you, or, if you're up for it, buy a couple of whetstones and watch some YouTube videos about sharpening by hand. Once you get acclimated, it can almost be a form of meditation, to be honest. Also, a few quick strokes on a ceramic honing steel will help maintain the blade in between sharpenings.

microplane brand graters

At home, I mostly use their fine rasp graters, ideal for zesting citrus and grating things like garlic as well as hard spices like nutmeg and cinnamon. Use the wider ribbon graters when you want to cover salad (like the Celery Salad on page 151) with soft cheeses, or for grating vegetables and fruits to a pulpy yet uniform consistency. They're cheap and sturdy, and I would have a tough time cooking without them. Buy a couple. And use the entire length to ensure they wear evenly.

wooden cutting board

Ditch the plastic ones and avoid the glass and hard bamboo varieties. All of these will just dull your knives. Look for a thick, butcher-block-style wooden cutting board. John Boos & Co. is kind of the go-to in this category. Avoid anything thinner than 1 inch (2.5 cm), as it'll be more likely to warp over time.

Never wash wooden cutting boards in the dishwasher; hand wash with soapy water and dry well before storing away. Every few weeks, put a little mineral oil on a towel and rub it over the dry cutting board in the direction of the wood's grain, then let the oil soak in before using the board again. This prevents the board from splintering, extending its life by years.

digital scale

Get a scale. Blah blah blah, "my grandmother didn't have a scale," blah blah blah. Just get a scale. If it was for just baking alone I'd argue that you have to get one. But it's not. If you want to cook good food consistently, you just need a scale. Five different people will likely measure "1 cup flour" five different ways, yielding totally different amounts. With weight, there's simply less room for error. Look for a digital model that can toggle between ounces and grams and register weights up to a few pounds.

suribachi and surikogi

The suribachi and surikogi are Japan's answer to the stone and olive-wood mortars and pestles (respectively) that you'll find in other parts of the world. Made of ceramic with fine grooves running throughout the suribachi, these things are ideal for pounding garlic to an even paste, crushing spices, and smashing herbs. We use ours every day to make infused oils, marinades, and sauces.

pepper mill

Look for a model that lets you easily adjust the coarseness of the grind. A lot of models are adjustable by means of a bolt on top. Better mills (like the Peugeot u'Select) are adjusted with a robust rotating ring at the bottom that is just more consistent, in my experience. Plastic pepper mills have a tendency to crack, so stick to wood and look for one that's about 7 inches (18 cm) tall. A small hand grinder made for coffee, like a Timemore Chestnut, can also work well.

towels

Buy a few soft tea towels for herbs and salad greens to rest on as they dry. Also, get a stack of ten or so thick, white kitchen towels. They're a critical restaurant staple that carries over very well to the home. Cooks always have a couple tucked into our apron strings, plus more on our stations. They're landing pads for hot pots and pans, quick spill catchers, and the best oven mitts. Don't mess with the silicone oven gloves: They make gripping dangerous and nearly impossible. Just use a dry kitchen towel folded over a couple of times. These things will get dirty, cleaned, dirty again, and wind up looking a bit ragged eventually, but even the very old ones will prove useful. They kind of do everything.

sheet trays and wire racks

Look for the quarter-sheet (13 by 9-inch / 33 by 23 cm) and half-sheet (18 by 13-inch / 46 by 33 cm) sizes of sheet tray, as these are best suited for home ovens. Beyond cooking with them, you can also marinate, season, and organize your mise en place with them. Try to get wire racks in sizes that fit your sheet trays, also. Use these racks for cooling cakes and pies, as well as resting meats (see page 258) to create airflow and prevent overcooking. They also serve as landing zones for various blanching, braising, and roasting projects, helping to keep your workspace clean. Get a few of each.

salad spinner

Unsung hero. Mueller makes my favorite. It has a little pull handle and makes quick work of wicking the water out of delicate greenery without beating up the leaves. Ours stands up to daily restaurant use, so it should last a home cook years. I'd avoid the ones with a rope you have to pull. Also, the type with a push mechanism in the center gets the job done, but isn't ideal—too fussy.

For how to handle your spun leaves, please read cleaning salad greens and herbs (page 48).

spice grinder

Basically, it's a coffee grinder. But get a cheap plug-in one dedicated to grinding spices only. You don't want your herbs to taste like coffee, and you don't want your coffee to taste like a bunch of toasted cumin and coriander. After each use, just wipe out the hopper and lid with a damp towel. I prefer the ones with a removable hopper, which makes it easier to transfer spices. I use one by Bodum at home; it's really reliable. Every now and then I just buzz some dry rice or stale bread to really clean out the nooks and crannies. If you don't want another appliance on your counter, just get a solid hand coffee grinder, like you might for black pepper (see page 51). They're pretty inexpensive and can fit easily in a drawer.

digital thermometer

Get a good pen-style digital thermometer. Lavatools makes one called Javelin that's really solid. Remember to test its accuracy every now and then by sticking it in a big glass of ice water. It should hover around 32°F (0°C). If it registers off that mark, it's time to recalibrate.

carbon-steel pan

If you wonder how restaurants get impeccable sears on crispy-skinned fish, or how professionals turn out steaks with those beautifully even mahogany crusts, the answer is usually a carbon-steel pan. They're cheap and durable. In addition to your heavy, expensive stainless pan that you don't really want to blast with that much heat, get one of these.

When you buy a new pan, make sure to season it following the manufacturer's instructions; the more you use the pan, the better seasoned it will become. To clean it, don't use soap, which can remove all the seasoning you worked for. Instead, dump in ¼ cup (40 g) kosher salt and rub it over the surface with an old kitchen towel (see? old towels . . .) to naturally scour and clean the pan, then rinse and immediately dry. It's really not much more work than scrubbing a pan with soap, and the extra effort is worth it. We use de Buyer carbon-steel pans at the restaurant; they're a classic for a reason.

a good peeler

Avoid anything gimmicky with serrated blades or a "perfect for asparagus" slogan. We go for Kuhn Rikon Y-shaped Swiss peelers, which have the most comfortable feel and comically simple design. They're incredibly versatile and a real workhorse in the kitchen. They're also crazy cheap and come in different colors.

parchment paper

A roll of parchment paper is great for baking cookies and for lining pans for cakes (like the Burnt Cheesecake on page 295). I also like to line sheet trays with parchment so foods don't take on any metallic flavors from the pan as they cook; ingredients high in acid, like tomatoes and marinated meats, are particularly susceptible. During summer months, we store fruits and vegetables on parchment sheets at room temperature to allow them to ripen further. You can also sift flour onto a sheet of parchment and then use it to transfer the flour to your mixer, avoiding spills.

SOME MORE ADVANCED STUFF

japanese mandoline

This is basically a single-beveled blade in the middle of a plank that allows you to cut very thin, even slices of fruits and vegetables. These things aren't expensive, but totally a pro move. Benriner has been my go-to for years. Beyond pretty knife cuts, a mandoline can help you with gratins, coleslaw, and shredded-vegetable salads, as well as photo-perfect rounds of radish and cucumber. A real time-saver. Warning, though—that blade is sharp, and a cheaply made mandoline can be a real fingertip modifier. Look for metal- or hard, rigid plastic-framed ones, and avoid anything made with thin and cheap plastic.

rice cooker

Please just make your rice in a rice cooker. Don't get worked up thinking you should make this particular item "by hand." We've had a Zojirushi unit at the restaurant since day one. Many family meals have been cooked with it, and I can fully endorse it. Do some research and see what fits your budget. And try to find a model that can cook a few different types of rice—long grain, sushi, brown, etc.

dutch oven

They're expensive. Super heavy. And they're totally worth it. A Dutch oven is far and away my most used pot at home. I've had the same one for years, and I really like how this worn-looking thing works exactly as well as it did the day I bought it. These lidded and (typically) enamel coated cast-iron workhorses cook evenly and stand up to high heat on the stovetop or in the oven. If you're only springing for one size, I'd suggest getting something in the 5- to 8-quart (5 to 8 L) range with the enamel finish. Le Creuset and Staub both make iconic versions that are built like tanks. There are also newer, flashier brands hitting the market—these are generally a bit cheaper. Nothing against them, but I haven't felt the need to deviate from the originals.

blender

Invest in a good high-speed blender. They're great for making sauces, purées, sorbets, and salad dressings. Beyond that, you'll get to drink the smoothest smoothies and milkshakes at home. Vitamix is the benchmark and worth the price tag if you'll be using it often, but Breville also makes a nice budget-friendly option.

food processor

Though not the ideal tool for delicate tasks (see Japanese mandoline . . .), a food processor makes quick work of chopping. And if you're looking to make something like hummus or romesco sauce, or even mayonnaise, from scratch, this thing will save you. I have a Breville model that came with all the gadgets: a really excellent multipurpose machine. It has these brilliant grating blade attachments—perfect for shredding cheeses, which means you can make dishes like lasagna and mac and cheese quickly without resorting to stale store-bought shredded cheese. And there's no reason to dread the cleanup: It's all dishwasher safe. Just a quick rinse and you're basically done. The parts just go in the dishwasher, so you won't hate yourself for using it.

stand mixer

My standard wedding-gift KitchenAid always works. If you're going with another brand, make sure you get one that has the dough hook, whisk, and paddle attachments. If you're doing a lot of baking, a stand mixer is indispensable. In addition to breads and pasta doughs, they're great for whipping cream, meringues, custards, and batters. You can buy attachments for rolling out and cutting sheets of pasta, grinding meat, even making ice cream. KitchenAid is the market leader for a reason—I've had one of mine at The Four Horsemen for seven years, and it's still plugging away after all that restaurant abuse.

a wood-burning grill

Humans like food cooked over live coals. The flavors are elevated and comforting at the same time. Absolutely Proustian. As an added bonus, your hands will smell like barbecue for hours.

Gas grills might seem easier, but if you know what you're doing, you can get a wood-burning grill ripping hot quicker. At The Four Horsemen, we use konro grills: tiny Japanese brick grills that fit in our comically small kitchen. At home, I use the Big Green Egg, which I can no longer imagine living without. For more details on wood-fired cooking, see page 230.

BULLES
TAVEL 2019
GOYO GARCIA MALVASIA
+
GOYO GARCIA ALBILLO+MALV
GLUCK
FREUDE
EX VERO III
MAXIME MAGNON CUVEE ROSE
+
16 VACCELLI
LARROUYAT JURANCON SEC
+
GIACOMETTI LE VIN COULE
WERLITSCH EX VERO
II
6 x 750 ml
NOT SELL
17 BARRAL FAGERES JADIS
+
TROUILLIER GUERILLEROS
PET NAT
CARTEROLE 'ESTA FETE'
+
MOSSE CAB FRANC
DO NOT SELL
HYDROPHOBIA
+
L'ENCLOS DES BRAVAS 'DURAS'EN..'
BRUYERE-HOUILLON
18 TROUSSEAU
19 PLOUSSARD
BERNADEAU
20 ONGLES
DO NOT SELL

WE ARE HERE TO DO THE THING

Throughout this book, I'll try to explain our approach to wine at The Four Horsemen while offering ideas and tips for drinking at home that have served me well over the years. This is not the *Oxford Companion to Wine*. This is a series of sections about seeking out, enjoying, and sharing wine written from the point of view of somebody who believes that the best way to learn about wine is by drinking it, preferably with other people. Hopefully this story will give you a sense of what I mean.

The first time James and I went to Racines in Paris, the restaurant was still operated by cofounder Pierre Jancou and opening chef Sven Chartier, two legendary figures in the bistronomy movement that started sweeping through France in the early 2000s. This will probably sound ridiculous, but the second I walked into that tiny dining room in the Passage des Panoramas, I knew it was where we needed to be. It felt like a Parisian Marlow & Sons, our Williamsburg haunt: full of charm yet super serious; a couple of guys in the kitchen with heads down, and servers who squeezed in between tables while cradling bottles of wine I'd never seen before.

While I waited for James to arrive, sommelier Ewan Lemoigne dropped a bottle of Andréa Calek's Blonde on the table. It's the first Calek vintage where the wine was still *pétillant* (or slightly bubbly), with just a little residual sugar. It was the PERFECT aperitif. A few minutes later, James walked in and sat down. I poured him a glass. Scanning the room, not saying a word, he smiled a very big smile. Then he just started to laugh. It is something hard to describe, but our friend Garrett Oliver refers to moments like these as "We came to do the thing." You could be the most domineering, OCD person on Earth and yet you instantly relinquish control and let the staff drive. Instead of opening the wine list, you ask your server, "What have you been drinking lately? Also, should we just order everything?"

Over the years, we've walked into many restaurants as strangers and walked out the door an absurd number of hours later as friends. The first time I went to Le Verre Vole in Paris I asked the server, "Is there anywhere else in this city where we can get food and wine like this?" He wrote me a list of restaurants and wine shops on the back of a receipt. Fifteen years later, I still go to some of them.

Nothing blows our minds more than knowing that The Four Horsemen is one of those spots that gets scribbled on the back of a receipt, a place where a good number of people have found that they can come in the door and just do the thing.

One thing we aren't going to do at the restaurant, or in this book, is try to teach you what you shouldn't drink. I've witnessed servers at some places laugh at a guest because of the wine they've asked for. To be honest, I used to admire that in the same way I had admired record-store clerks whose respect you had to earn by self-immolation. We decided very early on that we did not want to be confrontational. We don't hit people over the head with dogma, because dogma is no fun, and we don't roll our eyes when your mother-in-law asks for an oaky California chardonnay. We will totally find her an oaky California chardonnay.

I don't want anybody thinking that the following recommendations are hard and fast rules in any way.

Bianchino
SUCCÉS
BIM

GET SOME CANDLES BY AMANDA MCMILLAN

When I moved from Oklahoma to New York in the early aughts, I had only ever been to dive bars, "fancy" white-tablecloth restaurants, chains, and places with decent food and comic sans menus. I'd never even visited New York before. I had $1,000 in my bank account, and I thought I was rich.

At a bar around the corner from my Williamsburg apartment, I sat and had a late dinner by myself. Watching strangers eat, in a cozy room where every element was considered without being overly designed or fussy—this idea that every element in a restaurant could be compelling, the idea that dinner is the night out—I was just in complete awe. On that first night, I ate a perfect steak au poivre with a side of thoughtfully cooked greens. I had a glass of gamay, and a little chocolate pot de crème. In my mind, I feel like Neil Young's *On the Beach* played in its entirety as I ate. The bartender was cool, wearing his own clothes, not some weird uniform. The room felt like someone's home, someone with taste I could relate to. The lights were very, very low. It was a party, and it was dinner.

I ended up working at that place for years.

All of this is to say that when I started as general manager at The Four Horsemen, having already been there for a delicious dinner, I wanted to make it more of a party.

The first, and in my opinion biggest, contribution I ever made was to bring in candles. It's *incredible* how vital candles are to creating a vibe. It's so stupid to even say this, so obvious, but I can't tell you how many times I've gone to a restaurant that didn't have candles and just died inside. *Would it kill them to put some candles around?* When I have people over to my house, I always, always have candles. They make everything one hundred times dreamier, every time. You can serve chips and a can of Coke. If you light some candles, it's suddenly a romantic moment. Or the perfect setting for a good conversation.

The second thing I did right away as general manager was pack the room. When The Four Horsemen first opened, it was kind of a taboo to take reservations at a semicasual Brooklyn place. Almost everything around here was walk-in only. This meant you could maybe be a little spontaneous about your dinner plans, sure, but also that you'd sometimes find yourself waiting two hours to eat a piece of chicken. One real drawback I noticed about taking reservations was that your tables could sit empty between parties. I hate an empty seat; empty seats feel sad. So I tightened the turn times and packed the bookings so that, ideally, people would arrive right around the time the diners before them were paying their check. It's a risky way to live, but I think it's better. I personally don't mind waiting a minute or two for my table if the room feels right. It certainly beats being stuck eating dinner in a half-empty room at 7:30 p.m. Woof. It's a high-wire act, and the pressure is on, but that just gives you more reason to really pay attention . . . to take especially good care of everyone—the people finishing their meal, and the new ones arriving, ready to begin.

When considering how I got here and what we really do at The Four Horsemen, I thought a lot about what hosting a dinner entails and what makes an experience exceptional. I thought back to special days in my life. I thought about what really is the difference between a party, a holiday, and a dinner: Thanksgiving is a holiday because you have a special meal of things you probably only eat once a year (at least all on one plate!). Halloween is a holiday because you wear a crazy outfit. But so were the evenings when my mom would make breakfast for dinner. Sometimes, in my apartment, I will eat berries out of a very pretty, fancy bowl, and the difference between the fancy bowl and a regular bowl gives the act of eating berries a feeling of *occasion*.

Ultimately, what makes a dining experience, or any experience, memorable and special is incorporating as many elements as possible that are, in and of themselves, memorable and special.

My job is to try to tie those special things together. When we hit all the marks—the way the servers move around the room, pulling the perfect bottle for a guest, the menu on point and full of dishes we're excited to share, and how those dishes hit the table at the perfect pace, in the perfect sequence, where you want to dip in a bit of this to sop up a bit of that. Against the window, the fresh flowers are bringing just the right color and cheer, just as someone walks in, waves across the room at their friend, the music and lights working together to fill the space with warmth, the interactions in the room feeling effortless and lighthearted, whether meaningful conversation, or just some juicy gossip—it's magical. We try very hard to make every dinner here a holiday of sorts. And, of course, a party. A very nice house party.

295

TRUST THE WINE

When I started writing the list at The Four Horsemen, I was more concerned with representing winemakers and regions that I loved than with how those wines would work with Nick's food. I had never worked in a restaurant and didn't think about these things, which now are pretty obvious. As Nick and his team have evolved, so have my ideas about what wines are best for the table. Our salads can feature pretty assertive vinegars. There can be a fair amount of chile and citrus on the menu at a given time. Our desserts aren't just sweet—even the Basque cheesecake has a glug of sherry vinegar poured over it to cut the sugar. A lot of these twists and turns can make the traditional idea of wine pairings seem difficult, at least at first.

Nick's food doesn't stick to any specific regional ideas. It's very normal at The Four Horsemen for there to be a dish that leans toward Japan, one that leans toward the Mediterranean, and another with spices from North Africa all landing on the table at once. So where does that leave us when we talk about pairing wine with our food? It's best to zoom out and look at the meal as a whole. We tend to prefer wines with higher acidity, lower alcohol, and a sense of place in a wide range of styles, without geographic boundaries: very much in the same way our kitchen looks at food. A glass of sauvignon blanc from Styria can almost feel like two different wines as you switch between bites of Pan con Tomate (page 110) and Sugar Snap Peas with Calabrian Chile (page 138), but seamlessly work with them both.

And while I was hesitant at first, I've fully come around to the merits and pleasures of orange wines. Why was I skeptical? So many of them tasted alike, and it just seemed too trendy. I've since tasted many great examples, and they've become a core part of our wine list. The tannins, textures, and aromatics from the right white grape that has been fermented on its skins can work across an entire meal in ways that so many others can't match—from raw fish with a bit of heat and wild greens dressed in lemon and shaved cheese all the way to a fried chicken covered in Marsala. I didn't believe it until I experienced it myself with a bottle of skin-contact Muscat de Alexandria and Macabeo from the Côtes Catalanes. It was a wine that worked effortlessly over an entire meal. Moments like that are always humbling, and a reminder that the way the wines work with the food can be about more than just the name on the label.

Sure, maybe we'll suggest a bright, lemony aligoté with our bread and cultured butter; a creamy roussanne or Sylvaner with a couple of years of bottle age to push back on the acid in the starters, or to drink alongside a fresh pasta dish. But we tend to like to keep the styles as broad as possible. Maybe you are enjoying a chilled, carbonically macerated grenache that tastes like farmers' market strawberries, while your friend is on her second glass of an earthy, old-vines Nerello Mascalese from Mount Etna—and you're both eating the same cider-glazed pork chop. Don't worry so much about the pairings. Trust the wine, but most importantly, trust yourself.

THE CLOSEST I'LL GET TO PAIRINGS, CHAPTER BY CHAPTER

FRIED SNACKS

It's been discussed a bunch in recent years, and with good reason: Sparkling wine and fried food is honestly one of the greatest combos. A high-acid, low-dosage grower Champagne cuts through the crunch and oil in Chicken Karaage (page 93); the bubbles refresh your palate between each bite. A pét-nat wine cools the heat from the chipotle-tomato jam on the Patatas Bravas (page 87) or the spice on the Crispy Squid with Pimentón de la Vera (page 82) in ways that a simple white wine can't touch.

BREAD AND TOAST

We like putting fresher-styled, light, slightly chilled reds on the table with toasts. Village level Beaujolais, carbonically macerated grenache from the Rhône Valley, or something like old-vines babić from Croatia all deliver a wonderful combination of fruit and freshness that works with the yeastiness in the breads, while balancing the oils and seasonings of the toppings. This is also a great moment for orange wine—a skin-macerated zibibbo from Sicily alongside the Ham and Cheese Sandwich (page 100) or the Braised Leek Toast (page 113) would be great.

SALADS AND VEGETABLES

When it comes to salads, it's best to talk about white wines that can compete with the strength of the vinegars. The wrong wine will just get buried. We like to recommend a bright, fresh sauvignon blanc from the Loire Valley to push back against the dressing, or the stone fruit and beeswax flavors of an albariño from Rías Baixas for similar contrast. This is also a great time to go back to that bottle of sparkling wine that's been sitting in the ice bucket since you served your guests some when they arrived.

A BOWL OF . . .

While this chapter covers a variety of flavor profiles, the majority of dishes have an Italian bent. I love the light tannins and blackberry in a barbera from Piedmont. It's the old "if it grows together, it goes together" cliché, but it works every time. But don't get yourself backed into the Italian corner—look at the base ingredients in the dish and go from there: bright, acidic wines from Greece with oily fish; deeper tannic reds from the Languedoc with braised meats and ragù; Burgundy wines from a cool vintage. Chances are, something you've already got at home is going to work out perfectly, especially if you have started your wine pantry (see page 298).

SEAFOOD

Seafood is one of the core elements of the menu at The Four Horsemen. As Nick will tell you, at certain times of the year, we're basically a fish restaurant. We love a classic pairing, like white Burgundy with Fried Skate (page 217 and page 220) or Boston Mackerel (page 227): The saltiness, obviously, matches the fish, while the acid reins in the richness of the oil. The citrus elements in wines from the Savoie, like those made from jacquère and altesse, have become a favorite pairing at the restaurant, especially with freshwater fish. But don't sleep on chilled reds or darker rosé wines. We love to put a carbonically macerated grenache or a wine made from cofermented white and red grapes alongside seafood dishes all day and night. The red fruits are balanced out by the acid being slightly more pronounced after chilling the wine, which makes for very easy drinking.

MEAT

I mostly drink lighter-styled red wines, but dishes like Steak au Poivre (page 261) and Beef Short Ribs (page 255) are a great reason to break out the fuller-bodied options, like a Northern Rhône syrah or southwestern French carignan. Meanwhile, dishes like Chicken Liver Mousse (page 248) and Beef Tartare (page 252) call for something a little less concentrated, like a Cru Beaujolais or a mencía from Cantabria on the Spanish coast. There's also been an under the radar, unexpected natural-winemaking movement in Bordeaux of all places, and this is a good moment to show your guests that a wine made without additives can taste classical.

DESSERT

We really love dessert wines at the restaurant. We just don't like to drink them with dessert. I feel like they work best AS the dessert. It's just that sugar in the glass and sugar on the plate doesn't appeal to me; I prefer a brandy or eau de vie alongside a sticky toffee pudding. And while after-dinner drinks like chartreuse and amaro are certainly not short on sugar, the higher level of alcohol balances them and is said to help your body digest all the food you've put in it.

FRIED
OIL
FOOD
FIRE

FRIED SNACKS

FRIED SNACKS

I know it's not always 100 percent practical to make them outside of a restaurant kitchen, but fried snacks just go so well with Champagne, beer, wine, a spritz, sake, cocktails, weekend gatherings with friends, binge-watching television . . . anything, really. I'm especially into beginning a meal with them. When well executed, fried dishes are cozy and deeply aromatic, savory and satisfying. They can set the tone for the rest of the night. Shoulders drop, relax. You're just being taken care of here. Somebody loves you. Eat this little crispy bite. No big deal.

When I was a kid, my brother and I would fight over the calamari tentacles whenever our family went out and a basket hit the table. I don't remember when we clocked it was squid, actually. I still get a little excited whenever I'm fishing those little guys out from a pile of rings, off their wax-paper bed, all to myself. Fried foods make people happy, so I think they're worth the effort when you have friends over and you want them to feel at home.

The following recipes mark different moments in the restaurant's history, and each holds a special place in my heart. None of them is overly complicated, and I'll try to lay out some frying techniques and tools that should make the whole job a lot easier.

A FEW MOVES FOR FANTASTIC FRYING

Use a heavy-bottomed pot that's 4 to 6 inches (10 to 15 cm) deep for the best, and safest, results. At home, I use my trusty Dutch oven, and we sometimes even use one at the restaurant.

Canola oil is not only affordable and easy to find, it also allows for the most even frying. Peanut oil is another solid choice and is the favorite of most bistros.

Skip the spatter guard. As long as you add your ingredients to the hot oil carefully, they shouldn't send oil spitting all over the place, and none of the recipes calls for adding very wet ingredients that will cause serious spattering. For reasons we don't need to get into, the guard is just a nuisance.

Have a candy thermometer clipped to the side of your pot to monitor the oil temperature.

Keep the burner on medium to heat the oil. It'll take a little longer to heat up, but it'll be easier to catch and maintain the desired temp once you get there. Starting the oil on high heat gets you to the ideal temp faster, but there's a far greater chance you won't be able to hold it there for very long. Once you reach the desired temperature, drop the heat down to low until you're ready to fry.

Don't ever walk away from the kitchen once you've committed to the frying process. *Please.*

Invest in a spider (see page 49). This is the best tool for pulling foods out of hot oil. Tongs will work in a pinch, but have a tendency to break the crust you've just worked so thoughtfully to obtain. Slotted spoons tend to bring a lot of oil out of the pot along with the food you've fried. That's something you want to avoid, as excess oil can lead to soggy fried foods.

Have a sheet tray with a rack on top right next to your frying pot where you can transfer whatever you've fried to drain excess oil. If you're frying smaller items like herbs or anything that could fall through the rack setup, skip the rack and just line the sheet tray with paper towels. Sometimes, for more delicate fried foods, I'll even crumple the paper towels a bit to make a little nest to support them.

Jack up the heat a bit right before you start adding anything to the oil. With small amounts of oil, as I generally call for in these recipes, the oil temperature has a tendency to drop when cold or room-temperature foods are added to the pot.

tempura batter

MAKES 4 CUPS (1 L)

Our all-purpose batter for frying at The Four Horsemen is similar to a traditional Japanese tempura, except we don't use eggs. The goal should be to keep things crisp and light as opposed to soft and spongy. It's an extremely versatile recipe: We've had great results using it to fry vegetables and fish, really everything from shrimp and steamed sweet potatoes to asparagus and onions.

Note: You can substitute the sparkling water with beer for a denser, more fish 'n chips style coating when frying more robust ingredients, like onion rings or fattier fish.

- 2¼ cups (280 g) all-purpose flour
- 1¾ cups plus 2 tablespoons (225 g) cornstarch
- 1 tablespoon plus 2½ teaspoons onion powder
- 1 tablespoon plus 2 teaspoons garlic powder
- 1 tablespoon sugar
- 1 tablespoon plus 2 teaspoons kosher salt
- 2½ cups (600 ml) chilled sparkling water (see Note)

In a bowl, whisk together the flour, cornstarch, onion powder, garlic powder, sugar, and salt to combine. Add the sparkling water and whisk until the dry ingredients are incorporated.

Cover the batter, set it over a bowl of ice, and refrigerate until ready to use, up to 1 hour.

wax bean tempura with basil, parmigiano-reggiano, and lemon vinaigrette

SERVES 4

This is a good first fry for a novice, as the wax beans cook easily with minimal prep and fuss. Make sure to coat the ingredients well. The idea is to create a crunchy crust while steaming whatever is sealed inside. Be gentle with the battered beans in the early stages of frying. If you agitate them too much, you run the risk of breaking the crust and exposing the beans themselves to the oil, and the dish will wind up feeling a bit greasier.

Canola oil, for frying

1 batch Tempura Batter (page 71)

2 pounds (910 g) wax beans, stem ends snipped off

Kosher salt

¼ cup (8 g) fresh basil leaves

1 batch Meyer Lemon Vinaigrette (page 315)

1 (2½-ounce / 70 g) block Parmigiano-Reggiano cheese

In a heavy Dutch oven or deep stockpot, pour about 3 inches (8 cm) canola oil and heat the oil over medium-low heat until the temperature reaches 275°F (135°C). Adjust your burner as needed to maintain that temperature as you proceed with the recipe. Have a spider handy and set a sheet tray lined with paper towels nearby. Set the tempura batter over a bowl of ice on the counter near the fryer setup.

Place a small handful of beans into the batter and work them around with your hand to coat. This will be a little messy. (If you have some disposable rubber gloves at home, now would be the time to use them. Otherwise, the batter comes off pretty easily in the sink.) Once the beans are coated, carefully drop them one at a time into the hot oil. When you've got 8 to 10 beans in the pot, begin to gently stir them with the spider or a pair of tongs to try to separate them a bit. If a couple stick together, it's not the end of the world. You just don't want a huge mass of them stuck together. Fry the beans until they're lightly golden brown, then remove them with the spider and place them on the paper towel–lined tray. Season with salt and then transfer to a serving plate. Repeat to batter and fry the remaining beans, seasoning each batch with salt.

Tear the leaves of basil roughly and scatter them all over the beans. Drizzle with the lemon vinaigrette, then, using a wide-ribbon Microplane, grate the Parm over the top. Serve immediately.

nori fritters with yuzu sesame seeds and parmigiano-reggiano

SERVES 4

This recipe is inspired by Missy Robbins's cacio e pepe fritelle at Lilia, a brilliant restaurant just up the street from The Four Horsemen. I spent a summer eating countless plates of them, piping hot, with an ice-cold Aperol spritz. Our fritters were born one afternoon when our former sous chef Zach Frieling shaped the cheesy batter into long sticks, fried them, and covered them with finely grated Parmigiano-Reggiano. I added crumbled-up seaweed and some sesame seeds flavored with yuzu, and we had an instant guest favorite.

- 2 tablespoons unsalted butter
- 1½ teaspoons kosher salt, plus more for finishing
- ½ teaspoon sugar
- 1 cup (137 g) all-purpose flour
- ½ cup (50 g) loosely packed finely grated Parmigiano-Reggiano cheese, plus an extra block for serving
- 3 (7-inch / 17 mm) sheets nori, crushed by hand into ¼- to ½-inch (6 to 12 mm) flakes (about 4 tablespoons / 4 g)
- 2 large eggs, lightly whisked
- 1 tablespoon extra-virgin olive oil
- Canola oil, for frying
- 1½ teaspoons yuzu sesame seeds (store-bought is fine)

In a medium saucepan, combine ¾ cup (180 ml) water, the butter, salt, and sugar and bring to a simmer over medium heat.

Once the mixture reaches a simmer, sift the flour onto a piece of parchment paper, then pour it into the pot all in one go. Stir the mixture with a spatula, scraping the sides of the pot as you go. The dough will come together into a ball. When it does, cook the dough, using a kneading motion with the spatula, for an additional 5 minutes. At this point, some condensation should accumulate on the exterior of the dough.

Transfer the dough to the bowl of a stand mixer fitted with the dough hook. With the mixer running on medium-low speed, add half the grated Parm and mix, frequently scraping down the sides of the bowl with a spatula, for about 10 minutes, at which point the dough should have cooled to about room temperature. Add the remaining ¼ cup (25 g) Parm and 2 tablespoons of the crushed nori and mix until incorporated.

With the mixer on medium-low, add half the whisked eggs and mix until incorporated. Turn off the mixer, scrape down the sides, then turn the mixer back on and add the remaining eggs. Once the eggs are incorporated, transfer the mixture to a piping bag.

CONTINUED

Line a sheet tray with a piece of parchment paper and brush the parchment with the olive oil. Cut the tip of the piping bag to create a ⅜-inch (1 cm) opening, then pipe 9-inch-long (23 cm) strips of dough onto the lined tray. Place the tray in the freezer for 20 minutes.

While the dough is freezing, in a heavy Dutch oven or deep stockpot, pour about 3 inches (8 cm) canola oil and heat the oil over medium-low heat until the temperature reaches 350°F (175°C). Adjust your burner as needed to maintain that temperature as you proceed with the recipe. Have a pair of tongs handy and set a sheet tray topped with a wire rack nearby.

When the dough strips are firm enough to easily lift from the tray, carefully lower them into the hot oil and fry for 4 to 5 minutes, until golden brown. Remove the fritters with the tongs and place them on the rack. Season with a good pinch of salt, then transfer to a serving plate.

Using a Microplane, grate a ridiculous amount of cheese over the fritters, then sprinkle on the remaining nori flakes, followed by the sesame seeds. Serve immediately.

fried squash blossoms with goat's-milk gouda

SERVES 4

Squash blossoms are a harbinger of the coming summer vegetables: Corn, peppers, and eggplant will be just around the corner. The season for these delicate flowers is fleeting, so you buy them when you can, for as long as they last. We've put out a variety of squash blossom dishes, trying something different whenever we can get our hands on them. I feel like this recipe is one of our best.

If you have a reputable cheese shop nearby, pay them a visit. I like Brabander, a creamy, sweet, and rich goat's-milk Gouda. Also, don't skip straining the ricotta. You want to remove as much excess moisture as possible so your filling will be structured and tight.

FOR THE FILLING:

About 18 ounces (495 g) ricotta cheese, strained in a colander overnight

Heaping ½ cup (22 g) finely grated Brabander Gouda cheese (use a Microplane)

1½ teaspoons lemon zest (from about 2 lemons)

1 tablespoon finely chopped fresh parsley leaves

1 tablespoon very thinly sliced fresh chives, plus 2 teaspoons for finishing

1 tablespoon finely chopped fresh tarragon leaves

2 tablespoons plus 2 teaspoons finely chopped fresh chervil leaves (smaller stems are okay to include)

¾ teaspoon freshly ground black pepper

¾ teaspoon kosher salt

FOR THE SQUASH BLOSSOMS:

Canola oil, for frying

1 batch Tempura Batter (page 71)

20 small squash blossoms (2 to 3 inches / 5 to 7.5 cm long), plus some stem okay

Kosher salt

2 lemons, quartered and seeded

1 fist-sized chunk Brabander Gouda cheese

Freshly ground black pepper

MAKE THE FILLING: In a medium bowl, combine the ricotta, Gouda, lemon zest, parsley, chives, tarragon, chervil, pepper, and salt and stir with a rubber spatula to combine. Transfer to a piping bag or a zip-top bag. Set aside in the fridge. When ready to fill the blossoms, snip off the tip of the piping bag or one corner of the zip-top bag, creating an opening a little smaller than ½ inch (12 mm).

CONTINUED

MAKE THE SQUASH BLOSSOMS: In a heavy Dutch oven or deep stockpot, pour about 3 inches (8 cm) canola oil and heat the oil over medium-low heat until the temperature reaches 350°F (175°C). Adjust your burner as needed to maintain that temperature as you proceed with the recipe. Have a spider handy and set a sheet tray lined with paper towels nearby. Set the tempura batter over a bowl of ice on the counter near the fryer setup.

Pipe the filling into the cavity of one blossom until it feels plump and full, but not so full that you can't seal the flower petals around the cheese at the top. Set the stuffed blossom aside on a plate and repeat to fill the remaining blossoms.

Dip one stuffed blossom into the batter, swirling it gently to fully coat, then carefully place it in the hot oil. After about 15 seconds, batter another blossom and add it to the oil. (If you add too many too quickly, they can have a tendency to stick together in the pot due to the wet batter, but if you wait a little bit, the batter will start to form a seal and they won't stick together as easily.) Continue coating the stuffed blossoms in batter and adding them to the oil, but don't crowd the pot. Fry the first batch of blossoms until light golden brown, then use the spider to remove them from the oil and place them on the paper towel–lined tray. Lightly season with salt.

Repeat the process to batter, fry, and season the remaining blossoms.

Arrange the seasoned fried blossoms on a plate and squeeze lemon juice over them. Using a wide-ribbon Microplane, grate over copious amounts of the Gouda and finish with a few generous cracks of black pepper. Serve immediately.

how a dish makes it onto the menu

Growing up and beginning to cook in California, I felt lucky: all that relentless, beautiful produce and reasonable weather all year. But I believe you become a stronger cook once you're forced to pay close attention to what is thriving at any given moment. It wasn't until I moved out East that the fleeting nature of ingredients here, especially vegetables and fish, helped me fully appreciate cooking seasonally.

To be clear, no one moves to New York for the weather, but I think we're fortunate to have noticeable changes throughout the year: the full four seasons. At first I couldn't wrap my head around every chef freaking out over ramps when spring came. Why mackerel and uni wound up on almost every menu in early fall. Why black trumpet mushrooms were ogled over on their delivery day by entire teams of cooks. They were nice ingredients, *but I was from California*. We had everything all the time out there. After a few years, I finally got it. Scarcity, transformation, lack—these things can be inspirations. Now, when rhubarb or the first asparagus of the season start to pop up, I find myself getting excited. Something new is coming, and it's out of your control. The world is giving you an opportunity to change—forcing you. So you follow the seasons, which means you follow the ingredients.

I feel lucky to say that our suppliers are our trusted friends, and we look to them to bring us the best stuff they can get their hands on at any given moment. We rarely bother to dictate specifics—maybe ask them to prioritize the more unusual stuff that might not appeal to everyone else. By now they know we like to use offcuts, fish collars, interesting vegetables. They also know we'll only work with produce at its peak, so they don't bother bringing us citrus and chicories in the heavy heat of summer. Instead, they continually show up with the remarkable ingredients we need to make new dishes.

New elements in hand, we can begin asking ourselves some questions. What does the menu need? Are we going to bring back a favorite from last year, or can we do better? Is it maybe time for something lighter? Fresher? Does the menu seem too rustic

or simple and want something elegant? Or too subtle and refined and in need of a comforting and friendly dish? Is there a classic technique or presentation we can find an interesting way into? Beets are coming in . . . everyone will probably be doing cold salads with them. Can we make a warm root vegetable the envy of the person who ordered the steak?

All of our cooks and sous chefs get involved. I firmly believe this kind of open system leads to the best dishes, and makes for better, more resilient cooks on your team. My job is really to guide the process. Sometimes the ideas work, sometimes they don't. Honestly nine out of ten get shot down. It can be disheartening for the team at first, but once they experience the process, they get more comfortable with failure, and from those experiences, gain more actual confidence. I think failure is critical. If you never fail, you probably haven't really tried.

While we may embrace failure as an essential part of the *creative* process, we're absolutely uncompromising about the dishes we do finally send out. In the end, we're always proud of the results, because we trust our process and each other. Kitchen camaraderie is really one of the best reasons to work in a restaurant. Any honest chef will explain that they couldn't do what they do without their entire team, and I'm no exception.

In the end, it's as a unit that we deliver the new dishes that actually made the cut, sparked by ideas and arguments, curiosity, processes and flavor memories gathered over the years by our collective experiences. These years of practice, of making mistakes, of tasting, disappointment, recovery, and success. Sometimes the all-important moments of actual creativity are small and quiet, and happen only after all the care and technique and trust make them possible. But they make all the difference. I think this hard-won creativity is a central principle of our cooking at The Four Horsemen.

crispy squid with pimentón de la vera

SERVES 4

When dredging squid for frying, we set out our ingredients in large containers. Big mixing bowls work great. You want plenty of space to fully immerse the squid without crowding and clumping, as well as room to avoid splashing on your counter. Going back and forth between a seasoned dry dredge and sparkling water can make a surprisingly light crust on the squid. Just take your time, work clean, and be safe with the oil.

- Canola oil, for frying
- 3 cups (420 g) all-purpose flour
- ¾ teaspoon kosher salt
- 3 tablespoons cornstarch
- 1½ teaspoons Spanish paprika
- ¾ teaspoon cayenne pepper
- 1½ teaspoons onion powder
- 1½ teaspoons monosodium glutamate (MSG; optional, just add a bit more salt to finish if omitting)
- 8 cups (2 L) sparkling water
- 1½ pounds (680 g) squid, cleaned, bodies cut into ½-inch-thick (12 mm) rings, and tentacles left whole or split lengthwise if very large
- 1 teaspoon Pimentón de la Vera (Spanish paprika) or other sweet or smoked paprika
- 1 batch Aioli (page 305), for serving

In a heavy Dutch oven or deep stockpot, pour about 3 inches (8 cm) canola oil and heat the oil over medium-low heat until the temperature reaches 350°F (175°C). Adjust your burner as needed to maintain that temperature as you proceed with the recipe. Have a spider handy and set a sheet tray lined with slightly crumpled paper towels nearby.

In a large bowl, whisk together the flour, salt, cornstarch, Spanish paprika, cayenne, onion powder, and MSG, if using. If this dredge looks clumpy at all, feel free to pass it through a sieve or sifter. Pour the sparkling water into a separate large bowl. Set this bowl and the bowl of dredge on the counter near the fryer setup.

Working in batches, place a handful or two of squid bodies and tentacles into the dredge, then transfer them to the sparkling water, then back into the dredge. (We wear gloves for this at the restaurant.) Make sure to really move them around the second time you dredge them and do your best to separate them so they won't stick to one another as they fry.

Lift the coated squid from the dredge and give them a little shake to remove excess dredge, then carefully drop them in the oil. Move them around with the spider or a slotted spoon in the early stages of cooking

to prevent sticking. Maintain an even 350°F (175°C) to ensure the coating will be crispy; you may need to adjust the heat under the pot, as adding the squid can cool the oil. Fry until the squid are lightly golden brown, remove with the spider or slotted spoon, and transfer to the paper towel–lined sheet tray. Give the tray a little shake to distribute the squid and then sprinkle with the pimentón. Repeat to coat and fry the remaining squid.

Transfer the seasoned squid to a plate and serve with the aioli alongside.

salt cod fritters with spicy cilantro mayo

SERVES 4

Salt cod is a beloved staple of both Spanish and Portuguese cuisine, with the fish itself attaining some of the near divine status held by tuna in Japan. Because of the salting, the fibers and flakes of the fish become more noticeable, taking on a pleasing jerky texture with a deep and aromatic flavor.

Salt cod has gotten easier to find these days and will keep for years. But plan ahead. The fish needs to be soaked to remove excess salt before it can be used. Note that its shelf life is considerably shorter after soaking, so try to use it within a week.

1½ cups (272 g) coarsely chopped salt cod (½-inch / 12 mm chunks)

1½ cups (360 ml) whole milk

½ cup plus 2 tablespoons (140 g) unsalted butter, cut into 1-inch (2.5 cm) cubes

1 teaspoon kosher salt

1½ cups (180 g) all-purpose flour

5 large eggs

1 tablespoon cloves Garlic Confit (page 307), drained of oil

½ cup (40 g) finely grated Parmigiano-Reggiano cheese

¼ cup (16 g) finely chopped fresh chives

Freshly ground black pepper

Canola oil, for frying

1½ teaspoons ground cumin

1½ teaspoons pimentón (Spanish paprika)

Spicy Cilantro Mayo (page 304)

Place the salt cod in a bowl in the sink, rinse it with plenty of cold water, and then drain it. Fill the bowl again with cold water and let the cod soak overnight, changing the water once halfway through the soaking process. Transfer the soaked cod to another container and discard the liquid.

In a wide pot, warm the milk over medium heat. Add the cod to the warm milk and poach for about 10 minutes. Remove the fish with a spider and set it aside in a bowl.

Add the butter and salt to the milk. Cook until the butter has melted and the milk is just below a simmer, then add all the flour in one go, reduce the heat to low, and whisk to incorporate. When the mixture becomes stiff, switch to a wooden spoon. Stir until the flour has been completely absorbed, and the mixture begins to stick slightly to the bottom of the pan and looks a bit like mashed potatoes, 8 to 10 minutes.

Transfer the contents of the pot to the bowl of a stand mixer fitted with the paddle attachment. With the mixer on low speed, add the eggs

CONTINUED

one at a time, allowing each one to be incorporated before adding the next. Add the poached cod and the garlic confit, followed by the cheese and the chives. Add a few good cracks of pepper and then turn off the mixer.

Scrape down the sides of the mixer bowl with a rubber spatula and fold a few times to ensure all the ingredients are incorporated. Transfer the batter to a container and put it in the fridge, uncovered, until it has cooled, then place a lid on the container and keep the batter in the fridge (for up to 5 days) until you're ready to fry. It's better and easier to make the fritters when the batter is cold. (At this point, the batter can be stored in the freezer for up to 1 month. Thaw it in the fridge overnight before using.)

When you're ready to fry, in a heavy Dutch oven or deep stockpot, pour about 3 inches (8 cm) canola oil and heat the oil over medium-low heat until the temperature reaches 350°F (175°C). Adjust your burner as needed to maintain that temperature as you proceed with the recipe. Have a spider handy and set a sheet tray lined with paper towels nearby.

Mix the cumin and the pimentón and place in a little confectioners' sugar shaker or a small fine-mesh strainer, then set the shaker or strainer near your frying setup.

Using two small spoons and working right next to the pot of hot oil, begin scooping and carefully dropping little balls of batter into the oil. Scoop with one spoon, then use the other spoon to gently push the batter off the first and into the oil. Start with a few at a time until you get the hang of it. You're looking for shapes slightly smaller than a Ping-Pong ball. And don't worry about them being perfect spheres. The more organic the shape, the better, as long as they're all similar in size so they cook evenly.

Flip them over halfway through cooking and fry until golden in color, 4 to 5 minutes more, then remove the fritters with a spider to the paper towel–lined tray. Shake gently to remove any excess oil, then dust lightly with the cumin-pimentón mix. Allow to rest for about 5 minutes before serving. Repeat with the remaining batter.

Serve the fritters with the spicy cilantro mayo. If they get cool before you serve them, just warm them in a 350°F (175°C) oven for 3 to 5 minutes.

patatas bravas with chipotle-tomato jam and aioli

SERVES 4

This was one of the first dishes we put on The Four Horsemen menu. I always liked the casual grazing from bar to bar you can do in Spain—dropping into one local place after another where you can have a glass of wine or a gin and tonic and some snacks. Particularly in Madrid, you find sort of shockingly good patatas bravas, crispy cubes of fried potato with a spicy sauce.

With care and real attention to detail, you can turn out crisp and perfectly seasoned potatoes with sharp tomato sauce and a silky aioli.

2½ pounds (1.1 kg) russet potatoes, peeled and cut into ½-inch (13 mm) chunks

½ cup (80 g) kosher salt, plus more as needed

4 quarts (4 L) canola oil, for frying

1 teaspoon paprika

1 teaspoon ground cumin

1 batch Chipotle-Tomato Jam (page 310)

1 batch Aioli (page 305)

Rinse the potatoes in cold water for 3 to 4 minutes to remove excess starch. Place them in a large pot and cover with about 3 quarts (3 L) water. Add the salt and bring the water to a simmer over medium heat.

Reduce the heat to maintain a low simmer and cook the potatoes until very tender but not falling apart, 20 to 25 minutes. Set a wire rack on a sheet tray. Carefully remove the potatoes from the pot by wiggling in a spider and cradling them out and onto the rack. Place the tray in the fridge for an hour, until the potatoes are well chilled.

In a heavy Dutch oven or deep stockpot, heat the canola oil over medium-low heat until the temperature reaches 275°F (135°C). Adjust your burner as needed to maintain that temperature as you proceed with the recipe. Have a spider handy and set a sheet tray topped with a wire rack nearby.

Remove the potatoes from the fridge and carefully drop them into the oil (you may need to work in small batches). Fry until lightly golden, 8 to 10 minutes. Remove the potatoes with the spider and transfer them to the rack. (The potatoes can be prepared to this point 4 to 5 days in advance and stored in the fridge.)

For the final fry, bring the oil temperature up to 360°F (182°C) and have a bowl lined with paper towels nearby. Carefully drop the potatoes into the pot (or use the spider to lower them in for safer results—see how handy this tool is?!) and fry until golden brown, 3 to 5 minutes. Remove from the oil and place in the paper towel–lined bowl.

Remove the paper towels and toss the potatoes with a bit more salt. Mix the paprika and cumin in a small bowl, then sprinkle the mix over the potatoes as you flip them in the bowl to evenly disperse the spices.

Serve the potatoes immediately, topped with a few dollops each of chipotle-tomato jam and aioli.

on black pepper

Black pepper doesn't get enough credit. It's much more interesting and powerful than people think. Often just lumped without clarification into the "season with salt and pepper" formula (don't get me started on salt, page 108), black pepper is in fact a remarkably pungent and transformative spice that I believe should be used with intent. This element, once the most traded spice in the world and vital to both medicine and cooking, is without a doubt one of my favorite ingredients. I hope I can get you to see it a bit differently so that you can fully harness its potential.

What is black pepper, exactly? Pepper starts as the fruit of a vining plant (*Piper nigrum*) native to India; these days, most of the pepper we use comes from Vietnam, with India, China, Brazil, and Malaysia close behind. The berries are harvested at various stages of ripeness, depending on whether they're destined to be black, white, green, or red peppercorns. For black peppercorns, the fruits are picked when they've reached their full size but not yet ripened, and their skin is still green (those destined to become green peppercorns are harvested at the same point but processed differently). The berries are boiled briefly and then left in the sun to dry, turning dark black as they do from enzymes in their skins.

When finishing a dish with black pepper, always grind whole peppercorns fresh in a pepper mill (see Tools, page 51). Please don't use the pre-ground stuff here. Grinding fresh releases the most beautiful, woody, and floral aromas. It's just a really low-effort way to dramatically improve your flavors. There's nothing like the smell of freshly cracked black peppercorns hitting something warm. The spice and heat from fresh black pepper has a completely different flavor profile than the capsaicin in chile peppers—it's a more instantaneous tickling of the tongue, with a distinctly citrusy numbing quality. This attribute is expressed superbly in recipes like cacio e pepe, sauce au poivre, and chai.

Look for the Tellicherry and Sarawak varieties found in specialty shops. Both are ripened on the vine and allowed to dry quickly, which preserves the unique flavor profiles they're prized for.

chicken karaage with yuzu kosho aioli

SERVES 4

Izakayas in Japan serve these bites of remarkable fried chicken with bracingly cold draft beer, and often with a hit of the chile pepper seasoning blend shichimi togarashi for heat. We serve this karaage with a citrusy and rich yuzo kosho aioli. For extra credit, you can add refreshing lettuce wraps and Kewpie mayo. Stick with thighs. They have more fat and flavor, and will crisp up better.

1 pound 9 ounces (710 g) skin-on boneless chicken thighs, cut into 2-inch (5 cm) pieces

½ teaspoon grated peeled fresh ginger (use a Microplane), including any juice

1 teaspoon grated garlic (use a Microplane)

¼ cup (60 ml) soy sauce

1½ tablespoons sake

1 generous teaspoon toasted sesame oil

1 teaspoon sugar

2 quarts (2 L) canola oil, for frying

1 cup (130 g) all-purpose flour

1 cup (145 g) potato starch

2 teaspoons kosher salt

½ cup (60 ml) Yuzu Kosho Aioli (page 305)

Place the chicken thighs in a shallow baking dish. Add the ginger and any juice, garlic, soy sauce, sake, sesame oil, and sugar and massage the chicken lightly to combine the marinade. Cover and refrigerate for 2 hours.

In a heavy Dutch oven or deep stockpot, heat the canola oil over medium-low heat until the temperature reaches 350°F (175°C). Adjust your burner as needed to maintain that temperature as you proceed with the recipe. Have a spider handy and set a sheet tray lined with paper towels nearby.

Place the flour and potato starch in a mixing bowl and whisk to combine. Remove the chicken from the fridge and dip a few pieces at a time in the flour mix to coat, setting them on a plate or a small sheet tray as you go.

One piece at a time, place the coated chicken in the oil and fry until golden brown, 3 to 4 minutes. Remove them with the spider and transfer to the paper towel–lined tray. Season with the salt, then transfer to a serving dish.

Serve with yuzu kosho aioli for dipping.

BREAD + TOAST

BREAD + TOAST

The Humble Toast's charred edges and steamy interior provide a perfect platform for a bunch of different seasonal ingredients. This is why you'll always find one on our menu.

To make our toasts, we generally start with a cool, creamy cheese or pungent aioli-based sauce to contrast with the bread's hearty qualities. Then it's simply a matter of roasting or marinating vegetables, slicing some salty anchovies, or preparing a shellfish side to spoon over the top. You can purchase a classic rustic sourdough for most applications here. As an alternative, the Sesame Focaccia (page 103)—one of two versatile bread recipes I've also included—toasts up really well: Cover it in creamy burrata and grilled mushrooms.

Here are a few other simple combinations to consider beyond the full recipes.

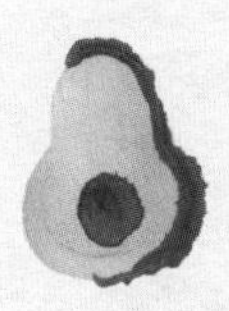

IDEAS FOR TOPPING TOASTS

Garlicky smashed broccoli

Sautéed greens (kale, arugula, spinach)

Stewed beans with crushed tomatoes and olive oil

Beef Bolognese and a poached egg with lots of Parm

Avocado with Garlic Chile Oil (page 306)

Crushed English peas with thinly sliced chorizo and mint

Blistered cherry tomatoes and basil

Salty French butter and thinly sliced ham

Whipped ricotta with homemade jams and black pepper

Dressed crab with tarragon and chives

Whipped charred eggplant with toasted sesame seeds

Juicy roasted mushrooms with a splash of sherry vinegar and herbs

grilled flatbread

MAKES SIX 8- TO 10-INCH (20 TO 25 CM) FLATBREADS

One good thing about this tangy and rich flatbread is you can start it in the morning and it'll be ready by the afternoon. Another is that it blisters nicely over coals. In the summer, try these flatbreads with marinated chicken or lamb skewers and lots of generously dressed cucumbers tossed with mint and cilantro. Match with Garlic Yogurt (page 307) or Spicy Cilantro Mayo (page 304), no matter what else you're serving.

- ½ teaspoon instant yeast
- 1 cup (240 ml) warm water (about 100°F / 38°C)
- ½ teaspoon honey
- 1 cup (125 g) whole-wheat flour
- 2 cups (265 g) all-purpose flour, plus more as needed
- 1 tablespoon plus 1½ teaspoons plain full-fat yogurt
- 2 teaspoons kosher salt
- Extra-virgin olive oil
- Maldon salt

In the bowl of a stand mixer, combine the yeast, warm water, and honey. Let stand at room temperature for 10 minutes to bloom the yeast.

Add the whole-wheat and all-purpose flours to the yeast mixture and mix with the dough hook on low speed for about 10 seconds, then add the yogurt and salt. Mix on medium speed for about 5 minutes, until the dough looks like a smooth ball. Lightly grease a container with olive oil. Place the dough in the oiled container, cover, and set aside at room temperature until doubled in size, about 2 hours. Note that the container should be at least twice as tall as the ball of dough.

Lightly grease a 9 by 12-inch (23 by 33 cm) baking dish with olive oil. With a bench scraper, transfer the dough to a lightly floured table. Portion the dough into six 3½-ounce (100 g) pieces and shape each piece into a ball. Place the balls in the oiled container, seam side down, leaving some space between each ball (they'll continue to grow). Cover and refrigerate for 1 hour.

Meanwhile, prepare a charcoal grill.

Use a rolling pin to roll out the balls of dough into roughly ¼-inch-thick (6 mm) rounds and place them on the grill. Cook directly over medium-high heat, until golden brown and slightly charred on the bottom, about 30 seconds. Flip with tongs and cook on the second side for 30 seconds or so. The flatbreads should be crispy on top but still light and pillowy in their thicker and puffy parts. Remove from the grill, drizzle with olive oil, and sprinkle with Maldon salt. Serve immediately.

our ham and cheese sandwich

MAKES 1 SANDWICH

There's a good chance this is the only recipe for a ham sandwich ever written that begins with a story about a global pandemic.

Everything changed when COVID-19 hit New York in March 2020. At The Four Horsemen, we had been riding high coming into that year. Business was better than ever, we finally got a review in the *New York Times*, and somehow our little Brooklyn restaurant wound up with a Michelin star. But when the virus started to take over the city, we had to shut down completely, laying off almost our entire team, sending them home to an uncertain time with boxes of groceries, toilet paper, and rubber gloves. Anyone who was in New York at that time can tell you about the sirens. Nonstop sirens. And the fear. It was a nightmare for the entire fragile food-service industry. It was a nightmare for everyone.

It's hard to keep a mental tally of all the false starts and sudden stops that followed. But I do remember vividly the moment we had the chance to start serving something, anything, again. Our sous chef Ben and I were the only ones in the kitchen when we "reopened." At first we portioned out and sold pantry goods: cookie dough, chile oil, spicy cilantro mayo, schmaltz, spice blends, vinaigrettes—staples of the restaurant that we figured home cooks could use. Everyone was cooking at home, and we were trying to keep ourselves as well as our suppliers in business until whatever was going to happen happened.

We eventually decided to try to do some takeout. People would order online, through a makeshift website we scrambled to set up ourselves. The menu had to stay simple, not just because there were only two of us to prepare it: We needed to make food that was approachable and traveled well, but still remained true to The Four Horsemen. We wanted our food to arrive and feel like a highlight of what was potentially a pretty brutal day. Housemade whenever possible, thoughtfully sourced whenever not. No unnecessary flourishes. No projects requiring our beloved prep team that wasn't there. Just straightforward cooking. Comfort food.

We settled on bright and sharp salads with lots of summer vegetables, and sandwiches like Nashville hot chicken, fried soft-shell crab, and burgers with cacio e pepe fries. We tried to keep it fun.

Somewhere along the way, I decided I needed to make a ham and cheese sandwich.

The idea came from a memory of traveling to Paris. Without fail, my first stop is always the nearest decent-looking boulangerie I can find, where I order a jambon beurre: sweet and juicy ham on a crusty baguette slathered with salty French butter. To me, it's perfect in its simplicity; entirely about the quality of the ingredients. Our sandwich wound up nothing like that quintessential Parisian staple (apparently over three million are sold in France each day!), but that's how these things go. I think they're supposed to happen that way. An idea starts as a memory and ends up as an invention.

We had long been making a focaccia that I was incredibly proud of, so we tried folding some toasted sesame seeds into the dough, which added a nutty aromatic complexity. This made us happy and immediately became the base for the sandwich. When I was a kid, my mom usually had a pack of decent Black Forest ham in the fridge, which she regularly threw into quick sandwiches to fend off her hungry, growing sons. Now, decades later and far from home, I wanted that flavor, and found a delicious Black Forest ham from a smokehouse in Connecticut. We sliced it paper thin, deli style, so we could really pile it high without it shooting out the side after a few bites. For the cheese, we found an aged and nutty Comté—my favorite of the Alpine cheeses. We whipped up some Dijonnaise and

CONTINUED

chopped some peperoncini and finished the whole thing with generous amounts of freshly cracked black pepper.

I'm writing this from the basement of The Four Horsemen. It's September 2022. We once again have a full team of incredible cooks from all walks of life working directly upstairs from where I'm sitting. The food they're making is precise and nuanced. The details and flourishes are back. But the ham and cheese sandwich stuck around. We've all become attached to it. So have our guests, who photograph it more than any other dish we serve, which I find funny. For the team, though, it's much more than just a good ham and cheese. It's a reminder of a dark time time when, over and over, we were inches from losing everything we had built here. It's a sign that we made it through. As a dish, this humble, unwieldy sandwich also represents a bridge between the "pre-pandemic" Four Horsemen and the restaurant we are today, because as happy as I am about the return of the flourishes, the truth is our food is more pared down than it used to be. There's less filler. While I certainly didn't expect it, COVID was the chapter in our story when we learned to care more than ever: about our work, about each other, and about serving what makes us and those around us feel good.

FOR THE DIJONNAISE:

½ cup (120 ml) Mayonnaise (page 304)

1 tablespoon Dijon mustard

FOR THE SANDWICH:

1 (5-inch / 12 cm) square piece Sesame Focaccia (page 103)

9 very thin slices Black Forest ham (7 ounces / 200 g), loosely pinched into bite-size rosettes

2 teaspoons pickled peperoncini, finely chopped, plus 2 teaspoons of their pickling liquid

1 (3 by 3½-inch / 7.5 by 9 cm) block Comté cheese, sliced into thin (about ⅛-inch-thick / 3 mm) rectangles

Freshly ground black pepper

MAKE THE DIJONNAISE: In a mixing bowl, add the mayonnaise and the Dijon mustard and stir to combine. Set aside.

MAKE THE SANDWICH: Slice the focaccia in half through its equator.

Spread the Dijonnaise on both halves of the bread with a spoon. Really make an effort to get it into the nooks, crannies, and corners.

Add the ham rosettes to the bottom half of the focaccia, over the Dijonnaise. Spoon over the peperoncini and their pickling liquid. Layer on the cheese and crack a generous amount of black pepper on both halves of the sandwich. Place the two halves together and slice in half to serve.

sesame focaccia

MAKES ONE 10 BY 12-INCH (25 BY 30.5 CM) FOCACCIA

Like I said, I'm proud of our focaccia. I'm proud of it even though it uses commercial yeast—or maybe partially because of that fact. At the moment I'm writing this, it's not particularly cool to use commercial yeast, but most things have their place, and I think focaccia is the perfect use case for this ingredient, ensuring a wide-open crumb and an expedited fermentation process. We also use a small amount of our sourdough starter for added flavor (see Note), but I'm not crazy about super-sour focaccia, so it's just a bit. In this particular case, I prefer allowing the yeast to help the dough rise. The dough can be mixed, shaped, and baked all in the same day. Almost any topping works.

Note: At the restaurant, we incorporate some of our sourdough starter into this focaccia dough. I've left it out here, but if you make bread consistently at home and happen to have some starter, omit ½ cup (66 g) of the whole-wheat flour, ½ cup (66 g) of the all-purpose flour, and ½ cup (120 ml) water from this recipe, then add 1 cup plus 2 tablespoons (264 g) of your active starter along with the salt.

1⅔ cups (405 ml) warm water

1 teaspoon instant yeast

1½ tablespoons extra-virgin olive oil, plus more as needed

2½ cups (322 g) all-purpose flour, plus more for the work surface

Scant 1 cup (116 g) whole-wheat flour

1 tablespoon kosher salt

¼ cup (75 g) toasted sesame seeds

Maldon salt

In a large bowl, combine the warm water, yeast, and olive oil and let stand at room temperature for about 10 minutes. The yeast will turn almost creamy when it's ready.

Add the all-purpose and whole-wheat flours and use your hands to aggressively combine them with the yeast mixture to form a dough. The dough will look wet and shaggy, but all the flour should be incorporated after about 5 minutes of mixing. Use a plastic bench scraper to scrape down the sides of the bowl every now and then while you mix. Cover the bowl with plastic wrap and let stand at room temperature for 30 minutes.

Add the kosher salt to the dough and mix it in by hand. Open your hands fully and squeeze the dough. It will go through your fingers and feel kind of fun. Do this for a minute or so and then start adding the sesame seeds, sprinkling a small handful at a time over the dough and mixing to

CONTINUED

incorporate before adding more. Keep doing this until all the seeds have been added.

Heavily grease a clear container with olive oil (the clear container will help you see the growth of the dough more easily). Place the dough in the oiled container, gather one side, and pull it up and over to meet its opposite side. Do this four times, once for each side, then flip the dough over so the folds are at the bottom of the bowl. The ball of dough should feel nice and taut, but don't fold so aggressively that you tear the dough. Cover and place in the fridge for the remainder of the folding process. Repeat this folding process every 20 minutes for an hour, then cover and refrigerate for about 2 hours, until roughly doubled in size.

Pull the dough out of the fridge. Using a bench scraper, carefully transfer the dough to a lightly floured surface. Again using the bench scraper, pull the dough toward you, scraping the counter, until it's nice and tight, then give it a quarter turn and repeat. Do this three or four more times, until you have a nicely formed ball of dough.

Grease a baking pan that is roughly 10 by 12 inches (25 by 30.5 cm). Place the ball of dough in the pan, seam side down, and let stand for 30 to 40 minutes to allow the dough to relax. Preheat the oven to 450°F (230°C).

Drizzle oil on top of the dough, then add a good pinch of Maldon salt. Rub a little oil on your fingers and then press your fingertips into the dough, all the way down to the bottom of the pan. Do this evenly all over the dough, then place the pan in the oven on the lower rack. Bake for 20 minutes, or until light golden brown in color. Remove from the oven and transfer the focaccia from the pan to a sheet tray topped with a rack (a fish spatula works well for this). Return the focaccia to the oven and bake for 5 to 10 minutes more, until dark golden brown. Remove from the oven and let cool for at least 45 minutes before slicing. To store, wrap in foil or plastic and keep for up to 3 days.

stracciatella toast with grilled peppers and onions

SERVES 2

I like to make this recipe in the summertime when we have access to the peak-season peppers: Corno di Toro, Lipstick, and Jimmy Nardello. I like to char them on the grill, for some smoky flavor. This also allows the tougher outer skin to come right off. If grilling's not feasible at home, just roast the peppers in the oven at 375°F (190°C). Either way, please don't char them over a gas range! It gives the peppers a really artificial flavor and an aroma of gas.

- 4 ounces (112 g) stracciatella cheese
- 6¼ ounces (175 g) sweet peppers (preferably Jimmy Nardellos, but other varieties, including red bell, will work, too)
- 3 tablespoons extra-virgin olive oil, plus more for serving
- 1 teaspoon kosher salt
- 1 small Spanish onion, cut into ⅓-inch-thick (6 mm) rounds
- 1 tablespoon red wine vinegar
- Maldon salt
- 2 (1-inch-thick / 2.5 cm) slices rustic country bread, cut to roughly 5 inches (12 cm) square
- Freshly ground black pepper
- A few fresh basil or oregano leaves, rinsed and patted dry (optional)

Prepare a charcoal or wood-burning grill for medium heat. Pull the stracciatella out of the fridge and set it on the counter to come up to room temperature.

Rinse the peppers, dry them with a towel, and transfer to a mixing bowl. Toss with 1 tablespoon of the olive oil and ½ teaspoon of the kosher salt. Once the grill is at a medium heat, place the peppers on the grill and cook, turning and adjusting the peppers to avoid flare-ups, until lightly charred and blistered. Try not to overchar them, as this could damage the flesh. Transfer the charred peppers to a mixing bowl and cover tightly with plastic wrap. Let them steam for 30 minutes.

Let the grill burn down to low. Place the onion rounds in a separate mixing bowl and, trying to keep them as intact as possible, gently toss them with 1 tablespoon of the olive oil and the remaining ½ teaspoon of kosher salt. Using tongs, place them on the grill and cook until lightly caramelized and tender, about 25 minutes. Remove from the grill and set aside. (Alternatively, roast the peppers and onions on separate sheet trays in a preheated 375°F / 190°C oven until blistered and lightly charred, about 25 minutes.)

Carefully peel the charred skin from the peppers, then split them in half lengthwise with your fingers and remove any seeds. If using Jimmy Nardellos or other smaller peppers, just leave the flesh whole; if using red bell peppers, cut the flesh into bite-size pieces.

In a bowl, mix the peppers with the onions and season them with the vinegar, remaining 1 tablespoon olive oil, and a pinch of Maldon salt.

Toast the bread—don't be afraid to get it nice and toasty with a little char. Working quickly so the bread stays hot, spoon the stracciatella cheese onto both slices of bread, followed by the marinated peppers and onions. Finish with a few cracks of black pepper, some more olive oil, and basil or oregano, if desired, then serve.

on the importance of salt

Salt is probably the most important element in food. From its abilities as a natural preservative we get Prosciutto di Parma, kimchi, capers, salted cod (page 85), and brined olives. In baking, its chemical properties tighten gluten strands, allowing more air to get trapped within breads and pastries, giving them structure. Its ability to bond proteins is crucial in the making of sausages and cheeses. Portuguese salt crusts can keep a fish impossibly moist and flaky while gently cooking it evenly. Oh, and it's also an essential nutrient for humans, without which we'd die. This is all to say that, before we even get into its impact on taste, salt has a massive influence on the way we make, preserve, and eat food.

I had a "formative experience as a young cook" (read: *green kid gets mind blown by experienced person with thing-he-should-already-know*) when I was blindly seasoning things according to recipe, not really understanding what salt, or anything else, did to the food. The head chef at the restaurant where I worked handed me two pieces of bittersweet chocolate, one of which was topped with sea salt, the other plain, and instructed me to try the plain one first. It was fine—what I expected. I ate the salted chocolate next, and it was an incomprehensibly different experience, opening up hidden treacle flavors seemingly undetectable in the original, subduing but not erasing its bitterness, and adding deep complexity. Salt changes your perception of all the other flavors—sweet, umami, bitter, sour—the way they balance and work. Small amounts can reduce bitterness and accentuate the sweetness of an ingredient, along with its sour notes. In higher concentrations, it can suppress that same sweetness, bringing up more umami notes. I highly recommend that you try that chocolate experiment to better understand how salt affects flavor. It's also pretty tasty, and a kind of sneaky move if you want a sweet treat in the kitchen late at night and you only have baking chocolate lying around . . .

There is a dizzying array of different types of salt you can buy. Table salt, kosher salt, pink Himalayan salt, Hawaiian black lava sea salt, Celtic gray sea salt, Trapani sea salt . . . Each type has its own salinity and texture, and, well, price. For sanity, we stick to two types of salt only at The Four Horsemen.

Our all around "ingredient" type is Diamond Crystal kosher salt. This was the kosher salt used to develop and test all the recipes in this book. The grains are even sized and not too fine, which lets you season consistently (finer-grained salts, in my experience, tend to make things saltier). Salinity is lower than that of other brands of kosher salt, such as Morton's, and it also weighs less, teaspoon for teaspoon, qualities that make over-seasoning less common and give you a little more room for error.

The "finishing" salt we use is Maldon. Harvested in Essex, England, Maldon sea salt is primarily about texture, and comes in trademark pyramid-shaped flakes that taste remarkably clean. These crystals break up easily between your fingertips, so you can decide how big you want your flakes. This is the salt you *see* on a dish—less salty and nicer in the mouth. Try to put some table salt on your tongue. It's not the best experience. Then try a Maldon crystal. It's much more balanced and pleasant in its pure form. Leave it really coarse on cooked steaks and pork chops to bring out their juiciness, or crumble lightly over raw fish with some super clean olive oil and a squeeze of lemon.

pan con tomate with fennel pollen, anchovies, and black pepper

SERVES 2

This toast is easy to make, but don't bother unless the tomatoes are ripe, juicy heirlooms, and you can find Cantabrian anchovies of the highest quality. The recipe is really and truly all about showing off the raw ingredients. We prefer to use our housemade focaccia for this recipe, but a more traditional baguette with an open crumb would do the job. If you opt for a baguette, just cut it into 5-inch (12 cm) lengths and then split horizontally. For the tomatoes, we use Brandywine, Cherokee Purple, or the best version of a beefsteak we can find.

Note: If you make a loaf of focaccia, you probably won't need all of it for this toast. The leftover portion will make some great sandwiches (like the Ham and Cheese on page 100) or overqualified croutons for a salad.

- Sesame Focaccia (page 103), sliced in half, then cut into 8 (2½ by 4-inch / 6.25 by 10 cm) pieces
- 2 ripe heirloom tomatoes (varieties mentioned above)
- A few cloves garlic, peeled
- 1 (3-ounce / 85 g) tin oil-packed whole Cantabrian anchovies
- Extra-virgin olive oil
- Maldon salt
- 1 tablespoon fennel pollen
- Freshly ground black pepper

In a toaster, or better yet, under the broiler, toast the bread cut side up until golden.

While the bread is toasting, cut about ⅓ inch (8 mm) off the bottom of each tomato to expose their flesh. Grate the flesh on the wider holes of a box grater, standing the grater in a bowl to catch all the juices. Discard any excess skins.

Arrange the toasts on a plate and rub each one generously with a garlic clove, being sure to scrape all the crustier bits with the garlic. Spoon the tomato pulp and some of the juice from the bowl onto the toasts. Lay 2 or 3 anchovies on each toast, drizzle with olive oil, then sprinkle with Maldon salt and the fennel pollen. Finish with a few cracks of black pepper and serve warm.

braised leek toast with whipped ricotta, oregano oil, and cantabrian anchovies

SERVES 4

This recipe originated with a few loaves of seeded sourdough bread baked one morning by our longtime prep cook Chantal. I fell in love with the toasty and nutty bread instantly. Later that same day, our sous chef Ben made some delicious braised leeks with ricotta for family meal, and as I sat there eating and getting ready for service, something clicked. I really just wanted those two textures and flavors together. That's the way these things happen sometimes. I wish I could pretend it was more like inspired genius, but it's often just, "I really wanna eat that."

You can prepare the leeks a day or two in advance, as long as you make sure to refrigerate them. Pull them from the fridge an hour before use so the oil doesn't congeal. If you can find a seeded loaf, great. If not, a good sourdough will do.

FOR THE LEEKS:

9 leeks (about 2½ pounds / 495 g)

2 teaspoons kosher salt

1½ teaspoons freshly ground black pepper

1 Spanish onion (about 6 ounces / 170 g), thinly sliced

10 cloves garlic, thinly sliced

1 cup (2 sticks / 225 g) unsalted butter, cut into 1-inch (2.5 cm) cubes

Peel of 2 lemons, cut with a peeler

2½ cups (600 ml) extra-virgin olive oil

1 tablespoon champagne vinegar

FOR THE OREGANO OIL:

½ cup plus 2 tablespoons (8 g) fresh oregano leaves

1 tablespoon Maldon salt

2 cups (480 ml) extra-virgin olive oil

FOR FINISHING:

4 (1-inch-thick / 2.5 cm) slices sourdough bread (seeded if possible)

8 ounces (225 g) ricotta cheese, strained in a colander overnight, then paddled in a mixer or pulsed in a food processor until smooth

8 oil-packed Cantabrian anchovy fillets, split lengthwise into long, thin pieces

1 tablespoon dried thyme flowers or fresh thyme leaves

Maldon salt

Freshly ground black pepper

CONTINUED

MAKE THE LEEKS: Preheat the oven to 350°F (175°C).

Trim the roots and the dark green tops from the leeks. Cut the leeks crosswise into 4-inch-long (10 cm) pieces, then split them in half lengthwise. Rinse with slightly warm water to remove any grit, but hold them securely as you do so the layers don't separate and fall apart. Place the rinsed leeks cut side down in a baking dish. Sprinkle on the kosher salt and black pepper. Scatter the onion and garlic over the leeks, then disperse the cubes of butter, the lemon peel, and the olive oil evenly over all.

Roast the leeks until they have no resistance when poked with a cake tester and the tops start charring a bit, 35 to 40 minutes. Remove from the oven, drizzle on the vinegar, and set the leeks aside to cool.

MAKE THE OREGANO OIL: Combine the oregano and Maldon salt in a mortar and pound with the pestle until the oregano gets a bit pulpy. Begin adding the oil 1 tablespoon at a time, pounding and smashing the oregano gently so as not to splash the oil. When you have added all the oil, allow the mixture to sit at room temperature for 30 minutes. Strain the oregano oil through some cheesecloth into a small jar or deli container, pressing on the herbs to extract all the liquid.

TO FINISH: In a toaster or, better yet, under the broiler, toast the bread until golden on both sides. Charring is welcome.

Spoon a thin layer of the whipped ricotta over the toasts, then spread the room-temperature leeks and some of their juices over the ricotta. Add a few spoonfuls of the oregano oil, then place the anchovies on top of the leeks and finish with the thyme flowers. Sprinkle on some Maldon salt and crack on some black pepper, then serve.

SALADS
+
VEGETABLES

SALADS + VEGETABLES

I'll never forget an observation the great David Tanis shared in one of his cookbooks about how garde-manger, the station at a restaurant responsible for cold dishes and appetizers, tends to command the least respect from young cooks, when actually, it should be the very opposite. Sure, everybody wants to jump onto the meat or fish station—to get scars up and down their arms, bags under their eyes, fingernails dirtied by wood, sweat, and fire. They want to become Real Cooks™. But firing a perfect Wagyu steak is a far easier proposition than conceiving—or even preparing—an excellent salad. You have to handle the greens with real care. You have to understand balance: how to make all the combined elements—the acid and oil, the crunch and fat—something greater than the sum of their parts. No Maillard reaction will save you. At The Four Horsemen, we really value vegetables, and here, that station has delivered many of our most important dishes.

"Salad" isn't a term we reserve only for greens with a vinaigrette. Marinated wax beans with pickled shallots and ricotta salata are just as much of a salad to us as a classic Caesar. I've included some favorites from The Four Horsemen that fit both bills. I've also tacked on a couple of warm vegetable dishes that certainly work on their own, but can also take a simple roast and elevate it into a spread you'd be proud to serve anyone.

When you bring your vegetables home, even (and maybe especially) from a farmers' market, give them a good rinse under running water before using them. We take a lot of pride in our cleaning, dressing, and storing salad greens properly (see page 130). And for things like potatoes, leeks, and some tomatoes, we'll use warm water to help dislodge any mud or dirt tucked away in their crevices. Some items will need to be split open to clean them properly; sunchokes and ginger, for example, have craggy surfaces where clumps of gritty soil like to hide.

In addition to the recipes in this chapter, there are some ideas for combinations that you can try (see opposite).

SOME FAVORITES AND HOW TO SERVE THEM

asparagus: pencil, jumbo, white, purple

Grilled jumbo asparagus with a sieved egg and whole-grain-mustard vinaigrette

Poached white asparagus with hollandaise

Early-season roasted pencil asparagus with lemon zest, thyme, olive oil, and thick shavings of Parm

beans/peas: yellow, burgundy, and green wax beans; haricots verts; green and yellow romano beans; snap peas, english peas

A simple plate of blanched wax beans with warm bagna càuda

Thinly sliced romano beans with tahini, fresh mint, and lots of fresh lemon juice

A huge bowl of freshly shucked English peas cooked in salty butter

Snap peas with flowering arugula, radishes, and pecorino ginepro cheese

beets: badger flame, forono, bull's blood, golden

Warm Badger Flame beets with beurre blanc and smoked fish

Forono beets with hazelnuts and chèvre

Golden beets with feta cheese, sesame seeds, and kalamata olives

cabbages: savoy, oxheart, caraflex, napa

Napa cabbage kimchi with cold fried chicken

Creamy savoy cabbage slaw with celery seeds, walnuts, and Honeycrisp apple

Shaved Red Beefheart cabbage with robiola cheese and pickled carrots

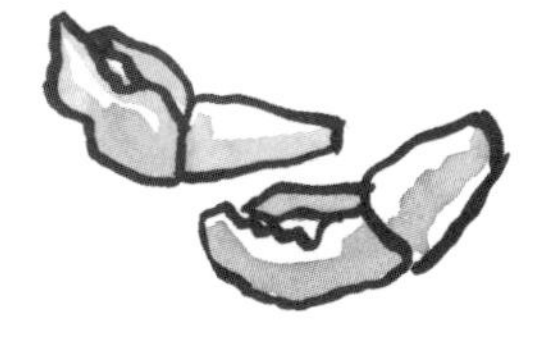

citrus: Cara Cara oranges, tangerines, mandarins, tangelos, Amalfi lemons, navel oranges, clementines

Various types of citrus in peak season with toasted pistachios, Calabrian chiles, and ricotta salata cheese

A deconstructed salad: chunks of ice-cold mandarins, sliced avocado, cilantro on the stem, and thin-sliced pickled red onion

A fancy plate of clementines and Bon Bon dates to end a meal

salad greens: arugula, Little Gems, romaine, puntarelle, frisée, Castelrosso, endive

Wild arugula with Marcona almonds, pickled golden raisins, and Piave Vecchio cheese

Little Gems with Italian vinaigrette, olives, peperoncini, and dried Sicilian oregano

Romaine hearts with buttermilk dressing, smoky bacon, fried onions, and blue cheese

Chicories with bandage-wrapped Cheddar and balsamic vinegar

tomatoes: Brandywine, Sungolds, Cherokee Purple, Sunray, Striped Cavern

Classic caprese salad: sliced tomatoes, slabs of mozzarella, torn basil leaves, olive oil

Chunks of juicy tomatoes tossed with shallots swimming in red wine vinegar, lots of fresh herbs (cilantro, chervil, parsley, chives), and freshly cracked black pepper

Tomatoes in a pool of olive oil and champagne vinegar with torn garlicky bread crumbs and anchovies

burrata with thinly sliced speck and grilled peaches

SERVES 4

There's little to "fix" about the combination of sweet fruit, cured ham, and burrata, so we're not reinventing the wheel here. Instead of prosciutto, we use speck, a slightly smoky ham from Alto Adige, the northernmost region of Italy. And instead of melon—at least, in the summer months—we go for ripe peaches.

A couple of things to keep in mind: When you're checking peaches out at the market, they should *give* a little bit when gently pressed with your finger. And at the butcher, the thinner the speck, the better, so go to someone who will slice to order carefully instead of chancing it in a grocery store aisle. If it's cut too thick, you won't experience the moment when the nearly translucent speck wraps around the warm peaches and basically begins to melt.

- 4 (2-ounce / 55 g) balls burrata cheese
- 1½ teaspoons extra-virgin olive oil, plus more for finishing
- 2 ripe peaches, halved through stem end (or quartered if large) and pitted
- ¼ teaspoon kosher salt
- Maldon salt
- 8 paper-thin slices of speck
- Freshly ground black pepper

Prepare a charcoal or wood-burning grill. Pull the burrata from the fridge and allow it to sit at room temperature for about 30 minutes to take the chill off.

Drizzle the olive oil over the peaches and sprinkle with the kosher salt. Once the grill's initial intense heat has dissipated and it's at a nice medium heat, place the peaches cut-side down on the grill. Avoid the instinct to move them around or flip them for the first couple of minutes. You want to get a good char on the bottom. Once they free easily from the grill when prodded, flip them over and cook for 1 to 2 minutes more. Transfer the grilled peaches to a cutting board and allow to cool for about a minute, then cut them in half.

Arrange the grilled peach quarters on a plate. Tear the burrata into small chunks and scatter those around the plate alongside the peaches. Drizzle on a little more olive oil and sprinkle with Maldon salt, then lay the slices of speck over the top, finish with a few cracks of black pepper, and then serve.

sweet corn salad with pine nut dressing, mint, and peppers

SERVES 4

Nico Villaseñor worked with us for years at The Four Horsemen (hi Nico!). He came to us a very good, albeit inexperienced, cook, with a contagious drive and curiosity. It's important to have motivated and positive people in a professional kitchen, and being around Nico's energy really pushed me to be more creative. This was the first dish we worked on together, and it began a long partnership that would turn out some of my favorite set lunches and desserts.

The dressing, with fish sauce and Thai chiles, torn mint leaves for sweetness and lime juice for brightness, is what holds everything together. I like cubanelles here because of their vegetal taste—not too spicy.

1 cup (120 g) pine nuts

4 cups (517 g) fresh corn kernels (from 7 ears)

1 cup (105 g) small-diced cubanelle peppers

½ cup (120 ml) Pine Nut Vinaigrette (page 313)

2 cups (20 g) fresh mint leaves, lightly chopped

2 tablespoons fresh lime juice

1 teaspoon Maldon salt

Freshly ground black pepper

Preheat the oven to 325°F (165°C). Arrange the pine nuts in a single layer on a sheet tray and toast in the oven, shaking the pan and swirling the nuts with a spoon every few minutes, until lightly browned, about 10 minutes. Once toasted, transfer the nuts to a plate and allow them to cool.

Place the toasted pine nuts, corn, cubanelles, dressing, mint, lime juice, and salt in a mixing bowl and stir with a spoon to combine. Plate the salad and finish with plenty of black pepper, then serve.

mandarins with cilantro, toasted sesame oil, calabrian chile, and kampot peppercorns

SERVES 4

When I was a kid, I thought mandarins were just weird, syrupy things that came in a can, and I wasn't super into them. But then I finally tried the real thing. Remarkably vibrant fruit, incredibly acidic, but still so sweet.

We ran this dish as a kind of snack; the kitchen team and I were very keen on it. Luckily, so was Pete Wells, the *New York Times* restaurant critic, who ended up including a positive mention of it in his review of our place. It's an uncomplicated dish that hinges on the quality of the fruit, as well as the somewhat unusual choice of Kampot peppercorns. Kampot is relatively easy to source and deserves a place in the pantry for the floral, almost tea-like notes it lends to fish and delicate salads.

3 (3½-ounce / 104 g) mandarins, peeled and separated into wedges

½ teaspoon Calabrian chile oil

¼ teaspoon toasted sesame oil

1 cup (40 g) loosely packed coarsely chopped fresh cilantro, plus 2 teaspoons finely chopped cilantro stems

¼ teaspoon Maldon salt

1 tablespoon extra-virgin olive oil

¼ teaspoon ground Kampot peppercorns

Arrange the wedges of mandarin on a plate, slightly overlapping them. Spoon over the chile oil, followed by the sesame oil. Sprinkle on the cilantro stems and salt, then drizzle with the olive oil.

Season the citrus with the Kampot pepper, then spread the chopped cilantro over the citrus and serve.

summer melon with pickled long hot peppers, prosciutto, and marcona almonds

SERVES 4

If you think we didn't deviate too far from the classic with our peach and burrata dish (page 122), here's the actual prosciutto with melon. We always have some iteration of this on the menu when the melon is in peak season. The fruit should be ripe and very fragrant upon initial inspection. Smell the ends of the fruit, as that's usually the best way to tell if it's ready. There should be a little bit of give when gently pressed also, but be careful not to let it get too soft—the texture can quickly turn from firm to spongy.

Keep the fruit well chilled until just before serving, and the addition of spicy pickled peppers and Marcona almonds gives a bit of a "Spain meets Italy on a hot summer day" thing.

- 2 ripe melons (4 to 5 inches / 10 to 12 cm in diameter), preferably cantaloupe or a similar variety
- 1 cup (100 g) somewhat finely chopped Pickled Long Hot Peppers (page 320; store-bought pickled piparras are a great substitute here)
- 20 slices Prosciutto di Parma (ask your butcher to slice it very thin)
- 2 cups (285 g) salted fried Marcona almonds (you can buy them this way . . . and you should!)

Halve and seed the melons, then cut them into 1½-inch-thick (4 cm) slices and remove the rind from each. Store in a shallow, covered container in the refrigerator until ready to serve.

Just before serving, arrange the chilled melon slices on a plate. Distribute the peppers and some of their juices over the melon so each bite will potentially have a little pop of pepper. Drape the prosciutto over the melon, allowing 1 or 2 slices per piece of melon. Scatter the almonds over the top and serve immediately.

real cooks make great salads

TO CLEAN SALAD GREENS

Always handle salad greens with care. That's rule number one. With that in mind, trim off a bit of the root end of a head of lettuce, then start to unravel the leaves, discarding any brown or damaged ones, as well as any too-sturdy or leathery bits. Once there are no more leaves left to remove, trim off some more root. Basically, you want to avoid tearing the leaves off their stems, which breaks down their cell walls and leads to oxidation, leaving you with rusty-colored salad greens. It also just looks sloppy.

Keep working your way through the head of lettuce, carefully peeling off more leaves and cutting more root until you reach the core. Transfer the freed leaves to a large container of cold water (no ice!) and gently swish them around with your fingertips. Let them sit in the water for a few minutes to allow any dirt to sink to the bottom, then carefully cradle them out and into a salad spinner. Do not crowd the spinner; note that you may have to work in batches, depending on the size of your spinner and the volume of greens you're cleaning. Spin the greens, then ditch the water, and finally spin one last time for good measure. Lay the greens out on a sheet tray lined with tea towels and set aside at room temperature for about 10 minutes. This will dry out any excess water before the tray goes into the fridge. You can wrap the greens in paper towels and store them just as you would fresh herbs: in a reusable zip-top bag or a bowl cloaked in a tea towel.

SALADS, SEASON BY SEASON

Here's a loose overview of some of the ingredients we use to build salads, organized by season—the vegetables and greens that hit the market during that time of year and the cheeses, nuts, and other accompaniments that get along very well with them.

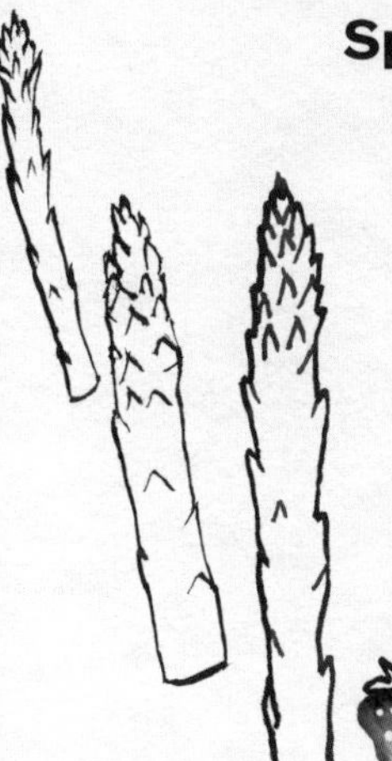

Spring

- Peas: snap, snow, English
- Asparagus: white and green
- Spring onions
- Green garlic
- Burrata
- Ricotta salata
- Fava beans
- Marcona almonds

Fall

- Porcini mushrooms
- Sun-dried tomatoes
- Parm
- Taleggio
- Cauliflower
- Leeks
- Arugula
- Radishes
- Hazelnuts
- Figs

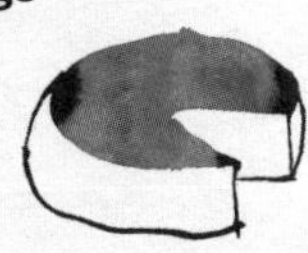

Summer

- Tomatoes
- Sweet corn
- Stone fruit: peaches, pluots, plums
- Cherries
- Melon
- Wax beans
- Feta
- Pine nuts

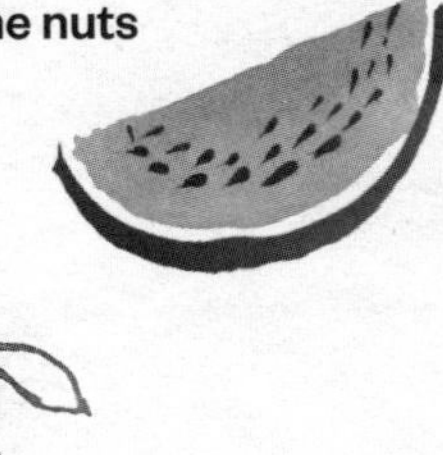

Winter

- Chicories: Treviso, Tardivo, radicchio, Castelfranco, frisée, puntarelle
- Citrus: mandarins, yuzu, tangerines, Cara Cara oranges
- Fuyu persimmon
- Apples
- Avocado
- Kale
- Little Gem lettuce
- Beets
- Prosciutto di Parma
- Comté
- Cheddar
- Walnuts

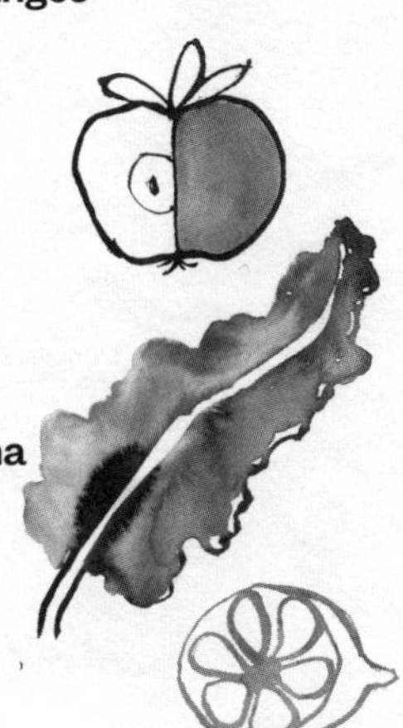

white asparagus with amontillado vinegar and idiazábal cheese

SERVES 4

The historical go-to methods for white asparagus are to poach them in a flavorful broth or cook them with an ungodly amount of butter. Both are great, but we wanted brightness to accentuate the vegetable's natural crisp minerality. At the restaurant, we slice the stalks on the bias and serve them raw, with an elegantly oxidative amontillado vinegar from Despaña (one of the best purveyors of Spanish food in New York), Marcona almonds (Spain again), and big leaves of parsley. If you don't have amontillado vinegar, any good sherry vinegar would work in a pinch. To balance the electric acidity, we also added some smoky Idiazábal cheese (from, you guessed it, Spain).

- 1 bunch white asparagus (8 ounces / 225 g)
- 1 tablespoon extra-virgin olive oil
- 1 tablespoon plus 1 teaspoon amontillado vinegar
- ½ teaspoon Maldon salt
- Leaves (with some stems) from ½ bunch parsley (about 1 loosely packed cup / 50 g)
- ⅓ cup (45 g) salted fried Marcona almonds (you can buy them this way . . . and you should!)
- 1½ ounces (40 g) Idiazábal cheese, rind removed

Peel the asparagus and trim off any woody bottoms. Slice the asparagus about ¼ inch (6 mm) thick on the bias so you end up with roughly 2-inch-long (5 cm) bite-size pieces. Place in a mixing bowl. Dress the asparagus with the olive oil and the vinegar. Add the salt, then toss a few times to coat the asparagus in the vinaigrette.

Spoon the salad onto a plate, along with most of the vinaigrette from the bowl. Add the parsley to the bowl with the residual vinaigrette and give it a few tosses. Spread it out over the asparagus, then scatter the almonds on top of the salad. Using a wide-ribbon Microplane or a peeler, shave pieces of Idiazábal over the salad and serve.

beets with hazelnuts, stracciatella, and fines herbes

SERVES 4

If you can find Badger Flame beets, just buy them. They are hands down my favorite beets. Whichever nice beets you find, this salad will be delicious. The "magic dust" is in the braising liquid.

Beets can take a surprising amount of seasoning during the roasting process. We like to roast them in a covered pot filled with vinegar, spices, aromatics, and lots of salt. Kind of our 4H de facto method.

- 4 large beets (2½ pounds / 1.1 kg), scrubbed under warm water
- ¼ cup (36 g) coriander seeds
- ¼ cup (35 g) whole black peppercorns
- 2 bay leaves
- 4 cups (1 L) cider vinegar
- 1 head garlic, split in half through its equator
- 2 or 3 cinnamon sticks (8 g)
- ¼ cup (40 g) coarsely chopped peeled fresh ginger
- 1 or 2 dried New Mexico chiles
- 1 orange
- ¼ cup (38 g) kosher salt
- ½ cup (75 g) hazelnuts
- ¼ cup (10 g) thinly sliced fresh chives
- ¼ cup fresh chervil leaves (some smaller stems are okay)
- ¼ cup fresh tarragon leaves
- ½ cup (140 g) stracciatella cheese
- Maldon salt
- 1½ tablespoons extra-virgin olive oil
- Freshly ground black pepper

Preheat the oven to 350°F (175°C). Place the beets in a baking dish and add the coriander, peppercorns, bay leaves, vinegar, garlic, cinnamon, ginger, and chiles. Cut the orange in half and squeeze the juice over the beets, then throw in the squeezed rinds as well. Sprinkle with the kosher salt and then add water to come up halfway on the beets, about 2 cups (480 ml) water (or more, depending on size of roasting dish). Cover very tightly with foil and roast for 1½ hours, then poke the beets with a small paring knife or cake tester. If it slips in with ease, remove them from the oven and allow to cool. (If they still feel firm, roast for another 30 minutes and then check again; continue roasting as needed until they're tender.) Keep the oven on.

Arrange the hazelnuts in a single layer on a sheet tray and toast in the oven, shaking the pan and swirling the nuts with a spoon every few minutes, until lightly browned, 12 to 15 minutes. Once toasted, transfer the nuts to a plate and allow them to cool, then crush them with the bottom of a pot. Try to keep the pieces on the larger side. If a few whole nuts sneak in, that's fine.

Once the beets are just warm to the touch, peel them by hand, using a small paring knife to scrape off the skin. Try not to dig into the flesh of the beets at all. You want to retain that round shape. Slice the peeled beets into roughly ¼-inch-thick (6 mm) rounds and set aside. You can discard the aromatic mix.

Finely chop the chives, chervil, and tarragon and mix them together in a small bowl. (I like to use my sharpest knife for this, as the herbs are particularly delicate and will bruise if they're cut with a dull knife.)

Let the stracciatella stand at room temperature for about 30 minutes before plating, then spoon it out onto a serving dish in a loose, even layer. Sprinkle on a bit of Maldon salt, then shingle the sliced beets on top of the stracciatella. Scatter on the toasted hazelnuts. Drizzle with the olive oil, then add the herbs and crack over some black pepper to finish. Serve.

on vinegars

Powerful and subtle in measure depending on their implementation, vinegars are a crucial part of a cook's toolbox. Build out your collection little by little. Vinegar keeps for a very long time, so as long as you have the space, you can explore and stock up. The following are some of my favorites.

THE TOP THREE

champagne vinegar

This is our workhorse at The Four Horsemen. It's made from chardonnay and pinot noir grapes (two of the famous Champagne region varieties), and we use it for pickling, salads, vegetables . . . everything. It's bright and has just the right amount of sweetness without being cloying. Go for the Beaufor branded one.

red wine vinegar

Another ingredient I learned to really appreciate while working at Camino. Chef Russ made his own in house and aged it in wooden barrels in the back of the kitchen. It was truly revelatory. If you can, try to find a red wine vinegar with some oak age; it can soften the inherent sharpness and add depth and character. Castello di Volpaia out of Tuscany is not oak aged, but makes up for it with gentle balance in the flavor. It's also not too hard to find.

cider vinegar

Cider vinegar is nice when you want a touch of extra sweetness and pleasant sharpness. It cuts through the richer preparations popular in winter months, breathing life and vibrancy into bitter chicories and roasted vegetables. I like the cider vinegars produced by Beaufor and O-Med.

OTHER OPTIONS TO CONSIDER

yuzu vinegar

Instead of lemon juice, try a splash of this vinegar to add sweet and floral citrusy notes to salads and fresh vegetables. O-Med makes a beautiful yuzu vinegar that really shines with fish.

sherry vinegar

I'm particularly fond of vinegars made from oloroso and amontillado sherries, but standard sherry is excellent as well. These vinegars have oxidative qualities that translate to a really rich and nutty finish. Try them on grilled meats or cheesy, vegetable-forward salads. Montegrato makes some beautiful sherry vinegars that you can purchase from Despaña in New York City (or via their online store).

rice vinegar

More delicate and slightly sweeter than white wine vinegar, rice vinegar is made by fermenting rice. It has a mild acidity that's great in marinades. Marukan makes an affordable one that you can find almost anywhere.

moscatel and banyuls vinegars

The moscatel and Banyuls wines are made from grapes that winemakers and drinkers prize for their sweetness. Those sugars produce vinegars that are ideal for summer salads and raw vegetables like cucumbers. I source them from La Guinelle.

infused vinegars

You can find many varieties of infused vinegar on the market, but it's also simple to infuse your own at home. We do a lot of that at the restaurant. We also like to make vinegar infused with the flavor of fig leaves, cilantro, sweet onions, ramps, or coriander—to name just a few. Generally, we warm some champagne vinegar slightly and then pour it over whatever we're hoping to flavor it with. Tuck it away in the fridge overnight, then begin to taste. It can be fun to play around with flavored vinegars—they will surely set your pantry apart, and you'll notice more vibrancy and a lot more nuance when you reach for one of these to spike a dish.

sugar snap peas with calabrian chile, mint, and ricotta salata

SERVES 4

When we did our friends-and-family opening dinners, I added this salad last minute as a vegetarian alternative to some meat thing I no longer remember. What I *do* remember is how stunned we all were by how well this dish was received. We put it on the spring menu that year, and then again the next, and the next. This one has Franny's written all over it: lemon juice, olive oil, salty cheese—simple, on the surface. There is a somewhat annoying (but oddly satisfying) task of taking all the strings off the snap peas. It's crucial—and you need to do both ends. We use a paring knife to kind of nip and pull the strings. Some peas have hardier strings than others; some have none. Either way, it's definitely worth the hassle. Cut the peas lengthwise on the bias, creating a little bowl shape to trap juices.

- 1 cup (86 g) whole cashews
- 4 tablespoons (75 g) kosher salt
- 1 pound (455 g) sugar snap peas, strings removed (see above for tips)
- ¼ cup (60 g) chopped Calabrian chiles
- ¼ cup plus 3 tablespoons (105 ml) fresh lemon juice
- 2 tablespoons extra-virgin olive oil
- Maldon salt
- 2 cups (30 g) loosely packed fresh mint leaves
- 1 (6-ounce / 170 g) block ricotta salata cheese

Preheat the oven to 350°F (175°C). Arrange the cashews in a single layer on a sheet tray and toast in the oven, shaking the pan and swirling the nuts with a spoon every few minutes, until lightly browned, 12 to 15 minutes. Once toasted, transfer the nuts to a plate and allow them to cool, then crush them with the bottom of a pot. Try to keep the pieces on the larger side. If a few whole nuts sneak in, that's fine.

Fill a large pot with 4 quarts (4 L) water and add 3 tablespoons of the kosher salt. Bring the water to a boil. Fill a large bowl with plenty of ice, add the remaining 1 tablespoon salt, and then add water. Line a sheet tray with tea towels and set it nearby.

Carefully drop the peas into the boiling water and cook for 1 to 2 minutes, until the peas are tender but still have a good amount of crunch. Immediately transfer them to the ice bath and allow to cool completely, about 5 minutes, then transfer to the towel-lined tray and place in the fridge to dry for about 30 minutes. (We spin them in a salad spinner at the restaurant; if you decide to use one, you can skip the refrigerating step.)

Slice the peas in half lengthwise on the bias and transfer them to a mixing bowl. Add the toasted nuts, chiles, lemon juice, olive oil, and Maldon salt. Coarsely chop the mint and add it to the bowl. Toss everything with a spoon and transfer to plates or a shallow bowl. Using a wide-ribbon Microplane, cover with ribbons of ricotta salata and serve.

chicory salad with fuyu persimmons, spiced walnuts, and tahini vinaigrette

SERVES 4

See if you can source good persimmons during the winter. You'll find two common varieties at markets in the US: Fuyu and Hachiya. We use Fuyu for this salad. This variety is crunchier and has an uncanny sweetness that's tough to place. (The Hachiya are also delicious, but they're prized for their jellylike flesh, not their snap, making them a completely different beast.)

Baharat is a warm spice blend (literally translates as "spices" in Arabic) that generally contains cinnamon, cumin, black pepper, and clove. If you end up with a jar, it's also great rubbed on meats before slow cooking or sprinkled into rice in the winter months.

1 cup (110 g) walnuts

1 teaspoon extra-virgin olive oil

1 teaspoon baharat

8 ounces (225 g) chicories (Castelfranco, Treviso, and Tardivo are all great options; about 2 heads)

Generous 6 ounces (180 g) Fuyu persimmons (2 to 3 persimmons)

3 tablespoons Tahini Vinaigrette (page 313)

3 tablespoons plus 1 teaspoon (50 ml) fresh lemon juice

Maldon salt

Preheat the oven to 350°F (175°C). Arrange the walnuts in a single layer on a sheet tray and toast in the oven, shaking the pan and swirling the nuts with a spoon every few minutes, until lightly browned, 12 to 15 minutes. Once toasted, transfer the nuts to a plate and allow them to cool.

In a mixing bowl, toss the toasted walnuts with the olive oil and sprinkle in the baharat. Stir and toss to combine and set aside.

Cut the chicories into quarters and remove the cores with a knife, then cut the leaves into bite-size pieces and pull them apart (chicories can cling together very tightly). Set aside in a large bowl.

Peel and quarter the persimmons, then remove any black seeds from the centers and the stems. Slice the persimmon quarters into thin half-moons and add them to the bowl with the chicories. Add the walnuts to the chicories along with the vinaigrette, the lemon juice, and salt. Toss the salad to combine, plate, and serve.

on olive oil

Olive oil with the official denotation "extra-virgin" is made by milling whole, undamaged olives to extract their oil. These olives have been carefully vetted and kept at a controlled temperature throughout the process to prevent any bacterial growth or off-flavors in the finished oil. A certification panel then evaluates the finished oil for bitterness, pungency, and fruitiness and then slaps the grade on it. A lot of labor, care, and choice ingredients go into making this stuff. Add that regulatory process, the excellent fruit, and the lower yields these standards imply, and you're looking at a more expensive final product than other types of olive oil. And it is entirely worth it: At the restaurant as well as at home, I only use extra-virgin olive oil.

We like the oils from Italy, particularly those from Liguria, where the salty ocean breeze might have something to do with the magic. This region's oils are buttery and rich, with a delicate and smooth finish. Sicily's volcanic soils produce more assertive and vibrant oils that stand up to grilled meats, fish, and vegetables. Tuscany, Umbria, and Lazio all bring different tones to the table as well. You really can't go wrong if you make any of these your olive oil of choice, but I'd encourage you to choose. Taste different oils and see which notes resonate with your palate and cooking style. Some of our favorite producers are Pianogrillo in Sicily, Laudemio in Tuscany, and Il Tratturello in Molise.

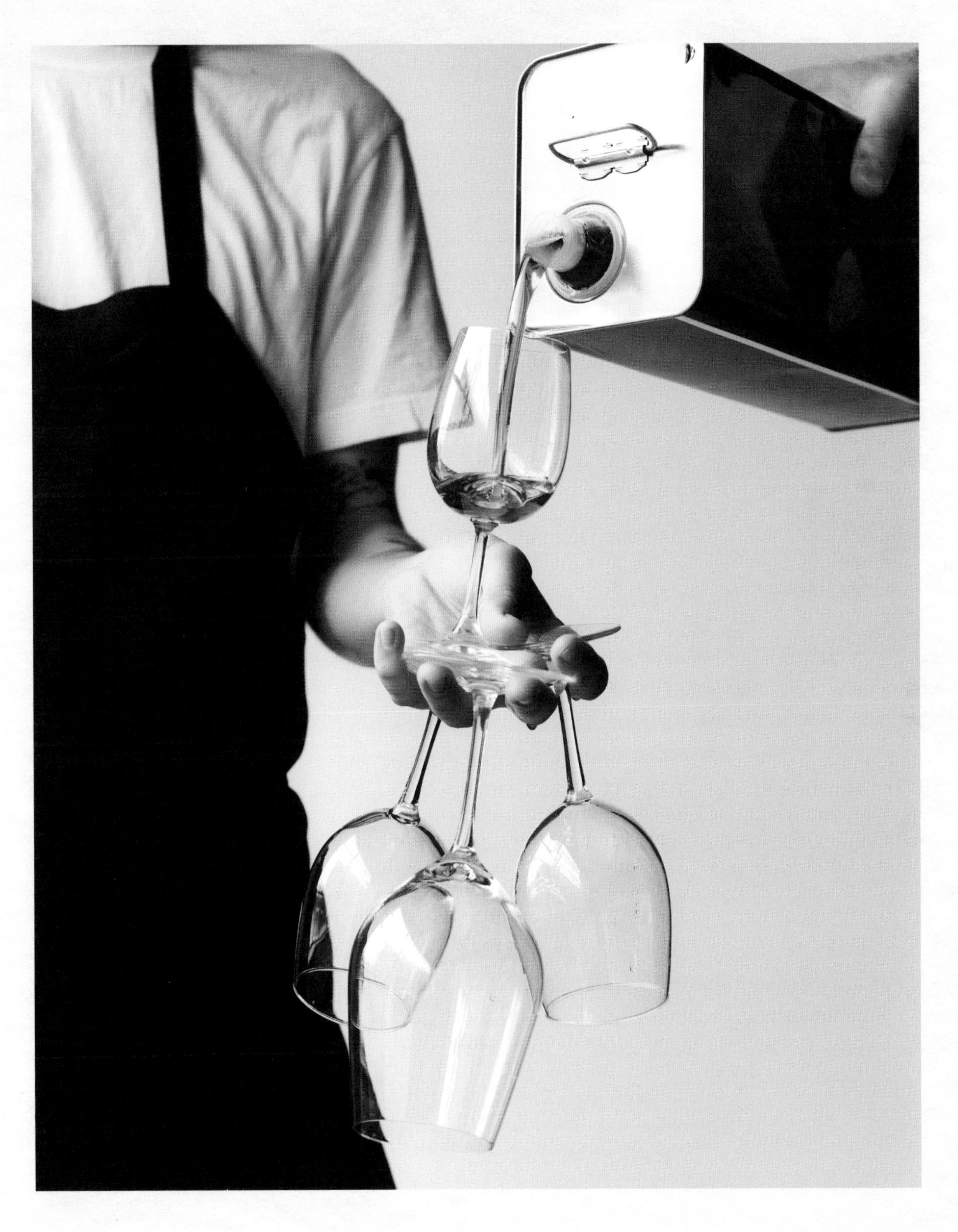

SALADS + VEGETABLES

red endive with honeycrisp apples, pistachios, vermouth vinaigrette, and cheddar

SERVES 4

We ran this salad at the restaurant during our first winter, then again the following year. The floral effect the pink peppercorn has on the pistachios . . . The bitterness of the endives and vermouth vinegar balanced by the fatty nuts and sweet Honeycrisps . . . Sure, it was a bit of a challenge, as not everyone thinks they want bitterness, but it's a real salad lover's salad. We kept having it back because we kept wanting that note on the menu.

We initially served this with Gran Pepe cheese grated on top. Pecorino pepato, though tough to come by, would be a good substitute. In case you don't have some master rare-cheese monger next door, we designed this iteration with a sharp Cheddar—here we like both Vermont and New York styles.

FOR THE PISTACHIOS:

1 cup (133 g) unsalted shelled pistachios

1 teaspoon extra-virgin olive oil

½ teaspoon finely ground pink peppercorns

1 teaspoon Maldon salt

FOR THE SALAD:

1 Honeycrisp apple

5 heads red endive, cut from their stems, leaves separated

⅓ cup (80 ml) Vermouth Vinaigrette (page 314)

½ teaspoon kosher salt

1 (4-ounce / 115 g) piece Cheddar cheese

MAKE THE PISTACHIOS: Preheat the oven to 350°F (175°C). Arrange the pistachios in a single layer on a sheet tray and toast in the oven, shaking the pan and swirling the nuts with a spoon every few minutes, until lightly browned, 10 to 12 minutes. Once toasted, transfer the nuts to a plate and allow them to cool.

In a mixing bowl, combine the toasted pistachios with the olive oil, pink pepper, and Maldon salt. Toss to combine and set aside.

MAKE THE SALAD: Quarter and core the apples, then slice the quarters into half-moons about ¼ inch (6 mm) thick.

Place the endive in a large bowl, followed by the apples, then the pistachios. Add the vinaigrette and kosher salt and toss to combine.

Plate the salad, then grate a generous amount of cheese on top with a wide-ribbon Microplane and serve.

little gems with green goddess, radishes, and fried croutons

SERVES 4

The dressing is so satisfying and the fresh gems are so alive, but fried croutons are kind of hard to compete with. Prepare them at the last minute so they're still warm when tossing the salad. The outsides should be crunchy, with a softer, chewy interior. If frying isn't feasible, you can oven-bake them. And if you can't find Little Gems, romaine hearts make a fine substitute. In general, better a fresh and crisp replacement green than some sad, limp gems.

Canola oil, for frying

4 loose cups (215 g) day-old Focaccia (page 103) or sourdough bread, crusts removed, bread cut into roughly ½-inch (12 mm) cubes

Kosher salt

5 large heads (about 1 pound / 500 g) Little Gem lettuce, leaves separated (tough outer leaves discarded)

1½ cups (355 ml) Green Goddess Dressing (page 312)

3 tablespoons anchovies, chopped (about 8 fillets)

1 cup (125 g) thinly sliced French Breakfast radishes

1 cup (125 g) pumpkin seeds

Freshly ground black pepper

In a heavy Dutch oven or deep stockpot, pour about 3 inches (8 cm) canola oil and heat the oil over medium-low heat until the temperature reaches 350°F (175°C). Adjust your burner as needed to maintain that temperature as you proceed with the recipe. Have a spider handy and set a sheet tray lined with paper towels nearby.

Working in batches if necessary, add the bread cubes to the hot oil and fry until golden brown, about 2 minutes. Transfer to the paper towel–lined tray with the spider or a slotted spoon and season with salt.

Put the Little Gem leaves in a large bowl, add the dressing and the anchovies, and toss gently, then add the sliced radishes and pumpkin seeds. Finally, add the warm croutons and toss to combine.

Plate the salad and top with plenty of black pepper, then serve.

chicory salad with anchovy and parmigiano-reggiano

SERVES 4

Puntarelle alla romana is a dish that's near and dear to my heart. We've put out some version of it at the restaurant every winter since we opened. Puntarelle is a sturdy and satisfyingly crisp chicory with a bracing bitterness and intense juicy quality. That being said, it can be a challenge to find outside of restaurants.

We did a bunch of testing and found some brilliant results using more frequently available chicories, such as radicchio, Tardivo, frisée, and Treviso. If you're at the market in winter and happen to find Castelfranco, La Rosa del Veneto, or Coraline, those in combination make for an impressive explosion of colors and textures.

FOR THE ANCHOVY DRESSING:

About 7 oil-packed anchovy fillets (1¼ ounces / 36 g total), finely chopped

1½ cloves garlic, grated with a Microplane

1 tablespoon Dijon mustard

4 teaspoons fresh lemon juice

¼ cup (60 ml) champagne vinegar

Freshly ground black pepper

1 teaspoon kosher salt

1 teaspoon chile flakes

1 cup (240 ml) extra-virgin olive oil

FOR THE SALAD:

10 ounces (300 g) chicories (a mix of varieties; see headnote), cut into 2- to 3-inch (5 to 7.5 cm) pieces

2 teaspoons fresh lemon juice

½ teaspoon kosher salt

1 cup (100 g) finely grated Parmigiano-Reggiano cheese, plus a small block for serving

Freshly ground black pepper

MAKE THE DRESSING: In a mixing bowl, combine the anchovies, garlic, mustard, lemon juice, and vinegar. Whisk to combine. Crack in 18 turns of black pepper and add the salt and chile flakes. While whisking, drizzle in the olive oil. Taste and adjust, if need be. (If you won't be serving the salad immediately, store the vinaigrette in an airtight container in the fridge for up to 1 week.)

MAKE THE SALAD: Place the chicories in a large bowl. Pour over ½ cup (120 ml) of the anchovy vinaigrette, reserving the rest for another use, then add the lemon juice and salt. Stir a few times, until the chicories are nicely coated with the vinaigrette.

Add the grated cheese and stir a few more times. Plate the salad, then grate more cheese over the top with a Microplane. Finish with a few good cracks of black pepper and serve.

SALADS + VEGETABLES

celery salad with toasted walnuts, medjool dates, and piave vecchio cheese

SERVES 4

This is a simple salad that we get a lot of questions about at the restaurant. Guests seem to think there's more to it . . . some kind of kitchen trick. Again, I think whatever magic there is just lies in the freshness of a few key ingredients (mainly the mint and the lemons), as well as the sharpness of your knife. If Piave Vecchio proves elusive, our old favorite Parmigiano-Reggiano will work well here. We've also had great success using smoky Idiazábal, though it's less of a 1:1 replacement, as it takes the salad in a totally different, albeit delicious, direction.

- Heaping ½ cup (65 g) walnuts
- 2 cups (200 g) celery, cut from core and sliced ¼ inch (6 mm) thick on the bias with a sharp knife
- ½ cup (75 g) Medjool dates, halved, pitted, and cut ¼ inch (6 mm) thick on the bias
- ½ teaspoon chile flakes
- 2 teaspoons kosher salt
- 2 tablespoons fresh lemon juice
- ⅓ cup (75 ml) extra-virgin olive oil
- ½ cup (25 g) loosely packed fresh mint leaves, coarsely chopped, plus more if needed
- 1 (3¼-ounce / 90 g) wedge of Piave Vecchio cheese, rind removed

Preheat the oven to 350°F (175°C). Arrange the walnuts in a single layer on a sheet tray and toast in the oven, shaking the pan and swirling the nuts with a spoon every few minutes, until lightly browned, 12 to 15 minutes. Once toasted, transfer the nuts to a plate and allow them to cool.

In a large bowl, combine the celery, dates, chile flakes, and salt. Add the toasted walnuts, giving them a slight crush as you sprinkle them in. Pour over the lemon juice and olive oil and stir well until the celery is glazed. The salad should look juicy and a vinaigrette should start to pool at the bottom of the bowl.

Add the mint leaves and give a toss or two—you don't want to beat them up too much or overdress them. They should remain very fresh in the salad.

Plate the salad, ensuring each dish gets a good amount of the nuts and dates. With a wide-ribbon Microplane or a peeler, grate a healthy amount of Piave Vecchio into long ribbons over the salad. The cheese should cover the salad almost completely, with bits of mint and celery and nuts poking out here and there, then serve.

romaine hearts with daikon radish and mint

SERVES 4

Good romaine. Its sturdy cups cradle dressings, herbs, everything so well. Try to use the really pale green inner leaves as they provide more juicy snap. This dish works best if the daikon is marinated overnight. If that's not possible, let it sit in the vinaigrette for at least an hour. You may not need all the vinaigrette, but the leftover portion will keep in the fridge for at least a week.

- 1 pound (455 g) daikon radish, peeled, quartered lengthwise, and very thinly sliced
- 1 batch Palm Sugar Vinaigrette (page 314)
- ½ bunch cilantro, leaves and stems reserved separately
- 4 romaine hearts, leaves separated
- 2 cups (60 g) fresh mint leaves
- ½ cup (75 g) sesame seeds
- Maldon salt
- Extra-virgin olive oil

Put the daikon in a small container with a lid and add enough of the vinaigrette to cover. Set aside in the refrigerator to marinate for at least an hour, but ideally overnight.

Right before serving the salad, slice the cilantro stems as finely as possible by lining them up together between your fingertips and cutting them into thin rounds. Set aside.

When you're ready to assemble the salad, place the romaine leaves in a large bowl. Drain the daikon and add it to the bowl. Add the cilantro stems, and a few spoonfuls of the vinaigrette and toss a few times, then coarsely chop the mint and cilantro leaves and add them to the bowl along with the sesame seeds and Maldon salt. Toss a couple more times, then plate, making sure the majority of the romaine is cup side up to catch all the juices. Divvy up the daikon and herbs among the plates, then finish each salad with a drizzle of olive oil and serve.

SALADS + VEGETABLES

tasters

We're constantly tasting food in The Four Horsemen kitchen. The entire team is involved in the creative process. We go over what we're working on, get into the ideas we want to explore, and push everyone to share their opinions and recent obsessions. Every night, even if we're busy, we'll put up dishes on the pass and each cook has to stop to taste, or "tuck" (kitchens really do have the dumbest lingo). In our industry, these scrums are called "tasters." To some of our newer cooks, it can feel a bit odd to be part of dish development and refinement, which in many restaurants happens entirely apart from the day-to-day operation.

Personally, I like to bring everyone in because I know from my own experiences that giving cooks as many opportunities as possible to taste is going to make them better at their jobs, which, in the end, is better for them, for the restaurant, and for me. Besides, it's more fun this way. It also helps me to hear a wide range of reactions from people of different skill levels and backgrounds. What if a dish reminds a new cook of a stew they used to eat back home that the rest of us have never heard of? There might be something to explore that you would have otherwise missed.

Even if you don't know what you're tasting for, taste. Then taste again. And try to identify what you're experiencing. This is how you'll learn the differences between bitter, salty, sweet, and savory, and how those flavors are brought about by different ingredients and techniques. The more you taste, the more you'll be in command of your cooking. That Meyer lemon pasta? Taste it before and after you add the lemon. What did it do to the dish? Did you add too much? Too little? If you went overboard, what can you do now to offset your heavy hand? Would a little butter help mute that acidity?

There's a lot of really interesting science on the subject of taste, but I'm partial to the idea that honing your palate is about conscious eating. With the memories amassed over many years working in a kitchen, a good professional cook can analyze food quite differently from most people, and will typically have developed an effective vocabulary to describe what they find, because they can quickly compare it to this Rolodex of previous experiences and flavors.

As mundane as this may sound, good cooking is about repetition. Sometimes (certainly in a professional environment) to a mind-numbing degree. But this repetition will lead to small "mistakes," which can either be brilliant surprises you'll want to repeat, or disasters you'll desperately try to avoid in the future. Developing a working palate is really just labor, attention, and time, after which your cooking will feel more and more natural and in your control. This well-earned sense memory then becomes the foundation of your creativity: Once you've built a library of flavors, techniques, errors and inspirations, surprises and horrors, you can let your mind wander as you work and see where your instincts lead. And all of it begins and ends with this simple task: *Taste it*.

roasted squash with brown butter and vincotto

SERVES 4

Dreary Winter Day therapy. It's basically all about the brown butter. We developed a way at the restaurant to kind of suspend brown butter solids in a very nutty and toasty sauce by stirring it over an ice bath. Typically, these solids will split when allowed to cool undisturbed, and you get left with an oily and kind of sad, separated butter. Our technique gives you a well-emulsified result, with a mix of fats and caramelized sugars in each bite. If you have leftovers, it's a great base for pastas with brown butter, finishing sauces, and gravies for meats. It can also be used in baking to add an extra depth of flavor to desserts.

- 1 pound (455 g) unsalted butter
- 2 tablespoons nonfat milk powder
- 1 (1½-pound / 680 g) Honeynut or butternut squash, split in half and seeded
- 1 tablespoon extra-virgin olive oil
- ½ teaspoon kosher salt, plus more if needed
- 1½ tablespoons vincotto
- Maldon salt

In a wide sauté pan, melt the butter over medium heat, then cook the melted butter until it starts to lightly brown, about 15 minutes. Add the milk powder and cook until you reach a golden brown hue. Immediately transfer to a mixing bowl and place the bowl inside a larger bowl of ice. Stir frequently until the butter begins to firm up and turns kind of a pale golden brown, about 5 minutes. (The browned butter can be stored in an airtight container in the fridge for a month or so or in the freezer for up to 2 months.)

Preheat the oven to 375°F (190°C). Place the squash cut side up on a sheet tray and drizzle with the olive oil. Sprinkle on the kosher salt and then flip the squash halves so they're cut side down on the tray. Roast for 30 to 45 minutes, until tender and slightly caramelized. Remove the squash from the oven and set aside to cool slightly. When it's cool enough to handle, scoop out the flesh and transfer it to a small pot. Smash it up a bit, but leave some nice chunks as well. It doesn't have to be perfect. Set the pot aside.

In a separate small pot, warm the brown butter.

Rewarm the squash, taste, and adjust with kosher salt, if need be, then divide among four bowls. Use the side of a fork to make some indentations in the top of the squash to catch the sauces. Spoon over the brown butter so it runs into all the nooks and crannies, then spoon over the vincotto. Finish with Maldon salt and serve immediately.

LES
AUNIS
GOURMANDISES

yellow wax beans with burrata, pine nuts, and oregano

SERVES 4

Hot take: I prefer yellow wax beans to green beans because there's something more delicate about them. It could also be the way they look, monochromatic but still summery. The pop of bright yellow beans against a creamy burrata backdrop is a good example. It is a simple and straightforward recipe, one that should be made when you can get some high-quality burrata and the beans are at their peak at the market—think midsummer backyard gatherings.

3 tablespoons pine nuts

¼ cup (75 g) kosher salt, plus more as needed

7 ounces (200 g) yellow wax beans, stem ends trimmed

4½ teaspoons fresh lemon juice

2 tablespoons extra-virgin olive oil, plus more to finish

1 (4-ounce / 115 g) ball burrata cheese, at room temperature

½ teaspoon Maldon salt

Leaves from 3 oregano sprigs (¼ cup loosely packed / 15 g)

Freshly ground black pepper

Preheat the oven to 325°F (165°C). Arrange the pine nuts in a single layer on a sheet tray and toast in the oven until lightly browned, about 10 minutes. Once toasted, transfer the nuts to a plate and allow them to cool.

Fill a large pot with 4 quarts (4 L) water, add the kosher salt, and bring to a boil. Fill a large bowl with plenty of ice, add some kosher salt, and then add water and line a sheet tray with tea towels; set both near the stove. Carefully drop the wax beans into the boiling water and cook for 1 to 2 minutes, until the beans are tender but still have a good amount of crunch. Immediately transfer them to the ice bath and allow them to cool completely, about 5 minutes. Remove the wax beans from the ice bath and transfer to the towel-lined tray. Place the tray in the fridge and let the beans dry for about 30 minutes.

When the beans have dried, transfer them with a spider or tongs to a mixing bowl. Immediately drizzle over the lemon juice, then add the olive oil and the toasted pine nuts. Toss to combine.

Cut the burrata into quarters and divvy them up among four plates. Top each plate with a pile of the wax beans and pine nuts. Finish the dish with the Maldon salt, oregano, and a few good cracks of black pepper. A little extra olive oil wouldn't hurt, either.

DRINKING WINE AT HOME

Little moves from restaurants are really easy to bring to your home table and can make a big difference. Here are some easy tips to serve wine the way we do at The Four Horsemen:

DECANTING AT HOME

I'm a big fan of decanting pretty much every bottle I drink: Pouring the wine into another vessel is a great way to soften the tannins and wake up a young wine, with the side benefit of bringing a little bit of drama and expectation to the table, which is never a bad thing. And in the case of many unfiltered wines, decanting leaves behind some sediment in the bottle, helping to avoid that dreaded last murky glass of grit.

The "decanter" I've used the most is a $1.99 water pitcher I picked up at a strip mall discount store in the mid-2000s. Nobody's ever raised an eyebrow when I've poured a sought-after Jura unicorn wine into it. A decanter is not something you need to spend a lot of money on, and it doesn't need to be glass, either. The classic Ricard and Pernod ones are ceramic. I've seen winemakers decant into bowls, watering cans, and, in one particularly rural case, a flowerpot. This is an opportunity to get creative and have something that tells a story on the table.

AGING AT HOME

For whatever reason, people continue to be surprised when I talk about aging natural wines. I imagine that this is because they don't think time helps inexpensive or low-intervention bottles, but that's definitely not the case. The Four Horsemen has off-site wine storage where we send bottles that we think will be better with time; it almost always pays off.

You can easily do the same at home. It doesn't matter if you don't have a EuroCave. I've stashed wines in the crisper of my fridge for a couple of months, even though I've been told that the extreme cold can compromise the cork and aromatics, leading to oxidation or leakage. I haven't had any issues. Other storage facilities in my home include under the bed, at the bottom of a closet, and in the basement. I put the wines there and then forget about them. Almost every single one improves. They become more open; the flavors less primary and more complex; the acids more integrated and, most importantly, more delicious.

One of the reasons aging can improve natural wine is that many of these bottles are sold very young–in some cases because they're designed for everyday drinking and ready enough soon after bottling, but mostly because the winemaker needs to sell this year's wines to have enough money and space to make next year's wines. I think people often think that aging means cellaring a bottle for decades, but I've found that just giving a wine six months to a year can pay dividends. It doesn't have to be a splurgy bottle. Try it with a $16 bottle of weeknight Côtes du Rhône, or a $25 sauvignon blanc from Austria–or, to really gain an understanding, buy a few bottles of something you already know and love and open a bottle of it every couple of months. Watching a wine evolve over time will give you an idea of where it's going and what that time really does. Just a few months can allow the wine to settle in itself, relax, and develop into something much more than it was when you brought it home from the shop.

THE RIGHT GLASS

Glassware is a surprisingly controversial subject. I came up in a slightly formalized wine world where wines and their regions were assigned their own specific type of glass. Situations where

a classical wine drinker might say something like, "Are you really pouring that red Burgundy into a barolo glass?" wasn't uncommon. For someone like me, on a budget, living in a small New York City apartment, it never really made sense. Thankfully, I can say that you can enjoy every wine in the same glass: 99 out of 100 of the wines we serve at The Four Horsemen are poured into glasses made by Korin that are officially sold as chardonnay glasses. We think they do more than that. They aren't the oversized balloon-shaped glasses that land on the table to announce the arrival of a blue-chip wine. They're thin but not fragile, about 8½ inches (22 cm) from base to rim, with a slender bowl and tapered opening that focuses the aromas.

There is plenty of incredibly expensive glassware on the market. It helps to remember that you will probably, eventually break whatever you buy. Yes, sure, the weightlessness of a $90 hand-blown piece of crystal stemware from Austria can be amazing, but there's a very intentional neutrality to the glasses we use at the restaurant. We like to think it's more about the wine than the glass anyway, and this can be a particularly welcome realization at home, when budgets and storage space are limited.

THE RIGHT TEMPERATURE

People don't seem to put enough consideration into what temperature they're serving their red wines. It's completely common, even in the home of someone that takes wine pretty seriously, to be given a glass of red that's at room temperature, or warmer. If they had just put that wine in the fridge for half an hour before popping the cork, the wine would be so much more enjoyable. Serving reds over 70°F (21°C) knocks the wine completely out of whack. The alcohol and the acids are exaggeratedly high, overwhelming the fruit and texture. But reds that are served cooler–say, somewhere between 60 and 65°F (15 to 18°C)–are balanced and much subtler. We keep our cellar at the restaurant at 55°F (13°C) and let the red wines warm up in the glass, on the table. Let them evolve. At home, I tend to keep all of the red wines I'm planning on drinking imminently in the refrigerator and just take them out 30 minutes before opening them.

On the other hand, everyone seems to agree that white, sparkling, and rosé wines should be served cold, but often they can be served too cold, like a truly icy, straight out of the refrigerator 35°F (1.6°C). We prefer serving these just a little warmer than you would think. Around 45°F (7.2°C) and the wine will thank you. The aromas will be there, the acidity will be more balanced, and the texture, depending on the weight of the wine, will be more opulent. All it takes is pulling the wine out of the fridge half an hour before popping the cork (just like the reds). Co-fermenting red and white grapes yields a fresh and juicy red, just a little darker than a classic rosé. These are great for casual drinking, and kill on a table filled with salads, vegetable dishes, and charcuterie.

When you start drinking wines at the right temperature, it's hard to go back.

A BOWL OF...

A BOWL OF...

A bowl can be a vehicle for a super clear and salty broth, packed with rich gelatin, a few satisfyingly cheesy tortellini floating around, waiting. Or maybe you have a bowl of fresh rice, topped with sticky glazed eel, its smoky juices working their way to the bottom on the journey to your table. The rice starts all dry and springy, distinct from the eel. By the end, each grain is coated in the sweet and savory sauce, and you end up with a whole new set of textures and flavors.

I have bowls in probably a dozen different styles and sizes tucked away in various corners of my home. Some I've collected from trips abroad to Japan and Italy; others have been made by hand by close friends. One of my favorite practices is to get new bowls, hide the old ones, then rediscover ones from years past and bring them back into rotation. In the restaurant, we have completely different bowls for various uses and presentations, as they can radically influence the taste and texture of the dishes they contain. No other plateware can have such an impact on the eating experience as a bowl.

The following pages feature some dishes best suited for whatever vessels you have around your house. A few of them (the raviolo, gnocchi, and lentils) call for a shallower bowl, but they'll be delicious no matter how you serve them.

POTATO GNOCCHI WITH FONTINA,
CHIVES, AND CRISPY SHALLOTS

potato gnocchi with fontina, chives, and crispy shallots

SERVES 4

I got really into potato gnocchi while cooking in Piedmont, Italy, some years ago. The food in the north can be much richer than it is in other parts of the country, especially when you start getting close to the Alps: the wild boar ragù, bowls of polenta with loads of Gorgonzola cheese, meat-stuffed pastas swimming in buttery sauces. It was an eye-opening experience. In particular, I fell in love with fonduta, a sauce featuring Fontina Val d'Aosta cheese.

Roasting the potatoes in their skins and drying out the cooked flesh as quickly as possible is crucial to the gnocchi's fluffy texture: Introducing water and steam means adding more flour later, which eventually means gummier gnocchi. Also, for this recipe, avoid the ridges sometimes found on gnocchi; this sauce doesn't require them, which makes shaping them a breeze. The crispy shallots are readily available at most Asian markets.

This recipe will make more gnocchi than you need for the dish, but they store really well in the freezer and are great for last-minute dinners.

FOR THE GNOCCHI:

5 pounds (2.3 kg) russet potatoes, rinsed

2 cups (115 g) finely grated Parmigiano-Reggiano cheese

2 large eggs, lightly beaten

2 teaspoons kosher salt

3⅔ cups (440 g) all-purpose flour, plus more for dusting

FOR THE FONDUTA:

2 cups (480 ml) heavy whipping cream

5 ounces (142 g) Fontina Val d'Aosta cheese, grated coarsely

1 tablespoon cornstarch

Kosher salt

TO FINISH:

3 tablespoons kosher salt

¼ cup plus 1 tablespoon (14 g) thinly sliced fresh chives

¼ cup (40 g) crispy shallots (see headnote)

Freshly ground black pepper

MAKE THE GNOCCHI: Preheat the oven to 400°F (205°C). Lay the potatoes out on a sheet tray and bake for 45 minutes, or until tender. Allow them to cool for 5 minutes.

Use a paring knife to peel the potatoes (place a tea towel in your hand to hold the potatoes for this step, as they'll still be hot). Pass the peeled potatoes through a ricer or food mill onto a clean countertop, then spread them out on the countertop and fan them for a minute or so with a bench scraper or similar tool.

Add the Parm, eggs, salt, and 1 cup (120 g) of the flour to the potato pile and use the bench scraper to chop and fold them into the potato. When most of the flour has been absorbed, add another 1 cup (120 g) of the flour and continue to chop and fold the flour into the potato. Add the remaining flour and start to really gather the dough into a mound. Knead it for a minute with your hands just enough to form a smooth and springy ball. Don't overwork it. Cover with a tea towel.

Line a sheet tray with parchment paper. Lightly flour a work surface. Cut off a portion of the dough (about one-eighth), keeping the rest covered so it doesn't dry out. Roll the piece of dough into an even snake shape roughly ½ inch (12 mm) in diameter. Cut the snake crosswise into 1½-inch-long (4 cm) pieces, then scoop them up with a bench scraper and lay them out in an even layer on the parchment-lined sheet tray. Repeat with the remaining dough, then place the tray of gnocchi in the freezer. Once they have frozen, transfer them to an airtight container and return them to the freezer. (The gnocchi can be stored this way for up to a month. They should be cooked straight from the freezer.)

MAKE THE FONDUTA: In a pot, bring the cream to a simmer over medium heat. Add the fontina and whisk until it melts. In a small bowl, mix the cornstarch with 1 tablespoon water to form a slurry. Whisk this slurry into the cheese sauce and bring to a bare boil, stirring continuously, then immediately turn off the heat. (Cornstarch is at its full thickening potential when the liquid it's in comes to a boil.)

Transfer the sauce to a blender and buzz on high speed until very smooth. Make sure when blending hot liquids that you always start on the lowest setting and work your way up to the higher settings slowly. Season with a pinch of salt, then strain into a pot large enough to hold the gnocchi. (Alternatively, pack the sauce into a container and let cool, then cover and store in the fridge. It will keep for about a week.)

TO FINISH: Fill a large pot with 4 quarts (4 L) water and add the salt. Bring the water to a boil. Meanwhile, warm the fonduta gently in a large, shallow pot over low heat.

Pull about half (1 pound 5 ounces / 600 g) of the gnocchi from the freezer (keep the rest frozen for another use). Drop the frozen gnocchi into the boiling water and adjust the heat to cook at a simmer for 2½ minutes. Remove them with a spider, reserving the cooking water, and transfer them to the warm fonduta. Swirl gently to coat the gnocchi, then cook them in the sauce for about 3 minutes. Add a splash of the gnocchi cooking water if they look too dry. You want the sauce to be nice and loose.

Carefully spoon the gnocchi and some sauce into each of four bowls. Sprinkle with the chives and crispy shallots and finish with lots of black pepper.

fusilli with slow-roasted beef ragù

SERVES 4

Fusilli is a favorite when I cook at home. It always retains a nice and pleasant chew. Plus, it's one of the best shapes at capturing sauces, like this well-balanced and wonderfully tomatoey beef ragù. Start this sauce on the stove and then transfer it to a low oven to slowly render for a few hours. This will give you time to work on other dishes without too much stress. I generally make more than I need because it freezes really well. With this recipe, you'll have about 1½ cups (360 ml) left over. It'll keep in the fridge for a week or so, and makes for a great Saturday breakfast: Toast a thick piece of sourdough, then spoon over some of the reheated ragù and top it with a fried egg. It's stupidly good.

Note: To save time, you can use a food processor to chop all the vegetables. I personally prefer the texture of the sauce when the vegetable prep is done by hand, but it's definitely not a deal breaker.

¼ cup (60 ml) extra-virgin olive oil

2 pounds (917 g) ground beef

5 tablespoons (40 g) kosher salt

4 tablespoons plus 2 teaspoons (65 g) unsalted butter

1 cup (130 g) finely chopped carrots

1 cup (130 g) finely chopped Spanish onion

1 cup (130 g) finely chopped celery

½ cup (75 g) finely chopped garlic (about 6 cloves)

2 tablespoons tomato paste

1 teaspoon chile flakes

1 cup (240 ml) dry white wine

1 (28-ounce / 794 g) can whole peeled San Marzano tomatoes

2 cups (480 ml) Roasted Chicken Stock (page 324), plus more if needed

4 bay leaves

½ bunch basil

1 pound (455 g) fusilli

Grated Parmigiano-Reggiano or pecorino cheese

Freshly ground black pepper

Preheat the oven to 275°F (135°C).

In a Dutch oven, heat the olive oil over medium heat. Add the ground beef and cook, stirring often, until the beef begins to brown, then add 1 tablespoon of the salt and use a potato masher or a wooden spoon to begin to break up the beef. Cook until it's nicely browned, about 10 minutes; by that time, it should be fairly fine and broken up without too many large chunks remaining. Transfer to a bowl.

In the same pot, melt the unsalted butter over medium heat, then add the carrots, onion, and celery. Raise the heat to medium and sweat the

CONTINUED

vegetables for a few minutes, stirring often. Add 1 tablespoon of the salt and cook until the onion turns a bit translucent with brown corners here and there. Add the garlic and stir for another minute or so, then add the tomato paste. Cook for about a minute, toasting the tomato paste in the oil to really accentuate its sweetness. Add the chile flakes, then add the wine carefully to avoid a flare-up and cook until the smell of alcohol has burned off, about 2 minutes.

Add the tomatoes, then pour the stock into the empty can to rinse it and add the stock to the pot as well. Add the bay leaves and basil and return the cooked beef to the pot.

Bring the sauce to a simmer, then cover the Dutch oven with its lid and transfer it to the oven. Cook for 2 to 2½ hours, checking at about the first hour mark to make sure it's not bubbling too hard or reducing. If it is, drop the oven temperature by a little bit and add some stock. The sauce is finished when it has thickened and tastes bright and rich, and the beef should be nice and tender. Remove from the oven and set aside on the stove.

Fill a large pot with 4 quarts (4 L) water and add the remaining 3 tablespoons salt. Bring the water to a boil. While the water is coming to a boil, transfer 4 cups (1 L) of the ragù to a separate pot and warm over low heat. Add the fusilli to the boiling water and cook for 2 minutes less than the manufacturer's instructions indicate. Drain the pasta, then transfer it to the ragù. Cook the pasta in the sauce for a minute or two, then scoop it into four bowls. Top with cheese and lots of freshly cracked black pepper.

poached chicken with jasmine rice and green garlic broth

SERVES 4

This is one of my all-time favorite comfort food dishes to prepare in early spring, when hints of greenery are beginning to poke their heads out but you're still in need of a bowl of broth to warm you up. Green garlic is one of those early signs that the bitter chill has passed: young stalks of garlic before it has grown into the bulbous form most of us are accustomed to. We bring the stalks in by the caseload and utilize both the tops and the bottoms in a variety of dishes. In this one, the bottoms get quickly sautéed, while the tops are steeped in the poaching broth to accentuate its singular flavor. The garlic's pungency mellows a bit after cooking and lends itself well to broths and stews.

We use a rice cooker for the rice, but you can prepare it in a pot on the stovetop if you don't have one. It would be very nice but not essential if you put the cooked rice in the fridge, uncovered, to dry overnight. This helps to give it a little more bite.

2 cups (370 g) jasmine rice

2 (10-ounce / 280 g) bone-in, skin-on chicken breasts

2 (4-ounce / 115 g) bone-in, skin-on chicken thighs

2½ teaspoons kosher salt, plus more as needed

8 cups (2 L) Roasted Chicken Stock (page 324)

12 ounces (113 g) green garlic stalks

4 thyme sprigs

2 bay leaves

2 tablespoons whole black peppercorns

3 green onions (21 g)

1 tablespoon extra-virgin olive oil, plus more for finishing

2 limes, cut into 8 wedges

1 cup (20 g) loosely packed fresh cilantro

Freshly ground black pepper

Rinse the rice in a colander under cold running water until the water runs mostly clear, then cook it, ideally, according to your rice cooker's instructions, or in a pot according to package instructions. Fluff the cooked rice and spread it out on a plate or sheet tray to cool, then refrigerate until ready to use.

Season the chicken breasts and thighs with 2 teaspoons of the salt and set aside.

In a stockpot, bring the stock to a simmer over medium heat. Separate the green tops from the lighter bottoms of the green garlic and set the bottoms aside. Wash the green garlic tops with warm water, then

add them to the stock along with the thyme, bay leaves, and peppercorns. Cut the darker green tops of the green onions from the lighter bottoms and add the tops to the pot of stock; set 3 of the bottoms aside for serving and reserve the remainder for another use. Carefully add the chicken breasts and thighs and adjust the heat to maintain a bare simmer. Cook the chicken breasts to about 155°F (68°C) and the legs to 170°F (77°C), about 12 minutes and 15 minutes, respectively.

Meanwhile, slice the green garlic bottoms in half lengthwise, then slice them crosswise into very thin half-moons. Transfer them to a bowl of warm water and swish them around. Wait a few minutes to let any dirt settle to the bottom, then carefully cradle them out onto a plate or sheet tray lined with a tea towel.

In a separate pot, preferably a Dutch oven or similar, heat the olive oil over medium heat. Add the sliced green garlic bottoms and remaining ½ teaspoon salt and gently sweat, stirring often to prevent browning, until soft and tender. Turn off the heat and set aside.

As the chicken breasts and then the thighs are cooked, remove them from the poaching liquid and set aside. Skim the surface of the poaching liquid with a ladle to remove any foamy bits. Strain through a fine-mesh sieve into the pot with the sautéed green garlic and bring to a simmer. Reduce the heat to low and cook for 30 minutes or so to infuse the flavors. Taste for salt and adjust if need be.

While the broth is cooking, pick the chicken meat off the bones and chop it into bite-size pieces; discard the bones.

Slice the green onion bottoms into thin rounds and coarsely chop the cilantro. Mix them in a small bowl and set aside.

To assemble the dish, add the chicken and rice to the pot with the green garlic broth. Bring to a simmer over medium heat, stirring often, then squeeze in the lime wedges; you may not need them all, depending on how juicy your limes are, so taste as you go. Throw in the green onions and cilantro, give a final stir, taste, and plate. Finish with a drizzle of olive oil and some black pepper.

on garlic

I'm not alone in thinking garlic is one of the pillars of flavor worldwide. Most food cultures would have my back here. Spanish sopa de ajo, a soup made with bread and spiked with aromatic sherry, is loaded with garlic. Garlic chile oils, with an insane variety of heat levels, line the shelves of Asian markets. Grilled crusty bread rubbed all over with a whole clove of garlic, then covered with olive oil and a pinch of salt is an archetypal snack for a Sunday in Sicily, or an ideal bed for a ladleful of Portuguese mussels cooked in a chouriço. We need garlic in our lives and in our kitchens.

Because of garlic's popularity and our basic human laziness, most supermarkets offer the cloves already peeled. Maybe steer clear of those, as they tend to be more astringent and have that kind of intensely pungent garlic flavor that's a real turnoff for a lot of people. I'm not saying a strong garlic flavor or smell is inherently bad, but fresher garlic has a pleasant sweetness and an intensity that mellows, when cooked, into something otherworldly.

To be perfectly clear, most garlic you buy, even when you buy it by the head, isn't exactly "fresh." Garlic, like almost everything else, also has a season, and farmers long ago figured out storage techniques to have it available year round. Think of the root cellars of yore: Potatoes, beets, cabbage, and more, picked during their peak season, got stored away at a safe temperature, preserving them so they could be used to feed your family during the remainder of the year. The same principles apply today: just swap out "root cellar" with "climate-controlled warehouse."

When buying garlic at the store, or better, at the farmers' market, look for firm heads with defined cloves. Avoid garlic with green shoots sprouting out of the top. This stuff has a very sharp flavor that will overpower any dish it's used in. Larger heads are great and make peeling easier, but pass over the "elephant garlic," as it is really more akin to onion, lacking the potency of traditional garlic.

In spring you'll find green garlic, the edible young stalk and bulb of a not-yet-matured garlic plant. Use it wherever you would garlic, especially in soups and broths.

When the garlic plant goes to flower, it produces beautifully colored buds that can be pickled using Our House Pickling Liquid (page 318).

One last note: Although ramps aren't specifically in the garlic family, they do have a potent garlicky aroma that is fun to add to dishes in the springtime. If and when they appear at your local market, you can absolutely try ramps in place of the garlic in most recipes.

A BOWL OF...

bucatini with toasted garlic, chile flakes, colatura, and egg yolk

SERVES 4

Somewhere between a decadent carbonara and a sharp aglio, olio, e peperoncino (pasta with garlic, oil, and chile), this dish comes alive with colatura di alici, an Italian fish sauce (the name translates to "anchovy drippings"). Cooking the garlic and chile flakes calls for a light touch, because you want the aromas to bloom, not burn. Later on, when it's time to add the eggs, take extra care that the yolks don't scramble as you coat the noodles with the sauce, which can happen if the heat is too high and there isn't enough sauce. A little pasta water should help. It'll also give the whole thing a lovely glaze.

- 1 pound (455 g) bucatini
- 3 tablespoons kosher salt
- ¼ cup (60 ml) extra-virgin olive oil
- ½ cup (53 g) thinly sliced garlic
- 1 tablespoon chile flakes
- ⅔ cup (155 g) unsalted butter, cut into ½-inch (13 mm) cubes
- 2 cups (50 g) finely grated Parmigiano-Reggiano cheese (use a Microplane)
- 2 tablespoons colatura di alici or other fish sauce
- 8 large egg yolks (120 g total), whisked quickly with a fork
- 2 cups (60 g) loosely packed fresh parsley leaves

Fill a large pot with 4 quarts (4 L) water and add the salt. Bring the water to a boil. Add the pasta and cook for 2 minutes less than the manufacturer's instructions indicate. You're aiming for a bit of that al dente chew, leaving wiggle room for the pasta to cook a bit more in the sauce.

While the pasta is cooking, heat a large skillet over medium-low heat. Add the olive oil, followed by the garlic. Let it sizzle gently until aromatic, about 3 minutes. Don't let the garlic get any color; we're just looking to infuse the oil with flavor and soften the garlic. Add the chile flakes, then turn off the heat and ladle in 1¼ cups (300 ml) of the pasta water to stop the cooking. Add half the butter and swirl it to melt and combine.

Drain the pasta, reserving about 1 cup (240 ml) of the pasta water, then add the pasta to the pan with the garlic, chile flakes, and butter. Return the heat to medium-low and add the remaining butter. Cook, stirring often with tongs, until the pasta is nice and glazed, then add the Parm and turn off the heat. Stir to combine.

Add the colatura, then add the egg yolks and stir continuously, allowing the residual heat of the pasta to cook the egg just until it binds the sauce. Be careful not to scramble the eggs. When it's ready, the pasta should be shiny and look very luxurious. Add the parsley, stir, and serve immediately.

raviolo with english peas and egg yolk

SERVES 4

This has become an annual classic for us after my longtime cook and sous chef Finn really dialed it in. He had always talked about a great egg yolk–stuffed ravioli, and we ended up workshopping this one for a couple of days to really nail the sauce and the filling. The beauty lies in the balance of the sweet peas and the rich, runny egg yolk. The sauce almost evokes a comforting and vibrant split pea soup. We finish it with an ungodly amount of chives, whose oniony flavor helps to cut the richness. Make this during those days leading up to summer, when the English peas are at their best.

FOR THE PEA FILLING:

1 cup (240 ml) heavy cream

2 cups (276 g) fresh English peas, plus more if needed

2 teaspoons kosher salt

½ cup (40 g) grated Parmigiano-Reggiano cheese

1 tablespoon cold unsalted butter

FOR THE RAVIOLI:

9 ounces (250 g) pasta dough (see page 183)

4 large egg yolks

Kosher salt, for the pasta water

FOR THE SAUCE:

2 tablespoons unsalted butter

1 tablespoon kosher salt

⅓ cup (15 g) sliced chives

MAKE THE PEA FILLING: In a medium sauce pot, combine the cream, peas, and salt. Bring to a simmer and cook for about 5 to 6 minutes, or until the peas become very tender and the cream thickens ever so slightly. Empty the pot into a blender and start blending, and add the Parm and butter and blend until very smooth. The filling should thicken up nicely but still be slightly pourable.

Taste the filling for salt, transfer to a mixing bowl, and cool while stirring over an ice bath. The finished product should be about the thickness of Greek yogurt. Reserve ½ cup (135 g) for cooking the sauce. Transfer the remaining filling to a piping bag and refrigerate.

MAKE THE PASTA: Divide the pasta dough in half and roll each piece so that it is thin enough to be delicate but thick enough to support a large amount of filling (on conventional pasta machines, this will be around a 6). Each strip of pasta dough should be about 30 inches (76 cm) long. Remove

CONTINUED

the tip of your piping bag and, on one strip of pasta dough, make 4 even piles of filling (about 2 tablespoons / 80 g per raviolo) in the center of the strip at least ½ inch (1 cm) from the edge of the dough, not exceeding an inch (2.5 cm) in height. Dip your finger in water and make a small divot in the center of each pile of filling. Place an egg yolk in each divot. Dip your finger in water once again and draw a very small line of water around each mound of filling. Carefully blanket the circles of filling with the other strip of pasta dough, making sure to align the edges neatly. Place a 4-inch (10 cm) ring mold around each mound of filling and carefully cut out 8 circles. After pressing gently to stick the pasta sheets together, you can pick up the ravioli and press your way around the edges to create a tight seal.

Drop the ravioli in salted, simmering pasta water for 2 minutes.

MAKE THE SAUCE AND TO FINISH: Meanwhile, get your sauté pan ready with the remaining filling, the butter, salt, and enough water to loosen it up, starting with ¼ cup (60 ml). Add a tablespoon of water at a time if it tightens. Cook the sauce on low heat until combined.

Transfer the ravioli from the pasta water into the sauce, bringing with it as little pasta water as possible. Cook in the sauce (facing up) for about a minute. You may need to add fresh water if the sauce gets too thick. Finish the sauce with chives.

Plate the ravioli carefully in the centers of the plates and spoon the sauce over. Serve immediately.

pasta coperta with grilled-eggplant ricotta, sweet corn, and herb butter

SERVES 4

We usually have some type of fresh pasta on the menu. Nine times out of ten, it's an incredibly involved shape that takes two people a couple of hours to produce for a busy night's service. But this one is simple—just sheets of pasta cut into squares. That's it. As delicious as they are boring looking. Somewhere between rich pappardelle and fresh lasagna, this dish is pretty remarkable considering how humble it is.

Note: If you like, after cutting the corn kernels from the cobs for the sauce, reserve the cobs to make corn stock by covering them in water and boiling for an hour or so. Use the stock in place of water in the sauce. Salva Cremasco is a salty cow's milk cheese from Northern Italy. If you can't find it, try ricotta salata instead.

FOR THE PASTA DOUGH:

1 cup (140 g) "00" flour

¼ cup (45 g) semolina flour, plus extra for dusting

7 large egg yolks

1 tablespoon extra-virgin olive oil

5 teaspoons tomato paste

FOR THE EGGPLANT RICOTTA:

1 small eggplant

2 teaspoons extra-virgin olive oil

2 teaspoons kosher salt, plus more if needed

8 ounces (225 g) ricotta cheese, strained in a colander overnight

FOR THE SAUCE:

2 cups (256 g) fresh sweet corn kernels (from about 3 ears)

½ cup (125 g) Herb Butter (page 322)

1 teaspoon kosher salt

TO FINISH:

3 tablespoons kosher salt, plus more as needed

4 scoops Eggplant Ricotta (3 tablespoons / 70 g each scoop)

Salva Cremasco cheese, for grating

1 teaspoon fresh thyme leaves

Freshly ground black pepper

Extra-virgin olive oil

MAKE THE PASTA DOUGH: Add the flours, egg yolks, olive oil, 8 teaspoons (40 ml) water, and tomato paste to the bowl of a stand mixer. Mix with your hands for 10 minutes. Knead with the dough hook for another 10 minutes until a smooth texture. Cover and let rest for at least 30 minutes before using.

MAKE THE EGGPLANT RICOTTA: Preheat the oven to 400°F (205°C). Prepare a charcoal grill.

CONTINUED

Drizzle the whole eggplant with the olive oil and season with 1 teaspoon of the salt, then grill it over medium-high heat until charred on all sides. If the charred eggplant is soft at this point, pull it off the grill. If it's still firm, place it on a sheet tray and roast in the preheated oven until soft; start checking after 10 minutes. Let the eggplant cool.

Meanwhile, place the ricotta in the bowl of a stand mixer with a paddle attachment and whip on medium-high speed for 3 to 5 minutes until creamy.

Line a colander with cheesecloth and set it over a bowl or in the sink. Remove the stem of the eggplant and peel off all the charred skin and burnt areas, then chop the flesh and place it in the colander. Let stand for about an hour, until a fair amount of water drains off. (If you want to speed up this process, you can squeeze the eggplant or place something heavy on top of it.) You should have about 1¾ cups (300 g) eggplant after pressing.

Put the whipped ricotta in a bowl and fold in the grilled eggplant. Add the remaining 1 teaspoon salt, then taste and adjust. Set aside.

FORM THE PASTA: Cut the pasta dough into two pieces. Working with one piece at a time, roll out the dough using a pasta roller into long, 5-inch-wide (12 cm) sheets. You want the dough thin, but not too thin (think of the thickness of a lasagna noodle); with this specific shape, going a bit thicker doesn't hurt. Trim the uneven ends of the long sheets and cut the sheets crosswise at roughly 5-inch (12 cm) intervals to form shorter, squarish sheets. You'll need 8 to 10 for this recipe. Store the sheets in the refrigerator on a sheet tray lightly dusted with semolina flour. Cover them with a tea towel or plastic wrap to ensure they don't dry out. They should keep like this for 2 days. Any leftover dough can be frozen for up to a month.

MAKE THE SAUCE: In a large pot, combine the corn, herb butter, and ¾ cup (180 ml) water (or corn stock). Cook over medium heat for about 4 minutes, then reduce the heat to maintain a very soft simmer. Season with the salt.

TO FINISH: Fill a large pot with 4 quarts (4 L) water and add the salt. Bring the water to a boil. Add the pasta sheets and cook for 2 minutes, then remove the sheets from the water and place them in the sauce. Cook the pasta in the sauce over medium-high heat for about 3 minutes more. You can add more water if the sauce gets too thick or dry. Taste and adjust for salt.

When you are happy with the flavor of the sauce, place a large dollop (about 3 tablespoons / 70 g) eggplant ricotta at the bottom of each of four bowls. Using tongs, drape 2 pasta sheets over the ricotta in each bowl. Spoon the corn sauce evenly over each bowl of pasta. Grate some Salva Cremasco over the top and finish with the fresh thyme leaves, black pepper, and a small drizzle of olive oil.

stone-ground polenta with puréed squash and pumpkin seed gremolata

SERVES 4

If you've never had coarsely milled polenta, try to seek some out and give this recipe a try. I totally get the appeal of instant polenta, given that a stone-milled polenta can take 2 to 3 hours to cook, but the flavor profiles and texture couldn't be more different. Coarse polenta has a nice, springy al dente chew and a toasty corn flavor that's really beautiful. I like polenta from Farmer Ground Flour, which is produced here in New York, but lots of regions have local mills now. You may find something really special closer to where you live.

Folding in puréed squash adds an earthy sweetness, but it's also absolutely delicious without. When hunting for squash, butternut will work well. If you find yourself at a farmers' market and they have some heirloom varieties, definitely grab those. Koginut is what we use at the restaurant.

FOR THE POLENTA:

5 cups (1.2 L) whole milk

2½ cups (600 ml) heavy whipping cream

2½ cups (455 g) coarse stone-ground polenta

Kosher salt

FOR THE SQUASH:

1 (3- to 4-pound / 1.4 to 1.8 kg) winter squash, split lengthwise and seeded

Extra-virgin olive oil

Kosher salt

FOR THE GREMOLATA:

1½ cups (170 g) pumpkin seeds

¾ cup (185 g) Salmoriglio (page 308)

Zest and juice of 1 lemon

1½ teaspoons Maldon salt

TO FINISH:

10½ tablespoons (150 g) unsalted butter, cut into ½-inch (12 mm) chunks

2½ cups (150 g) finely grated Parmigiano-Reggiano cheese

Kosher salt

MAKE THE POLENTA: In a heavy-bottomed stockpot or Dutch oven, heat the milk and cream over medium heat, stirring occasionally, until you begin to see slight bubbles and steam rising. While whisking steadily, begin to pour in the polenta in a thin stream.

When all the polenta has been added, bring the mixture to a simmer, then reduce the heat to low. Season with kosher salt, but keep in mind that the polenta will cook down a bit and the salt level may increase. Adding fats and cheese can also accentuate "saltiness" in a dish, so just be aware that your initial seasoning should be a little on the lighter side. Cook, whisking

CONTINUED

A BOWL OF...

frequently until you can no longer whisk the polenta due to its thickness, then switch to a wooden spoon or rubber spatula and stir every now and then for the next 1½ to 2 hours. After 45 minutes, begin tasting the polenta. You're looking to lose that chalky and almost raw flour taste as well as any perceived grit or toughness. The polenta when fully cooked will still have a little chewiness, which is part of its appeal. You just want to make sure to cook out the starch. When it's close, it will begin to taste like sweet corn. Feel free to add water here and there if it starts getting really stiff before it's fully cooked.

MAKE THE SQUASH: Meanwhile, preheat the oven to 350°F (175°C).

Place the squash cut side up on a sheet tray or roasting pan and drizzle with olive oil. Season generously with the kosher salt, then flip the squash halves cut side down. Roast until the squash is tender when poked with a fork, about 30 minutes (this can be longer depending on the size and denseness of the squash). Don't be afraid to overcook it. You're looking for it to be nice and soft. Remove the squash from the oven and set it aside to cool slightly. Keep the oven on.

Scoop the flesh of the cooked squash into a mixing bowl and mash it. It's up to you how smooth or coarse you want your final product. At home, I would just attack this with a fork and call it a day. If you're showing off for friends, though, grab a standing blender and buzz it up a bit. Either way, once it's mashed, set it aside at room temperature.

MAKE THE GREMOLATA: Spread the pumpkin seeds on a sheet tray and toast in the oven until lightly golden brown and aromatic, about 15 minutes. Remove from the oven. Lightly crush the seeds on the sheet tray with the bottom of a small pot. Transfer the seeds to a colander and sift out any dusty bits (making sure to save them for future salads—they're a go-to ingredient for family meals at The Four Horsemen).

In a bowl, stir together the toasted seeds, salmoriglio, lemon zest, lemon juice, and Maldon salt to combine.

TO FINISH: When the polenta is fully cooked, remove from the heat, then add the butter and stir until completely melted and incorporated. Add the cheese and then stir in the mashed squash. You may not need all the squash—I'd say add most of it, stir, taste, and then decide if you want to add more or if you're happy with the flavor and texture. I like this polenta slightly loose, like porridge. Taste again and adjust the seasoning with kosher salt if need be. Spoon the polenta into bowls, top with the gremolata, and serve.

a kedgeree, kind of

SERVES 4

My wife first turned me on to kedgeree years ago. She worked at Fergus Henderson's restaurant St. John in the early aughts and had me dig out the recipe from one of their old books we had around the house. I loved it then and I still love it today.

The version of kedgeree served in the UK generally consists of long-grain rice, smoked haddock, parsley, boiled egg, and curry powder. We don't stray too far from that. We do like to smoke our own fish, which I'll include instructions for, but feel free to skip this step if you can get your hands on fish that's already smoked—and really, any smoked fish will work here. If haddock proves elusive, a fattier white fish like sablefish would work. Trout and salmon could fit the bill, too. All are fairly common here in the US, whereas haddock might require a bit more searching. Well worth the effort, though, considering how its very large and meaty flakes really stand out in this dish.

FOR THE SMOKED HADDOCK:

4 teaspoons kosher salt

8 ounces (225 g) haddock fillet, pin bones removed

Handful applewood chips

FOR THE SPRING ONIONS:

5 cloves garlic, thinly sliced

⅓ cup (75 ml) extra-virgin olive oil

7 spring onions, halved lengthwise and thinly sliced (2½ cups / 170 g)

1 teaspoon kosher salt

1 teaspoon saffron threads

FOR THE RICE:

1 cup (180 to 190 g) white rice (basmati or jasmine)

1½ cups (360 ml) Savory Fish Stock (page 325)

2½ tablespoons Curry Butter (page 322)

3½ tablespoons (50 ml) fresh lemon juice (from about 1 lemon)

½ cup (15 g) fresh cilantro, coarsely chopped

½ cup (41 g) thinly sliced green onions

Kosher salt

MAKE THE SMOKED HADDOCK: Salt the haddock all over, then place in the fridge for 20 minutes. After 20 minutes, rinse the fish and place back in the fridge.

Start a smoker. (Alternatively, prepare a very low fire on a grill and soak the wood chips in water for 10 minutes. When the grill is warm, line a small sheet tray with aluminum foil, then scoop the wood chips out of the water and place them on the tray. Place the tray on one side of the grill, then light the wood chips using a blowtorch, getting them nice and smoky.)

CONTINUED

Line a sheet tray with parchment paper and place the haddock on the parchment. Place the tray in the smoker or on the grill next to the tray with the wood chips. Close the lid and smoke for about 20 minutes, until a thermometer inserted into the fish reads 125°F (52°C). Remove the haddock and allow it to cool slightly.

Flake the smoked fish into large chunks and place them in a bowl. Spoon in any of the juices left behind on the tray, cover, and place the bowl in the fridge. (The smoked fish will keep for about a week.)

MAKE THE SPRING ONIONS: In a sauté pan, toast the garlic in the olive oil over low heat until lightly golden in color. Add the spring onions and the salt and let them sweat gently.

Place the saffron in a bowl with 2 teaspoons water. When the onions are translucent and soft, 3 to 4 minutes, add the saffron and water and stir to combine. Remove from the heat. (This can be made a few days in advance and packed away in a jar or a small deli container.)

MAKE THE RICE: Rinse the rice in a colander under cold running water until the water is mostly clear, then cook it, ideally, according to your rice cooker's instructions, or in a pan according to package instructions. When the rice is finished, fluff it with a rice paddle.

Combine the spring onions, stock, and curry butter in a 2-quart (2 L) sauce pot and warm the mixture over medium heat until simmering. Add the cooked rice and the smoked haddock and cook until just warmed through, no more than 3 minutes.

Remove from the heat and add the lemon juice, cilantro, and green onions. Stir a couple of times, taste for seasoning, and adjust with salt, if need be, then divide among four bowls or serve in a single large serving dish.

really good butter beans

5½ CUPS (1.4 KG) COOKED BEANS

I really like beans. I think beans can surprise people when thoughtfully cooked and correctly seasoned. Our kitchen gets pretty excited when we hear that a guest feels like the beans were the unexpected highlight of the meal. This happens more often than you might imagine. I like that. I also like that the road to really delicious beans isn't through some super rare specimens of hard-to-get varieties, planted exclusively during the vernal equinox on the southfacing hillsides of Tuscany or something. As usual, I think the process for making truly exceptional beans is just that: a process. It's really just a couple of vital things that are commonly overlooked, even by a good deal of professional chefs.

It starts with dried beans. Canned beans serve their purpose, but we're aiming for mind-altering beans here, so skip the cans. I'm sticking with butter beans here because they've been a staple at The Four Horsemen for years, but gigante, zolfini, borlotti, and flageolet beans are a few more of our favorites. No matter which you chose, the procedure is always the same.

We always soak dried beans overnight in plenty of water before cooking them. They expand, so we generally use enough water to cover them by at least a few inches. Soaking ensures even cooking, as dried beans can otherwise be a bit unpredictable. And without the soaking, you can end up with a lot of exploding beans and murky water. Avoid recipes selling shortcuts. They may yield OK results, but we want excellent ones.

After a night of soaking, ditch the water, transfer the beans to a pot, and cover with at least a few inches of fresh water. We season the water with salt moderately at the beginning, then fine-tune later in the cooking process. Make sure the water is nicely seasoned from the get-go so the beans absorb the salt as they cook. Otherwise, you're just adding salt to the broth at the end, and the center of the beans will taste bland.

Next, layer two pieces of cheesecloth on top of one another. Place some thyme, garlic, bay leaves, and peppercorns in the middle of the cheesecloth and bring up the corners. Tie the top with a piece of kitchen twine to make a sachet and then add it to the pot of beans.

Bring the water up to a simmer. Lower the heat and skim any foam that rises to the top with a ladle. You don't want violent bubbles, just a nice, delicate, steamy heat.

CONTINUED

After the first 30 minutes, taste the beans often and top up the water if you notice that it has reduced. You want to end up with about the same amount of liquid as when you started, as the beans can get too salty if you allow the liquid to reduce too much. After about 2 or 2½ hours, when the beans are getting close—meaning they don't feel chalky or starchy when you try one—evaluate the cooking liquid. Does it need a touch more salt? Now's your chance to add it. Continue cooking and tasting. When you think they're finally done, taste the beans again. Not just one—taste ten. There shouldn't be any question about their doneness. The texture should be creamy. The broth should be rich and savory, and the skins silky. If you have any doubts, cook for another 15 minutes, and *keep checking*. The benefit of cooking the beans slowly is that it leaves you a wider window to catch them at the perfect time. This isn't like meat, where assessing doneness means accounting for carryover cooking—once the beans are done, they're done, so get them where they need to be before you pull them off the heat.

Take the pot off the heat and leave the beans in their broth to cool. If you pull them out of the liquid right away, the skins will peel right off and the beans will partially disintegrate. If you agitate them too much or dump them into a colander at this point, you might as well use them to make some hummus. Let them relax. Once they've cooled, transfer them carefully, with their liquid, to a storage container. Avoid storing them in tall containers, as the weight of the beans on top can crush those on the bottom. They'll keep in the fridge for about a week.

To cook the beans, you'll just need the few ingredients listed below. And after they are done, you can use them in any number of dishes. I'm especially fond of the two recipes on the following pages, Butter Beans with Salmoriglio (page 195) and Butter Beans with Kimchi and Salt Cod (page 197).

1 pound (455 g) dried butter beans

2 tablespoons kosher salt, plus more if needed

3 thyme sprigs

8 cloves garlic, peeled

3 bay leaves

1 tablespoon whole black peppercorns

butter beans with salmoriglio

SERVES 4

Beans are the perfect platform for salmoriglio, the bright Southern Italian herb-heavy sauce that commonly accompanies meaty fish in Sicily and Calabria. We like to add some buttery anchovies to the sauce as well as some chopped Calabrian chiles for heat, and we sneak in some vinegar-macerated shallots that really pack a lot of acidity. These elements play really well with the grassy herbs and the hearty beans. I think this dish has a lot of elegance, despite how rustic it may seem on the surface. Serve it on its own or with grilled swordfish, braised artichokes, or charred slices of medium-rare steak.

3 cups (540 g) Really Good Butter Beans (page 192)

1¼ cups (300 ml) Salmoriglio (page 308)

Kosher salt

Drain the beans, reserving 2 cups (480 ml) of their liquid.

In a medium pot, gently warm the beans in the reserved liquid over low heat. Remove from heat and add the salmoriglio. Taste and season with salt as needed.

Use a slotted spoon to scoop the beans into individual bowls, then spoon over the desired amount of broth (ideally, the broth should come halfway up the beans) and serve.

butter beans with kimchi and salt cod

SERVES 4

My friend Sunny Lee is an incredible chef who has taught me a great deal about Korean food. During a pop-up she did at The Four Horsemen a few years ago, she showed me how to use kimchi as the base for stews. It added brightness and just the right funky note, irresistible when paired with cod. It's the perfect soul-warming dish to enjoy during the transition from winter to spring. I particularly like daikon kimchi, which we make at the restaurant on occasion, but any good store-bought variety will do. Just make sure it's not white kimchi, since that doesn't incorporate the chile powder gochugaru. We add ramps when they're in season, but the dish could easily be made without: Substitute some thinly sliced Spanish onion.

- 1 bunch ramps (about 24), trimmed
- 1 tablespoon extra-virgin olive oil, plus more as needed
- 1 teaspoon kosher salt, plus more if needed
- 3 cups (540 g) Really Good Butter Beans (page 192)
- 2 cups (480 ml) Roasted Chicken Stock (page 324)
- 2 cups (300 g) kimchi (any type will work—cabbage, daikon, ramp, etc.)
- 1 cup (175 g) 1-inch (2.5 cm) cubes salt cod, soaked (see page 85)
- 2 teaspoons pimentón (Spanish paprika)
- 2 tablespoons fish sauce, plus more if needed
- 1 tablespoon tamari
- Freshly ground black pepper
- 2 cups (80 g) coarsely chopped fresh cilantro leaves (with some stems)

Separate the ramp bulbs from the green tops; coarsely chop the tops and set aside. Thinly slice the bulbs.

In a large pot, heat the olive oil to medium-high. Sauté the sliced ramp bulbs and salt until soft, about 1 minute. Add the beans, stock, kimchi, and salt cod. Decrease the heat to medium and bring the stew to a simmer, then reduce the heat to maintain that simmer and cook for 30 minutes or so, tasting the stew along the way. The flavors should start to meld together, and the natural gelatin in the cod will add a nice richness. The beans should break up slightly, and the fish should flake into the broth, thickening it along the way. The kimchi should mellow in flavor and add a gentle acidity to the broth. Once you've reached this state and you're happy with the results, add the pimentón, fish sauce, ramp greens, and tamari and stir to incorporate. Taste and adjust with more salt or fish sauce, if need be. You may find you don't need to add any, depending on the salinity of the salt cod and kimchi.

Portion the stew into four bowls. Top with a good drizzle of olive oil, a few cracks of black pepper, and the cilantro, and serve.

lentils with fried bread crumbs and mozzarella

SERVES 4

Lentils make for such a delicious chilled marinated salad. We like to cook them with a mix of carrots, onions, and celery and some herbs like bay leaves and thyme. For this dish, it's important to make sure there's plenty of water during the cooking process. Cooking the lentils in too little water crowds them, which has a tendency to create mushy, overcooked lentils. Sometimes that can be fine, too. We're into slightly overcooked lentils with chorizo and lots of olive oil. But for a salad, you want the lentils to maintain their shape.

We're trying to channel some semblance of an Italian antipasti situation here. A few pieces of torn creamy mozzarella, some crispy fried bread crumbs, and some pickled green tomatoes for brightness turn this dish into a really nice accompaniment to roasted meats and grilled swordfish. You can play around with add-ins here. Sun-dried tomatoes, basil, oregano, sautéed peppers, and zucchini would all be welcome.

FOR THE LENTILS:

½ cup (65 g) small-diced Spanish onion

½ cup (65 g) small-diced celery

½ cup (65 g) small-diced carrots

1 tablespoon extra-virgin olive oil

1 tablespoon kosher salt

1½ cups (320 g) dried black beluga lentils

1 thyme sprig

2 bay leaves

FOR THE BREAD CRUMBS:

¼ cup (60 ml) extra-virgin olive oil

2 cups (130 g) panko bread crumbs

1 teaspoon chile flakes

Zest of 1 lemon

½ teaspoon Maldon salt

TO FINISH:

½ cup (100 g) chopped Pickled Green Tomatoes (page 319), with their juices

2 tablespoons extra-virgin olive oil

1 tablespoon sherry vinegar

1½ teaspoons Maldon salt

1½ cups (225 g) torn fresh mozzarella cheese

MAKE THE LENTILS: In a pot, sweat the onion, celery, and carrots in the olive oil with the kosher salt for 2 to 3 minutes over medium heat. Add the lentils and toast them for 2 to 3 minutes. Add 4 cups (1 L) water, the thyme, and the bay leaves and simmer for about 40 minutes, stirring occasionally. Remove from the heat, drain off any excess liquid, and let cool completely.

MAKE THE BREAD CRUMBS: In a pan, heat the olive oil over medium heat. Add the panko and toast, stirring continuously so it doesn't burn, until almost fully golden brown. Add the chile flakes, lemon zest, and Maldon salt and toast, stirring, for another 2 minutes, then transfer the crumbs to a plate to cool.

TO FINISH: In a bowl, mix 3 cups (700 g) of the cooked lentils with the green tomatoes, olive oil, vinegar, and Maldon salt. Adjust for seasoning. Spoon a pile of the lentil mixture onto each of four flat plates. Tear pieces of mozzarella and scatter them over the lentils. Scatter 1½ cups (100 g) of the bread crumbs over the plates, dividing it evenly, and serve cold.

SEA
FOOD

SEAFOOD

As kids, my brother and I loved taking the hour-and-a-half drive down to Monterey: walking through the famous aquarium, exploring the town with its fishing boats, seafood stalls, the old cannery signs straight out of Steinbeck, our entire experience permeated by the salt smell of the sea. These memories are all tied for me to the startling bounty of local seafood that would blow us away when we'd finally stop for lunch: plates of fish and crustaceans, and almost endless lists of "catches of the day," images of which bubble up in my lizard brain whenever I get my hands on beautiful, fresh seafood—either as a dish I get to eat, or as an ingredient I'm lucky enough to work with.

Truly great seafood isn't always easy to get your hands on (see Finding Fresh Fish on page 210), especially the sashimi-quality fish we serve at The Four Horsemen. For this reason, I opted to focus mostly on some easier to find species. There are a few classics that most of our regulars and friends will recognize, as well as a couple of fun, larger party-style dishes with more common specimens.

yellowfin tuna with yuzu kosho, tonnato, and smoked dulse

SERVES 4

This is one of our most well-known dishes at The Four Horsemen. It was an early breakthrough that marked a turning point in our food, and has held a place on our menu (and in my heart) for the better part of the past six years. It exemplifies many of the qualities we strive for—balance, frugality, beauty, good sourcing, focused creativity—and it pulls from so many of the formative experiences I personally had on my way to The Four Horsemen. Even though it falls toward the more difficult end of the preparation spectrum, I felt we needed to include it here.

The tonnato sauce is something I learned about while working in Piedmont, Italy, in the early 2000s. It's integral to the dish vitello tonnato, thinly sliced veal topped with a sauce made from buzzing up mayonnaise and tuna confit. I hadn't seen much of it in the States at the time, and it stayed with me.

Years later, in 2016, one of our purveyors brought in a beautiful top loin of yellowfin tuna from Montauk. We knew we didn't just want to do a tartare, really, or anything featuring thick chunks of the fish; those raw seafood preparations could be found all over the city at the time. My mind wandered back to vitello tonnato. *What if we swapped in tuna for veal?* We tried freezing the loin and passing it through a slicer, and most people still imagine that's how we would do it today. But pounding the tuna after a quick cure in salt, sugar, lemon zest, and bay leaf turned out to be the best method. We also removed all the sinewy pieces, which can be tough when raw, and poached them in olive oil to make the tonnato, ensuring that there was barely any waste. Since you might not want to do this at home, purchasing a jar or tin of fatty ventresca (tuna belly) packed in water is the next best thing.

Once we had the tuna dialed in and the sauce in mind, I started to think about how we could bring balance to a dish that was on its way to becoming dangerously rich. I grabbed some yuzu kosho and some yuzu zest from the pantry and rubbed a thin layer of each on the pounded tuna; the yuzu kosho added salty heat, while the zest foregrounded sweet citrus notes. To lighten things up further, we charged the tonnato sauce in an iSi siphon, a technique I had seen Phil Krajeck, chef of Rolf & Daughters in Nashville, use for his tonnato sauce just months prior at a pop-up we did together. A siphon is an insulated bottle with a

CONTINUED

nozzle that uses nitrous oxide to turn denser creams and the like into light, airy, almost ethereal sauces (your local coffee shop likely uses one to top drinks with whipped cream), and they came into popularity with the foam craze of the early 2000s.

With the tonnato sauce on the plate and the spicy, citrusy tuna draped elegantly over the top, we finished the dish with a good squeeze of lemon, Sicilian olive oil, and some flakes of smoked dulse we happened to have on hand.

I feel like it's all there in this dish: the benefits of a well-stocked pantry, the insights from experiences like pop-ups, the reason we care so much about sourcing, and the constant, conscious effort to make something that is first and foremost delicious while thoughtful and technically sound.

FOR THE TONNATO SAUCE:

½ cup (120 ml) warm water

½ cup (120 ml) Mayonnaise (page 304)

¾ tablespoons water-packed ventresca (tuna belly)

2 anchovy fillets

FOR THE CURE:

1 cup (150 g) kosher salt

¼ cup (66 g) sugar

2 teaspoons lemon zest

2 bay leaves, thinly sliced

FOR THE TUNA:

10 ounces (284 g) yellowfin tuna fillet, trimmed of its blood line

1 teaspoon yuzu kosho

2 teaspoons finely chopped yuzu peel (pith removed before chopping)

4½ teaspoons extra-virgin olive oil

1 teaspoon fresh lemon juice

2 teaspoons Maldon salt

2 teaspoons smoked dulse flakes

MAKE THE TONNATO SAUCE: Place the warm water and mayonnaise in a blender, then add the tuna belly and the anchovies (having the looser ingredients on the bottom helps with the blending process). Buzz on high until very smooth, 2 to 3 minutes, then pass the sauce through a fine-mesh strainer. Transfer the sauce to a whipping siphon and charge the siphon with 2 nitrous oxide cartridges. Refrigerate for at least 6 hours before use.

MAKE THE CURE: In a mixing bowl, combine the kosher salt, sugar, lemon zest, and bay leaves and stir to incorporate evenly. (The cure can be made up to 2 weeks in advance and stored in an airtight container at room temperature.)

MAKE THE TUNA: Place the tuna in a dish and cover it with the cure, turning it to coat completely. Put the tuna in the fridge for 40 minutes, then remove it and rinse it with very cold water to remove the cure.

Place a rack on a sheet tray. At the restaurant, I use towels made from a nonwoven fabric (the kind of material used to make surgical gowns) to line the rack; they're ideal for handling fish, as they prevent any reaction with the metal rack and inhibit off-flavors. At home, paper towels work just fine. Set the tuna on the towels and refrigerate for 2 hours to allow it to dry a bit, until the surface is somewhat tacky.

Line a sturdy work surface with plastic wrap. Use a wet knife to split the tuna in half against the grain (from top to bottom). Then cut the tuna into 2-ounce (57 g) pieces and place them on the plastic, spacing them 6 inches (15 cm) apart. Place another layer of plastic wrap on top of the tuna, then, using a mallet or heavy-bottomed pot, pound the tuna evenly until it's about 5 inches (12 cm) square and thin enough that it's almost transparent. Using a knife, cut the plastic between the tuna pieces so each sits between its own two layers of plastic. Wrap the plastic over the edges of the fish to cover, then stack in an airtight container. Refrigerate until ready to use, up to 1 day.

TO FINISH: Chill four plates in a freezer. Lay the tuna portions out on a counter and remove the top layer of plastic. Using an offset spatula, spread a thin layer of yuzu kosho onto each piece of tuna. Using the same offset spatula, scatter some yuzu peel onto each piece.

Give the tonnato sauce a shake and squirt out a golf ball–size pile onto the center of each chilled plate. Lift up a piece of tuna in one hand, then use your other hand to carefully remove the remaining plastic wrap, starting with one corner and slowly working the tuna off the wrap. Drape the tuna over the tonnato, zest and kosho side down, covering the sauce completely and giving the fish a nice organic shape. Repeat to plate the remaining tuna.

Drizzle a bit of olive oil onto each piece of tuna. Finish with the lemon juice, Maldon salt, and dulse, and serve immediately.

scallops with daikon radish and leche de tigre

SERVES 4

A few summers ago, this guy pulled up to the restaurant in a van and asked if we had a minute to check out his fish. We were pretty hectic, not to mention obviously skeptical of some random person dropping in with a bunch of seafood, but I have a pretty well-defined weak spot: *What if?* It turns out Jason Miller from Big Water had extraordinary scallops, among other local fish. He explained that the scallops he brought had been harvested on various dayboats in and around the waters of Montauk less than 12 hours before their arrival at our doorstep. We bought a bit of everything, but the scallops really blew our minds and inspired us to develop this simple dish to show off their texture and flavor.

Leche de tigre (Spanish for "tiger's milk") is the acidic, sweet, and pleasantly fishy sauce left over from making ceviche. We fake it a bit here by macerating cilantro, jalapeño, and onion in citrus juice and then adding fish sauce to mimic that flavor.

FOR THE LECHE DE TIGRE:

½ cup (120 ml) fresh lime juice (from 4 to 5 limes)

¼ cup (60 ml) fresh orange juice (from 1 orange)

¼ cup (25 g) sliced seeded jalapeño (½-inch-thick / 12 mm slices; about ½ jalapeño)

½ cup (51 g) sliced red onion (¼-inch-thick / 6 mm slices; about ¼ onion)

1¼ cups (38 g) loosely packed fresh cilantro sprigs

¼ cup (60 ml) fish sauce

FOR THE SCALLOPS:

8 (10/20-count) dry scallops

4 cups (1 L) ice water

2 tablespoons kosher salt

4 cups (1 L) cold water

TO FINISH:

1 (3-inch / 7.5 cm) piece daikon radish

2 cups (480 ml) ice water

1 teaspoon Maldon salt

Lime zest (optional)

MAKE THE LECHE DE TIGRE: Combine the lime juice, orange juice, jalapeño, onion, and cilantro in a container and massage them with your hand for a minute or so until they start to macerate. Cover and refrigerate for an hour. Strain the mixture through a fine-mesh sieve, discarding the solids, and add the fish sauce. Taste and adjust, if need be, with more acid or salt, then cover and refrigerate until needed. (It will keep for 2 to 3 days.)

MAKE THE SCALLOPS: Remove the abductor muscle from the scallop. Otherwise known as the "foot," this is a small, rectangular, opaque piece

that runs along the outside of the scallop. In a bowl, combine the ice water and salt and stir until the salt dissolves to make a quick brine. Fill a separate bowl with the cold water. Add the scallops to the bowl of brine and swish them around, then transfer them to the cold water.

Line a sheet tray with a tea towel. Remove the scallops from the water and lay them out on the tray, then place in the fridge. The scallops prepared in this manner should keep in the fridge for 2 days.

TO FINISH: Peel the daikon, then cut it into quarters lengthwise and round off two of the edges so it has a sort of tombstone shape when you're looking at it head-on. Using a mandoline, cut each daikon piece into 1⁄16-inch-thick (2 mm) slices. Place the daikon pieces into the ice water to crisp for 10 minutes, then remove them and place them on a sheet tray lined with a paper towel.

Slice the scallops into ½-inch (12 mm) pieces and place them in a small bowl. Add the leche de tigre and stir a few times with a spoon. Split the scallops among four bowls and disperse the leche de tigre evenly among them. Cover each dish with shingles of daikon and sprinkle with the Maldon salt. Grate a bit of lime zest, if using, over to finish, then serve.

finding fresh fish

It's all been said before: Look for bright red gills, clear and shiny eyes, no fishy smell, and flesh that's resilient to the touch. And it's all true, except that it's hard to evaluate these characteristics from behind a pane of glass, and I don't recall too many fishmongers who were keen on letting loads of customers touch their fish before deciding whether or not to buy.

At our restaurant, we're lucky to not have to worry about this. We've forged relationships with a core group of about five purveyors who know and respect our standards, so they would never think to bring us anything even remotely questionable.

We also have very specific storage and aging rules at the restaurant when it comes to fish. Whenever possible, we opt to get the fish whole so that we can control and monitor quality; they're then scaled, gutted, and filleted by the team and used in whatever application we see fit.

Almost three-quarters of our menu highlights seafood. It's central to our style, and I really enjoy the challenges and rewards of working with fresh fish. That being said, I didn't want to load up this book with recipes that can't be cooked outside The Four Horsemen. I don't expect everyone reading this to be able to source shima-aji, live spot prawns, geoduck, madai, tilefish, fluke, and king crab without a ton of work. They're all amazing, but I've maybe only seen one of those species at a neighborhood fish market. I'd like to make sure that the recipes in this book can be used, so I'm primarily sticking with fish that I see in the shops I frequent here in New York.

Going back to spotting quality: I think the best ways to get good fish outside of a restaurant are to hit farmers' markets, order online from trusted retailers who ship fresh, or build a rapport with your local grocery store. A lot of Asian grocery stores stock incredible fish. Many keep live fish in tanks to ensure quality, but if they don't stock fresh, then they have some pretty nice flash-frozen stuff that will work in a pinch. As long as the flesh is frozen as quickly as possible after the catch, it should

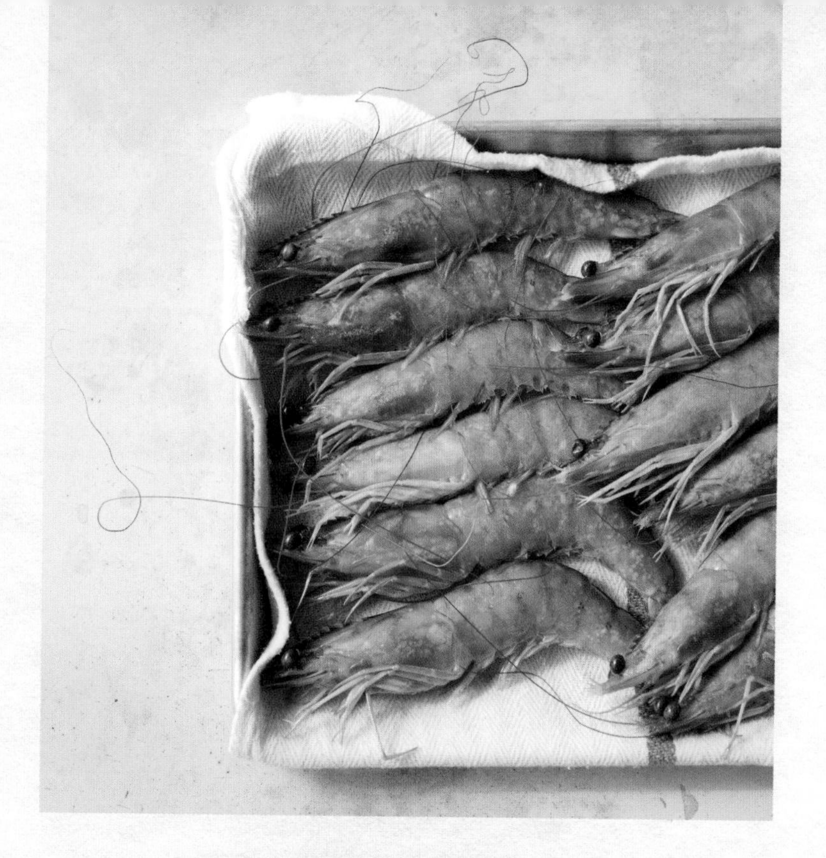

be fine: Consider that most fish used for sushi and sashimi is actually flash-frozen. Whichever shop you end up visiting, whole fish should be stored upright (as if it's swimming in the water with its spine parallel to the floor) and well iced. Fillets should be neatly separated in clean trays on ice. Cutting boards and workstations should be pristine, free of fish debris, guts, and blood. And there shouldn't be an overall off-smell of fish. Fresh fish doesn't really have an odor.

One final suggestion: Instead of inquiring about something specific, try asking your supplier or fishmonger what they're really liking at that moment. What's landed most recently? What's been coming in looking better than everything else? Believe it or not, most fish have a season, a certain part of the year when the fish is more sustainable to catch and of better quality than it would be out of season. Show real interest and make them feel like it's on them. They may take great pride in pleasing you, even stopping you next time you come in to tell you about some great fish that just arrived. Stay open to improvising last minute based on their guidance. You never know where that might lead.

marinated mussels with onion vinagreta

SERVES 4

The idea for this recipe—and the majority of the work that went into making it real—should be attributed to one of our amazing previous sous chefs, Finn O'Hara. Finn came back from a family vacation in Spain itching to do something with the overload of inspiration he brought home. He mentioned one dish, a simple plate of mussels with a generous amount of raw onion on top. The concept was great, he said, but he felt we could execute it in our own way, really "make it sing." Here's what we came up with.

Note: Your mussels should be tightly closed and lacking any "fishy" aromas. The smell of fresh, clean ocean water is great. If any are open, give them a gentle squeeze. If they slowly close back up, they're still okay. If they spring back open, discard them. One bad mussel can ruin the whole batch. Mussels attach themselves to surfaces with what is called a beard, which looks like a stringy bit of seaweed along the seam of the shell. In most cases, the beard should be removed before cooking (I like to remove it after if the mussels are to be shucked: after cooking and before serving), as it is rather unpleasant to eat. Use a pair of needlenose pliers to pull them out, then give the mussels a quick rinse with cold water to remove any debris. The beard can tear easily, but the trick is to make sure you get a good hold of its mass before giving it a careful, smooth pull.

FOR THE MUSSELS:

⅓ cup (80 ml) extra-virgin olive oil

2 cups (250 g) thinly sliced Spanish onion

1 teaspoon kosher salt

½ cup (63 g) smashed garlic cloves (about 10)

Peel of 1 medium orange, cut with a peeler

Peel of 2 medium lemons, cut with a peeler

3 bay leaves

1 tablespoon coriander seeds

2 cups (480 ml) dry white wine

1½ pounds (675 g) thumb-size mussels (3 dozen or so total), cleaned (see Note)

FOR THE VINAGRETA:

1 cup (80 g) very small-diced Spanish onion

2¼ tablespoons champagne vinegar, plus more if needed

¾ teaspoon kosher salt, plus more if needed

1 tablespoon extra-virgin olive oil

⅔ cup (35 g) chopped fresh parsley

TO FINISH:

Extra-virgin olive oil

Maldon salt

CONTINUED

MAKE THE MUSSELS: In a pot, heat the olive oil over medium heat. Add the onion and kosher salt and cook until the onion starts to soften, about 5 minutes. Add the garlic and cook for another 2 to 3 minutes. Add the orange and lemon peels, the bay leaves, and the coriander and toast slightly, about 1 minute. Add the wine and cook until the smell of alcohol has burned off, then add the mussels. Cover and cook until the mussels open, then cook for another 2 to 3 minutes.

Remove from the heat and use a slotted spoon to transfer the mussels to a dish, discarding any that don't open. Strain the cooking liquid through a fine-mesh sieve into a separate container and cover. Place the mussels and the strained cooking liquid into the fridge to cool.

Once cool, pick the meat carefully from the mussel shells, trying not to tear it. Separate the shells, discarding any broken ones and keeping all the nice ones for serving. Scrape off any remaining meat with a small offset spatula, then rinse the shells and set aside.

Debeard the mussels with a pair of scissors and pull out any stray coriander seeds or other debris. Transfer the mussels to the cooking liquid. Swish them around, then, using your fingertips, cradle them out and place them in an empty container.

Using a fine-mesh strainer, strain the cooking liquid over the mussels again. Repeat the swishing process one more time, again removing them from the cooking liquid and then straining it over the mussels. Cover, and refrigerate until ready to use, preferably overnight, as the mussels get plump and juicy in their liquid after cooking. (They can be stored like this for about 5 days.)

MAKE THE VINAGRETA: Combine the onion and vinegar in a bowl and stir. Set aside for 1 hour.

Add the kosher salt, olive oil, and parsley and stir to combine. Taste and adjust the salt and vinegar. It should be bright and highly seasoned.

TO FINISH: Place a handful of mussel shells cupped side down on a platter. Set the remaining mussel shells cupped side up on top. Spoon a mussel into each shell along with a few drops of the cooking liquid. Spoon some of the vinagreta onto each mussel, along with some of the precious juices. Finish with a few drops of olive oil and a few flakes of Maldon salt, and serve.

mussels with stewed leeks and garlicky broth on toast

SERVES 4

Quickly steamed-open mussels on toast can make a great impromptu meal . . . one that can be assembled quickly with a little foresight, as well. The only real "do ahead" task would be to have some fish stock on hand. Beyond that, this is a one-pot deal. If you don't have any fish stock in your freezer (see page 325), check with your seafood purveyor, as many tend to make stock of their own with the leftover bones they have from butchery. And if you're planning ahead, make some aioli, then put a little plop of it on each toast before spooning over the mussels as a delicious bonus.

2 large leeks

¼ cup (60 ml) extra-virgin olive oil, plus more for finishing

Kosher salt, if needed

6 medium cloves garlic, sliced very thin

2 cups (480 ml) Savory Fish Stock (page 325)

¼ cup (60 ml) dry white wine

Pinch saffron threads

1 pound (455 g) thumb-size mussels, cleaned (see Note, page 212)

2 tablespoons unsalted butter

Leaves from ½ bunch parsley, finely chopped

Sourdough bread, cut into ¾-inch-thick (2 cm) slices

Aioli (page 305; optional)

Trim the roots and green tops from the leeks (reserve for a vegetable stock, if you'd like) so you're left with the white portion. Split them in half lengthwise, then slice them into ½-inch-wide (12 mm) half-moons; you should have about 2 cups (170 g). Fill a large bowl with warm water, add the leeks, and swish them around, letting any dirt sink to the bottom. Let them sit in the water for a few minutes, then carefully cradle them out onto a plate lined with paper towels, leaving any dirt behind in the bowl.

In a heavy-bottomed pot, heat the olive oil over medium-low heat until it just begins to shimmer. Add the leeks and a pinch of salt and sweat them, stirring often, until translucent with slight tinges of caramelization, 4 to 5 minutes. Add the garlic and cook for a few moments to allow its flavor to infuse the olive oil, then add the stock and the white wine.

Increase the heat to medium and bring the stock to a gentle simmer. Pinch the saffron threads between your fingers and add them to the broth. Simmer for about 10 minutes, then taste the stock. The fish stock recipe in this book is nicely seasoned, but if you used store-bought stock, you may need to add a pinch of salt at this point. Just be careful not to add too much, as the mussels bring a bit of their own salinity to the dish.

CONTINUED

Add the mussels to the simmering stock and cover the pot. Cook until all the mussels open, about 2 minutes. If one or two remain closed, remove those with a pair of tongs and discard them. Add the butter and stir to melt and incorporate it. Add the parsley and turn off the heat.

Toast the bread in a toaster oven or under the broiler until quite dark on both sides with some charred bits here and there. Divvy up the bread among four bowls and spoon on some aioli, if desired, followed by the mussels. Try to get a bit of leeks and garlic into each dish. There may be some residual sand or grit in the bottom of the pot, so try to avoid using that last quarter inch or so. I like to use a large spoon and then tilt the pan slightly to scoop out the mussels. Then I kind of tip the pot at an angle and spoon out the leeks and garlic to finish plating. Finish with a good drizzle of olive oil and serve.

fried skate wing with cabbage salad, mint, and lime vinaigrette

SERVES 4

I'm kind of mindlessly into fried fish. Cod, haddock, hake, smelt—I'm not too picky. Even so, I think skate is the true winner. This underdog's thin strands of flesh have an almost crablike richness to them and remain incredibly juicy after cooking. My two favorite recipes for it follow, but honestly, you can try out all sorts of combinations on your own. With skate, sometimes all it takes is a squeeze of lemon and some aioli. Skate can be found all over the world, but it can still be a little difficult to source. That's the only challenge. If you happen upon some good stuff, buy a little extra. The fillets keep surprisingly well in the freezer.

If you've ever had dinner at my house, you've probably feasted on one of my favorite kitchen moves: the shredded cabbage salad. I love massaging finely sliced strips of this sturdy brassica with salt to really help marinades and vinaigrettes permeate its squeaky flesh. Seasoning in advance only benefits the salad, which makes it ideal for meals that involve some multitasking. Look for savoy cabbage, which has tons of tiny little nooks that are great for soaking up flavor without wilting. Lots of mint and a bright lime vinaigrette pair absurdly well with crispy fried fish. Just make sure that you spoon all those Precious Juices™ from the cabbage over the dish.

FOR THE SKATE:

1 pound (455 g) boneless skate wing, cut into 4 equal pieces

1 tablespoon kosher salt, plus more as needed

2 cups (480 ml) egg whites (from about 14 large eggs)

1½ cups (300 g) cornstarch

2 cups (250 g) all-purpose flour

3 cups (225 g) panko bread crumbs

FOR THE CABBAGE SALAD:

7 ounces (200 g) cored green cabbage (about ½ head of cabbage, thinly sliced)

½ teaspoon kosher salt, plus more as needed

½ clove garlic, grated with a Microplane

1 tablespoon lime zest (from about 2 limes)

½ cup (120 ml) fresh lime juice (from 4 to 5 limes)

½ teaspoon honey

¼ teaspoon ground coriander

¼ cup (60 ml) extra-virgin olive oil

1½ cups (220 g) diced pineapple

2 cups (30 g) loosely packed fresh mint leaves

1 cup (70 g) sliced red onion

TO FINISH:

Canola oil, for frying

1 teaspoon kosher salt

1 tablespoon Maldon salt

CONTINUED

BREAD THE SKATE: Before breading, I like to quickly rinse the skate wings in cold water, then salt them lightly for about 15 minutes to draw out moisture and firm up the fish's flesh. This also ensures more even seasoning. Finally, I rinse them with cold water again and then, to dry them, I place the fillets on a sheet tray lined with absorbent towels and put them in the fridge for an hour.

In a blender, combine the egg whites and cornstarch and blend on high speed until smooth. Transfer to a shallow baking dish. Put the flour and a pinch of salt in a second baking dish and stir with a fork to combine. Put the panko in a third dish.

One at a time, dredge the skate wing pieces in the flour, then dip in the egg white mixture, and finally coat with the panko. At the bread crumb stage, really press the panko into the fish and crumble some of it in your hands to make a mix of finer and coarse crumbs to get every bit of flesh covered. This will create a barrier that protects the fish from the hot oil, allowing it to steam in the crust and keeping it juicy. Set the breaded skate pieces on a sheet tray and place in the fridge.

MAKE THE CABBAGE SALAD: In a mixing bowl, toss the cabbage with the kosher salt, massaging the cabbage with your hands to release some of its water.

In a bowl, combine the garlic, lime zest, lime juice, honey, coriander, and a pinch of salt. Whisk in the olive oil, then taste and adjust if necessary.

Add the dressing to the cabbage along with the pineapple, mint, and onion and stir with a spoon until incorporated. Set aside.

TO FINISH: In a heavy Dutch oven or deep stockpot, pour about 3 inches (8 cm) canola oil and heat the oil over medium-low heat until the temperature reaches 350°F (175°C). Adjust your burner as needed to maintain that temperature as you proceed with the recipe. Have a spider handy and set a sheet tray topped with a rack nearby.

Carefully slip each piece of breaded skate into the hot oil, being careful not to overcrowd the pot (this can drop the oil temperature, which leads to soggy fish). Cook until golden brown, about 4 minutes, then remove with the spider and place on the prepared rack. Season with the kosher salt on both sides and the Maldon salt on the side you're serving up, then arrange each piece of skate on a plate. Spoon over the cabbage salad and its juices and serve right away.

fried skate with sungold tomatoes, garlic, and opal basil

SERVES 4

One of the annual favorites of The Four Horsemen. The feature is a simple sauce of bright orange Sungold tomatoes, blistered open with garlic and olive oil, then deglazed with white wine and finished with a knob of butter. The bright, savory liquid from the tomatoes is balanced by the butter to create a luxurious summer sauce, paired here with the crispy skate wing. This sauce works equally well with a fried chicken cutlet or spooned over some grilled bread with slabs of mozzarella cheese.

FOR THE SKATE:

1 pound (455 g) boneless skate wing, cut into 4 equal pieces

2 cups (480 ml) egg whites (from about 14 large eggs)

1½ cups (300 g) cornstarch

2 cups (250 g) all-purpose flour

1 tablespoon kosher salt

3 cups (225 g) panko bread crumbs

FOR THE TOMATO SAUCE:

2 tablespoons extra-virgin olive oil

5 medium cloves garlic, thinly sliced

1 teaspoon Aleppo pepper

¼ cup (60 ml) dry white wine

2 pints (625 g) Sungold tomatoes

3 tablespoons unsalted butter

½ teaspoon sugar

1 tablespoon kosher salt

TO FINISH:

Canola oil, for frying

¼ teaspoon kosher salt

¼ teaspoon Maldon salt

1 cup (40 g) fresh Dark Opal basil leaves, finely shredded

BREAD THE SKATE: Follow the instructions on page 219.

MAKE THE TOMATO SAUCE: In a sauté pan, heat the olive oil over medium heat. Add the garlic and let it sizzle and cook gently until fragrant and slightly toasted (but not browned or burnt). Add the Aleppo pepper, then add the wine and cook until the smell of alcohol has burnt off, a minute or so.

Put the tomatoes in a mixing bowl, then set another mixing bowl on top and press down to crush the tomatoes between them. Add the crushed tomatoes to the pan and reduce the heat to medium-low. The mixture should be just gently bubbling away with a nice amount of liquid from the wine, the olive oil, and the juices from the tomatoes. Add the butter to the sauce and move the tomatoes around. You're looking for some of them to be kind of smashed and some to be whole, but cooked and juicy. The smashed ones will leach their juices into the sauce. Cook until the sauce has a nice

sheen from the butter and good acidity from the wine and tomatoes, 3 to 4 minutes. The fat from the butter and oil should be emulsified and lend balance to the sauce; it shouldn't be broken or too tight. Add the sugar and the kosher salt and stir, then turn off the heat and set aside.

TO FINISH: Fry the skate, then arrange on your serving plate, per the instructions on page 219. Add the Opal basil to the warm tomato sauce, then spoon the sauce over the fish and serve.

manila clams with fennel and pastis

SERVES 4

One of my favorite stews, this simple dish comes together quickly and packs a very flavorful punch. The rich broth, the citrusy notes from the lemon peel and yuzu kosho, and the sweet anise flavors from fennel and pastis all work together effortlessly.

If you can't find Manila clams, which are a bit more delicate, littlenecks would work just fine. Either way, I encourage you to purge the clams before cooking them: A few hours before you plan to cook them, fill a bowl with water and add 3¾ teaspoons kosher salt per 4 cups (1 L) water (or 30 g salt per 1 kg water). Add the clams and soak for about 30 minutes. Scrub and rinse, then pack them away in the fridge until you're ready to prepare the dish. You could use a store-bought fish stock or chicken stock here, but I highly recommend you try making your own fish stock for this particular dish. If you have any left over, you can warm it up with some rice to make a nice soup the next day.

- 2 tablespoons extra-virgin olive oil, plus more for serving
- 1 cup (100 g) small-diced fennel bulb (about 1 bulb; green stems discarded)
- 1 cup (100 g) small-diced Spanish onion (about ½ large onion)
- 1 teaspoon kosher salt
- Pinch saffron threads
- ¼ cup (60 ml) pastis
- 2¾ cups (660 ml) Savory Fish Stock (page 325)
- 4 medium cloves garlic, thinly sliced
- 1 lemon peel, white pith removed, sliced into very thin 1-inch-long (2.5 cm) strips
- 2 pounds (910 g) Manila clams, purged (see headnote)
- 1 cup (½ stick / 225 g) unsalted butter
- 1 teaspoon yuzu kosho
- 1 cup (57 g) fresh chervil leaves, coarsely chopped

In a wide, shallow pot, heat 1 tablespoon of the olive oil over medium-low heat until it shimmers slightly. Add the fennel, onion, and salt and cook, stirring often, until the vegetables are tender but not browned at all, about 5 minutes. Add the saffron, then add the pastis and cook until most of it has evaporated and the smell of alcohol is replaced with a sweet aroma of fennel. Add the stock and bring to a simmer. Adjust the heat to maintain a low simmer for 20 minutes to allow the flavors to infuse. Remove from the heat and set the broth aside. (This can be allowed to cool and then stored in an airtight container in the fridge up to 3 to 4 days in advance.)

CONTINUED

In a separate pot, heat the remaining 1 tablespoon olive oil over medium heat. Add the garlic and allow it to sizzle gently for a minute or so while stirring, then add the lemon peel and stir for another 30 seconds. Add the broth, making sure you get some of the fennel and onions into the mix, then add the clams. Bring to a simmer and cover. Cook until the clams open, about 3 to 5 minutes, discarding any that don't. Add the butter and the yuzu kosho, reduce the heat to low, and cook, stirring, to melt the butter and incorporate both ingredients into the broth.

Add the chervil, give everything a quick stir, and immediately spoon the clams into bowls. There may be some residual sand or grit at the bottom of the pot, so try to avoid using that last quarter inch (6 mm) or so. I like to use a large spoon and then tilt the pan slightly to scoop out the clams. Finish each bowl with some olive oil and serve immediately.

SEAFOOD

boston mackerel with piparra peppers, sweet onions, and aioli

SERVES 4

Mackerel is easily one of my favorite types of fish. The Atlantic or "Boston" variety is smaller than its more common Spanish cousin, and its flesh, when cooked to a nice medium-rare, is fatty, rich, and delicious.

A lot of people wrongly dismiss mackerel as "fishy," but that reputation was born out of poor seafood hygiene. Mackerel is full of amazing healthy oils and fats that contribute to its beautiful flavor and texture, and it's those very fats that can make it go bad earlier than something like a cod. Buy this fish from a trusted source, as you want it really fresh.

1 small sweet onion (Vidalia or Walla Walla)

16 pickled piparra peppers, pickling liquid reserved

2 Boston mackerel, 10 to 12 inches (25 to 30 cm) in length, filleted and pin bones removed

Kosher salt

Extra-virgin olive oil

Maldon salt

Aioli (page 305)

Peel the onion and cut it into quarters through the stem. Remove a couple of the petals and slice them lengthwise into ¼-inch-wide (6 mm) strips. Place them in the piparra pickling liquid and set aside in the fridge to marinate for at least 1 hour or up to 1 day.

Prepare a wood-burning grill, getting it to a nice medium heat (you should be able to hold your hand 6 inches / 15 cm above the grate for 4 to 5 seconds).

Line a sheet tray with parchment paper and arrange the fish on the tray. Season lightly with kosher salt on the flesh side only. Flip the fish over and brush lightly with the olive oil. Place the fish skin side down on the grill and cook for 1 to 2 minutes, until the skin is crispy but the flesh is still bright pink on top. Remove the fish from the grill with a spatula and transfer each fillet to a warmed plate, skin side up. (If you're using a small grill with an easily removable grate, you can just remove the grate and place a sheet tray or plate on top of the fish, then flip the grate and plate over together so the fish falls right onto the plate.)

Spoon a few of the pickled onions and a bit of their juices over each fillet, followed by 3 or 4 of the piparra peppers. Sprinkle on a few flakes of Maldon salt and spoon a good dollop of aioli next to the fish. Serve right away so the skin stays nice and crispy.

rainbow trout with asian pear and kohlrabi

SERVES 2 TO 4

If you come across good trout at your local fish market, pick up a few and have a go at this recipe. A key step here is to butterfly the fish, which your butcher should be happy to do. I like to let the fish dry out overnight in the fridge, skin side up, to ensure the skin will crisp when cooking. The trout's fatty flesh pairs well with a juicy slaw of Asian pears and kohlrabi, the cabbage-flavored champion of crunchy raw salads.

FOR THE TROUT:

2 whole trout (1½ pounds / 680 g total), butterflied

1 teaspoon shio koji

1 teaspoon yuzu kosho

Extra-virgin olive oil

FOR THE SALAD:

1½ cups (90 g) kohlrabi, peeled

1½ cups (90 g) Asian pear, peeled

4 cloves garlic, finely grated

Fresh lemon juice

1 teaspoon Maldon salt, plus more as needed

2 tablespoons olive oil, plus more as needed

1 tablespoon yuzu vinegar or apple cider vinegar

½ cup (14 g) shiso, coarsely chopped

1 cup (30 g) loosely packed fresh parsley, picked

PREPARE THE TROUT: Using a pastry brush, brush the flesh of the fish (not the skin) with the shio koji and yuzu kosho. Line a sheet tray with parchment paper and arrange the fish on the tray, skin side up. Allow to marinate, covered, in the refrigerator for at least 2 hours or up to overnight.

When you are ready to cook the dish, prepare a wood-burning grill, getting it to a nice medium heat (you should be able to hold your hand 6 inches / 15 cm above the grate for 4 to 5 seconds) and brush the skin of the fish with olive oil.

PREPARE THE SALAD AND COOK THE TROUT: Slice the kohlrabi and Asian pear into 1½-inch-long (4 cm) strips. In a mixing bowl, combine the garlic, kohlrabi, Asian pear, 1½ tablespoons lemon juice, the Maldon salt, and olive oil and stir. Add the vinegar, give it a few more tosses, and set aside.

Place the fish skin side down on the grill and cook for 3 to 4 minutes, until the skin is crispy but the flesh is still bright pink on top.

TO FINISH: Sprinkle a little extra Maldon salt, olive oil, and lemon on the kohlrabi and pear. Add the shiso and parsley to the bowl, toss, and divide the salad between two warmed plates. Remove the fish from the grill with a spatula and transfer each trout to a plate, skin side up, over each nest of salad. Sprinkle with lemon juice and serve immediately.

OPINEL
INOX

grilling over wood and charcoal

I'm lucky to have done a lot of grilling in my life. I've worked with massive hearths and wood-burning ovens, roasted whole petrale sole, juicy porcini, craggy knobs of celery root, and Dungeness crabs next to glowing embers that perfumed each item with a light, sweet smoke you can't get any other way. I've cooked thousands of pizzas inside a brick oven in Brooklyn. I once got to prepare whole lambs, splayed out on handmade iron crosses, that cooked low and slow over a massive firepit. That was probably the most fun I've ever had cooking.

As much as I'm into all of these primal methods, they're fairly impractical in either a Brooklyn restaurant or your typical home. But you can still get a stand-alone grill. I use a Big Green Egg kamado-style ceramic grill at my house, which I love. It's fantastic for low-and-slow cooking and really shines when cooking steaks, pork chops, and burgers. At the restaurant, we have a smaller Japanese konro grill made of bricks with a simple metal grate on top. It's reliable, sturdy, easy to use, and relatively cheap.

We like to use binchotan wood in the restaurant kitchen. Preburned in low oxygen until it becomes pure carbon, this beloved Japanese charcoal burns at a very high temperature and emanates minimal smoke. It's perfect for quick grilling, which is what I do at The Four Horsemen. At home, I opt for a larger-chunk preburned charcoal. It's a bit smokier and burns longer. It's also significantly cheaper than proper binchotan. I usually incorporate chunks of dried hardwood that don't give off a lot of heat if I'm slow cooking and want to incorporate a good amount of smoke.

Regardless of what kind of grilling you like to do, please avoid briquettes and lighter fluid—they're loaded with chemicals and can affect the flavor of your food. Try natural fire starters made from compressed wood chips or thin pieces of wood that

have been spun together. A couple of tools that will help you along the way are a chimney starter and a small blowtorch. If you're committed to doing a lot of of grilling, these aren't too pricey and make quick work of starting a fire without you spraying a pile of gnarly uniform lumps with gasoline like a fifties dad.

TO LIGHT A GRILL

Place a layer of charcoal at the bottom of your grill and put three or four fire starters in the center. Then place the chimney starter on top and load it with a few pieces of charcoal, then a couple of fire starters, then more charcoal, until it's almost full. Aim the blowtorch at the base of the chimney starter and hit it. Once the fire starters at the bottom catch, kill the blowtorch. Allow the charcoal to burn until the top pieces begin turning to embers. Carefully grab the handle of the chimney starter—you might want to have a towel in your hand to be safe—and tip the coals into the grill bed. With tongs, scatter them evenly for a single-level grill. Alternatively, scoot them over to one side for a two-tiered grill. The latter option is best suited for larger grills: You'll now have the space to start something on high heat on one side, then move it to the side with fewer coals for a more indirect heat. This technique, with the lid closed, is akin to a smoky oven.

grilled head-on shrimp with pounded cilantro and thai chiles

SERVES
4 TO 6

In addition to being one of the best things you can put in your face, grilled shrimp are an absolute dream to prep and cook. We've prepared them all sorts of ways, and this is definitely a kitchen favorite. The sneaky hit is the Thai chile and herb sauce, best made in a suribachi (see page 51), whose thin indentations aid in the pounding process. The result is a vibrant sauce with more character and texture. You could make this in a food processor, but honestly it kind of loses a little something. Plus, using the suribachi is fun.

I like head-on fresh shrimp for this dish, but get what you can. Your next-best option would be high-quality frozen shrimp. Just thaw them in the fridge the night before. Make sure to remove the digestive tract (also called the vein) from each shrimp; cut a small slit down the back with scissors or a knife, then pull out the brown (or sometimes orange) stuff. It won't kill you if you eat it, but it can be a bit gritty, which weirds some people out.

15 large shrimp (1 kg), peeled (heads left on) and deveined

3½ tablespoons (52 ml) extra-virgin olive oil

¾ tablespoon kosher salt

1 cup (240 ml) Thai Chile and Herb Sauce (page 309)

4 cups (66 g) chopped fresh cilantro

4 cups (50 g) chopped fresh mint

1 pinch Maldon salt

Lime wedges

Prepare a wood-burning or binchotan grill.

When the grill is hot, toss the shrimp carefully with the olive oil and kosher salt. Place on the grill and char on one side for about 1 minute, until they are opaque and pink. Flip and cook for another minute or so. Remove the shrimp from the grill and place in a mixing bowl. Add the Thai chile and herb sauce, the cilantro, mint, Maldon salt, and a good squeeze of lime. Plate and serve immediately with lime wedges on the side.

a whole roasted sole for a special occasion

SERVES 4 TO 6

Dover sole is the ideal fish to serve whole. Turbot is arguably a better fish but requires a bit more technique and finesse, and can be wildly expensive. Sole, on the other hand, has become more readily available.

Sole is a flatfish, meaning it swims on the ocean floor with eyes on the top of its head. It lurks in the sand, camouflaged by its skin, and consumes mollusks and crustaceans all day long. This diet makes its flesh incredibly rich and fatty. When cooked, it has a very fine, flaky texture with loads of natural gelatin that keep it moist and help the fish essentially baste itself during the cooking process.

You are looking to buy a whole fish that has been scaled and gutted by your fishmonger; if you can't find Dover sole, look for lemon sole or petrale sole. Now, you could, in theory, just roast it as is. The results would be great, though you'd have a fair number of small bones to deal with. And if you've ever ordered this at a restaurant where it is deboned tableside, you know that some small fin bones always remain. If you're moderately handy with a knife, we developed a way to serve the sole boneless so every square inch of it is perfect.

To debone the sole, all you need are a pair of scissors and a sharp, thin knife: Take the scissors and trim off the little wings on either side of the fish, working from tail to head. (These line both sides of the body and are the fins that help propel the fish with a serpentine movement. Called *engawa* in Japanese, these are actually incredible grilled, so feel free to save them and give that a try, or freeze them and add them to a fish stock down the line. They're high in gelatin.) With the wings removed, position the fish dark side up on a cutting board with the head facing away from you and the tail closest to you. Hold the knife parallel to the fish and make an incision above the bones all along where you just removed the fins. Work about 1½ inches (4 cm) into the fish until you almost hit the spine. Stop there and do the same on the other side. Flip the fish over and repeat the process, working above the bones, parallel to the cutting board.

Once you've almost reached the spine on all 4 fillets, use the scissors to remove the small set of bones that are about ½ inch (12 mm) wide. You'll basically see two sets when you peek into the fish. The smaller set is what we're looking to remove; the larger set is the spine, and we want to save that for roasting the fish (it will help keep the flesh juicy). You should see a clear delineation between the two sets. Cut right at that line on both sides. Once you have those bones removed, the fish is ready to cook.

FOR THE DASHI:

1 (4 by 6-inch / 10 by 15 cm) piece kombu, rinsed with cold water

Peel of 1 lemon (about 10 g), cut with a peeler

1½ cups (15 g) katsuobushi (bonito flakes)

FOR THE FISH:

1 (1½-pound / 680 g) Dover sole, deboned as described opposite

¼ teaspoon kosher salt

2 tablespoons unsalted butter, at room temperature

1 cup (75 g) hon-shimeji (beech mushrooms)

2 teaspoons fresh lemon juice

½ teaspoon Maldon salt

½ teaspoon fennel pollen

1 (2-inch / 5 cm) piece fresh horseradish, peeled

MAKE THE DASHI: In a pot, combine 4 cups (1 L) water, the kombu, and the lemon peel and bring to a low simmer over medium heat. Cook for 30 minutes, then turn off the heat and add the katsuobushi. Allow to steep for 10 minutes, then strain through a fine-mesh sieve. Refrigerate until ready to use (it will keep for up to 5 days).

CONTINUED

MAKE THE FISH: Preheat the oven to 375°F (190°C).

Season both sides of the fish and inside the cavity with the kosher salt. Pour the dashi onto a sheet tray just big enough for the fish, then place the fish on top. Spoon the butter onto the fish, spreading it evenly. Roast the fish for 7 minutes, then pull it out of the oven and spoon over the precious juices (see page 272) from the pan to baste the fish. Scatter over the mushrooms and return the fish to the oven for another 7 minutes, or until an instant-read thermometer inserted toward the spine, right near the head, reaches 140°F (60°C).

Using two spatulas, transfer the fish to a serving platter. With a knife, make an incision all the way down the spine. Use a fork to hold the fish in place, then use a flat palette knife to slide the flesh off one side of the spine. Do the same for the other side, then use a pair of scissors to cut the spine right near the head and then the tail. Starting with the tail, begin to pull up the spine with your fingers while holding down the flesh it's clinging to with the palette knife. As you move your way toward the head, keep adjusting the palette knife farther and farther up the spine to prevent the spine from taking too much flesh with it. If the fish is cooked perfectly, it should just pop right out.

Spoon some of the cooking juices left in the pan over the fish, along with the mushrooms. Sprinkle over the lemon juice, Maldon salt, and fennel pollen, then grate the horseradish over the fish using a fine Microplane and serve.

SEAFOOD

THE LIST: HOW WE BUILD IT AND SHARE IT

We have hundreds of wines on our list. Here's how we decide what to serve and how we try to share this in an approachable way with our guests—as well as a few ideas for how this might help your drinking situation at home.

THE WORK

People often ask me how I go about finding wines for the restaurant. I get the sense that a lot of them picture me somewhere in rural France, tasting with a legendary winemaker while the sun sets across gorgeous ancient vineyards. Okay, maybe that does actually happen from time to time, but usually I'm posting up at the empty bar of the restaurant in the morning, waiting for the first person to roll in their wares for me to try. You may not know that restaurants in New York State are legally forbidden to buy directly from a winery, so having deep relationships with small, passionate importers and distributors is so important for what we do. These folks work with the winemakers, ship their wines to the US, and sell them to us.

In 2003, when wine was beginning to become my job, there were maybe three or four importers specializing in low-intervention wines; maybe a few hundred of those wines were brought to New York. Now there are literally thousands of natural wines available and dozens of enthusiastic importers trying to set appointments with us or just optimistically showing up at the door at random times. *Hello, is Justin here?* I may not have the time in my schedule to accommodate a cold call—or

JAVA
MURI

it may just be that I don't have to taste the wines they represent to know it won't be a fit–but I tell everybody on staff to treat everyone who shows an interest in adding to our offerings with kindness and respect. I really cannot stand seeing restaurants shoo away folks that are just trying to do their job.

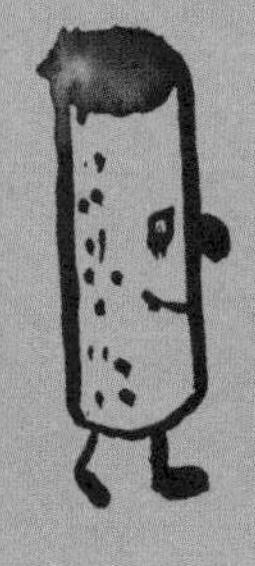

My first sales visit is usually around 9:30 a.m. The restaurant is closed, the chairs are still upside down on the tables, and our head prep cook, Chantal, is baking bread in the oven. Down in the basement, her team is rolling out fresh pasta for the night's service. Each distributor will usually bring me somewhere between six and ten wines to taste. They pour me about an ounce of wine in the glass, I swirl it around, smell it for a second, take a sip, swish it around in my mouth, and dispose of it into a spit bucket. Rinse and repeat, literally. I take some notes throughout. We also get to catch up, maybe trade a little gossip about the industry. At the end, I let them know if we'd like to order anything and then they're off to their next appointment and the next salesperson comes through our doors, and I do it again. On some days, I will have tasted around forty or so wines by noon, of which maybe two or three make it onto the list.

These visits are just as important, if not more so, than those postcard perfect moments in the Loire. Seeing what the wine feels like in our glasses, at our place, gives us a very honest impression of what's there when the romantic backdrop fades. Several of the sales-people I work with have been doing this longer than me. I've tasted wine with them hundreds of times throughout the years. We've seen the industry change and each other's tastes evolve, so they know what I like–and they can identify openings to push me out of my comfort zone.

Why am I telling you all of this? Why would I want you to picture me spitting into a bucket on a

Wednesday? My point is that these salespeople are a crucial part of our restaurant family, and we couldn't do it without them.

THE FAIRS

Another way that I find wine for the restaurant is by traveling to wine fairs. The first weekend in February is Super Bowl Sunday for natural wine fans around the world (it is also, coincidentally, actually Super Bowl Sunday in the States). That's when wine aficionados descend into the Loire Valley villages of Angers and Saumur and surrounding towns for a long weekend of tasting a sea of the most recent vintage from hundreds of the greatest natural winemakers from around the world at several wine fairs, among which are La Dive Bouteille, Les Pénitentes, Les Anonymes, and Salon du Grenier Saint Jean. Hundreds of winemakers, thousands of wines, much-needed camaraderie. I've been going for fifteen years. By now, it never fails: After a week of too many bottles, too many miserable attempts at speaking some childish form of French, and too many incredibly late nights, I'm hungover on the plane back to New York, saying to myself "never again." Two weeks later, I'm Googling flights for next year's fairs.

There are also weekends in Barcelona, Vienna, London, Los Angeles, and New York as well as smaller tastings in dozens of other regions happening almost every month. It is now impossible to attend them all, so I mostly stick to the Loire in February and Karakterre in Vienna in May. Each one has its own culture and crowd, some serious, some more of a party. Everyone has their favorites.

All of them have gotten more crowded over the years. Even though the lines at the tasting tables can be long, there's just nothing like being face to face with the people that actually make the wines we love so much—wines that our guests want to try so badly that they'll go through the trouble it takes to get into our small restaurant. It's amazing to get even five minutes with a winemaker once a year to ask how the harvest was, or get some details about the process, or even just taste some things that are so rare they won't make it to the US. It's something that we, as a team, will always look forward to.

THE CHOICE OF THREE

After visiting the fairs and tasting my way through the portfolios of the importers and distributors, we have access to a vast, curated selection of wines. But a big part of the challenge is to give our guests access to these wines in a way that is approachable and fun. In a restaurant with a list as large as ours, it's pretty normal for a guest to just look at the server and ask, "So, what do you think we should drink tonight?" We don't have sommeliers at The Four Horsemen. Your server tells you about our food, talks with you about our wine, clears your table, runs your food, refills your water, and does pretty much everything else related to your evening: a style influenced by our friends in Paris, more specifically the incredible Parisian bistros Le Verre Volé and Le Baratin. Until just a few years ago, Le Verre Volé had no wine list at all. You would have a quick chat with your server about what you liked, wanted to spend, and maybe how many bottles the night might have in store for you. The server at Le Baratin, on the other hand, will just bring you a bottle they feel you deserve and that is what you will be drinking tonight. We've kind of turned that into our "choice of three" presentation tableside.

Guests come in, ask the server what they think they should drink, and we ask a few questions to get a sense of the parameters. We come back from the cellar with three bottles of different styles and prices that we think will fit the food and the moment and talk a little bit about why. We love being able to get this personal. Our guests seem to like it, too, because more often than not, they get a few bottles into dinner and wind up never opening the wine list.

MORE IS MORE

Listing two wines by glass from the same winery seems to be a no-go for most restaurants and wine bars. I've never understood this. When I'm checking out wines for the restaurant, I often taste six or more from each winemaker in a row. That's how I learn about their winemaking style, what grapes they grow, what the vintage was like, everything. For this reason, I occasionally offer a couple glass pours by the same winemaker (say a white and an orange, or a sparkling white and still red) on our list.

It also, occasionally, makes having a drink more than just a glass of wine. Many guests who order wines by the glass aren't looking at the winery name at all. They tend to order based on the price or the name of the grape. But if we see them enjoying one of the options from a winemaker listed twice, there's an opening: "Oh, I see you enjoyed the Keltis sparkling rosé. You should check out their orange wine, which we also are pouring." It is a great way to help bring attention to new wineries or generally lesser-known regions. The guest ends up learning something through experience rather than being lectured to. This is something to consider at home as well. If you find a wine you like, it can be fun to seek out other offerings from the same producer and try them side by side, or over the course of a few days.

POULTRY
BEEF
PORK

MEAT

MEAT

When you go out to dinner, do you ever have the experience where the meal starts out brilliantly—fried bites, pungent cured meats, bright raw fish, and tasty salads—but then quietly begins to fade when it comes to the mains? Sometimes it can seem like there isn't as much focus and attention to detail—a mishmash of ingredients crammed on a plate in a manner that feels substantial in volume, but less enjoyable for eating.

With this in mind, we turn to special ingredients or techniques that I can highlight with minimal fanfare. This style of cooking suits us at The Four Horsemen. Less fuss, more focus. Don't worry about getting multiple components on a dish; instead, truly prioritize only what's necessary. An excellent professional chef will look at a dish and think more often about what can be taken away than what can be added. Try to do the same. And, important: Special doesn't always mean expensive.

Beyond classic main dishes from the restaurant, I've also included a couple of smaller bites, along with larger preparations designed for gatherings and occasions.

ben's chicken liver mousse and fennel pollen crackers

SERVES 4 / MAKES 16 CRACKERS

There was a solid two-year stretch at the restaurant when this mousse was available in some way, shape, or form. It was like catnip for the cooks in the kitchen, and almost every table ordered it. My sous chef Ben Zook, a Brooklyn boy through and through, spent a lot of time finessing our version.

You're going to want to use a blender for maximum smoothness. You'll also need a little duck fat. We like to melt it down and, once the mousse has set in the fridge, pour a thin layer of the fat on top. This keeps it pleasingly pink and prevents oxygen from tainting the mousse, so it will keep for up to two weeks. Feel free to omit this step if you're going to eat the mousse within a day or two.

Here it's served with fennel pollen crackers, inspired by the thin lavash crackers we made in the wood-burning oven during my time at Camino, but it's just as good with some toasted sourdough bread.

FOR THE FENNEL POLLEN CRACKERS:

1⅓ cups (200 g) all-purpose flour

½ teaspoon kosher salt

½ teaspoon sugar

1 large egg yolk

⅓ cup (75 ml) warm water (80°F / 27°C)

2 tablespoons unsalted butter, melted and cooled slightly

Water, preferably in a spray bottle

½ teaspoon fennel pollen, plus more if needed

½ teaspoon Maldon salt, plus more if needed

FOR THE CHICKEN LIVER:

2 cups (525 g) chicken liver (trimmed of any sinew)

1 teaspoon kosher salt

¼ teaspoon Insta Cure #1 curing salt (optional)

¼ cup (55 g) duck fat, melted

FOR THE PAN SAUCE:

½ cup (50 g) thinly sliced shallots

¼ cup (60 ml) fino sherry

1 cup (240 ml) Roasted Chicken Stock (page 324)

TO FINISH:

¾ cup (180 ml) heavy whipping cream, at room temperature

1 cup plus 2½ tablespoons (262 g) unsalted butter, cut into 1-inch (2.5 cm) cubes and chilled

2¼ teaspoons sherry vinegar

1 teaspoon kosher salt

¼ cup (55 g) duck fat, melted

CONTINUED

MAKE THE FENNEL POLLEN CRACKERS: In the bowl of a stand mixer fitted with the dough hook, combine the flour, salt, and sugar and mix on low speed to combine.

Increase the speed to medium and add the egg yolk, then stream in the warm water, followed by the melted butter (it should still be warm, but cool enough that it will not cook the egg). Mix until the dough comes together and creates a ball, 3 to 4 minutes. The dough will be slightly sticky. Wrap the ball in plastic wrap and let stand at room temperature for an hour.

Preheat the oven to 350°F (175°C).

Line a sheet tray with parchment paper. Cut the dough ball into 4 equal pieces; set one on your work surface and leave the rest covered. Roll out the dough with a rolling pin into a sheet about ⅓ inch (8 mm) thick. Using a pasta roller, start on the widest setting and roll the dough once through each setting until you get to the thinnest setting. As it goes through the last few settings, allow the dough to become taut and stretch slightly as it's going through the machine. Repeat with the remaining dough.

Using a metal bench scraper or a knife, cut the sheets of dough into roughly 5 by 12-inch (12 by 30.5 cm) crackers and transfer to the parchment-lined tray. Spray generously with water, then sprinkle on the fennel pollen and Maldon salt. Cover with another piece of parchment and bake for about 10 minutes. Remove the parchment and cook until a pale golden brown, about 3 minutes more. Ovens differ, so you may need more or less time, depending. Remove from the oven and transfer to a container to cool, then cover tightly. (Stored this way at room temperature, the crackers will stay crispy for about a week.)

CURE AND COOK THE CHICKEN LIVER: In a ceramic or glass baking dish, combine the chicken liver with the kosher salt and pink salt, if using. Place in the fridge for 3 hours.

Line a sheet tray with paper towels. Rinse the liver under cold water, then place on the sheet tray. Pat dry with another paper towel, then leave in the fridge, uncovered, overnight.

The next day, line a sheet tray with parchment. In a heavy-bottomed skillet, heat the melted duck fat over medium heat until shimmering. Add the cured liver and sear on one side until golden brown and slightly crispy, then flip and cook lightly on the other side. The liver tends to pop and spit a bit of fat at this stage, so just be mindful. Remove the liver, reserving the pan, and set on the parchment-lined tray. Set aside.

MAKE THE PAN SAUCE: Add the shallots to the pan you cooked the liver in and sweat them over medium heat in the leftover fat until they're transparent. Carefully pour in the sherry and cook until the smell of alcohol has burned off, then add the stock and cook for 2 to 3 minutes. Remove from the heat and set aside.

TO FINISH: In a blender, combine the cooked liver, the pan sauce, half the cream, and ¼ cup (60 ml) water. Blend on medium speed, then, with the blender running, slowly begin to feed in the butter one piece at a time, adding the remaining cream and another ¼ cup (60 ml) water in between adding pieces of butter. Increase the speed to high and purée until very smooth.

Strain the liver mousse through a fine-mesh sieve, then season it with the vinegar and salt. Transfer the mousse to a couple of small containers like Mason jars or deli containers. Cover the surface of the mousse with some of the melted duck fat, then close the jars or containers and store in the fridge overnight. The mousse should keep for a couple of weeks when covered by the fat; if you break the fat layer to serve some of the mousse, be sure to finish the rest within a day or two.

To serve, remove the mousse from the fridge for 1 hour. Remove and discard the fat layer and spoon the mousse into a little crock. Break the crackers up into roughly 3- to 4-inch (7.5 to 10 cm) pieces and serve the mousse directly from its storage container or spread some on a serving plate alongside the cracker pieces.

beef tartare with pickled cabbage and sesame crackers

SERVES 4

Kill your darlings, the saying goes. Apparently, our staff, regulars, and partners don't agree, because they gave me a whole lot of grief when I took our tartare off the menu. I loved it, too, *so* much; night after night, I never got tired of tasting it for quality control as it went out. But, in the immortal words of the great George Harrison, all things must pass. I've always made an effort to resist the temptation to stay in our comfort zone for too long. Whenever it looks like an item has earned a permanent place in the lineup, I start to think about getting rid of it.

The decision to say goodbye to this one was far from arbitrary. For one thing, it's pretty phenomenal, if I do say so myself. Beyond that, beef tartare is an iconic wine bar staple, and early on, we embraced that mantle—until we decided to break free and grow. Still, I held on to the tartare well past that realization: After dispensing with the cheese plates and charcuterie, it was the last of the opening dishes to exit the repertoire. I hope it can live on in your homes.

FOR THE SESAME CRACKERS:

½ cup plus 2 tablespoons (100 g) all-purpose flour

½ cup (90 g) whole-wheat flour

¼ cup almond flour

1 teaspoon kosher salt

Water, in a spray bottle

¼ cup plus 1 tablespoon (50 g) white sesame seeds

¼ cup plus 1 tablespoon (50 g) black sesame seeds

1¼ teaspoons Maldon salt

FOR THE THICKENED BUTTERMILK:

1 (3 g) sheet unflavored silver-strength gelatin

Ice water

¼ cup (60 ml) heavy whipping cream

¼ teaspoon kosher salt

¾ cup (180 ml) buttermilk

FOR THE PICKLED CABBAGE:

2 cups (480 ml) Our House Pickling Liquid (page 318)

1 cup (70 g) finely chopped savoy cabbage

FOR THE RENDERED BEEF FAT:

8 ounces (225 g) beef brisket

FOR THE TARTARE:

1 (8-ounce / 225 g) eye round roast, trimmed of silver skin and excess fat, slightly frozen for an hour (this makes it easier to slice)

2 tablespoons crushed toasted sunflower seeds

2 tablespoons crushed toasted pumpkin seeds

1 teaspoon Maldon salt

1 tablespoon Garlic Chile Oil (page 306)

MAKE THE SESAME CRACKERS: In the bowl of a stand mixer fitted with the dough hook, combine the all-purpose, whole-wheat, and almond flours, the kosher salt, and 6 tablespoons (90 ml) water. Mix on medium speed until a ball of dough forms and pulls away from the sides of the bowl.

Remove the dough from the mixer bowl and knead by hand for about a minute, then wrap in plastic wrap and let stand at room temperature for about an hour.

While the dough is resting, preheat the oven to 350°F (175°C). Line three 13 by 18-inch (33 by 46 cm) half-sheet trays with parchment paper.

Cut the dough in half. Roll one piece through a pasta roller set to the thickest setting. Fold the dough over and pass it through the widest setting again, then continue rolling the dough through each setting until it's the thickness of a credit card. Repeat with the remaining dough.

Cut the dough sheets into 18 by 5-inch (46 by 13 cm) pieces and lay two pieces side by side on each parchment-lined tray. Working one tray at a time, spray the rolled-out dough generously with water and immediately

CONTINUED

sprinkle with the white and black sesame seeds (1 tablespoon of each per cracker). Divvy up the Maldon salt among the crackers, then bake for about 15 minutes, until lightly golden brown. Remove from the oven and let cool, then store in an airtight container. (They should keep at room temperature for about 5 days.)

MAKE THE THICKENED BUTTERMILK: Soak the gelatin in ice water.

Meanwhile, in a pot, warm the cream over low heat until it starts to bubble, then turn off the heat. Squeeze out excess water from the gelatin sheet and add the gelatin to the cream. Stir to dissolve the gelatin. Add the salt, then pour the buttermilk into the cream and whisk to combine. Transfer to a small jar or deli container and let the buttermilk cool in the fridge, preferably overnight, before using. Be sure to cover it after about an hour or so. (It will keep for about 5 days.)

MAKE THE PICKLED CABBAGE: In a small pot, bring the pickling liquid to a boil, then pour it over the cabbage and allow to cool to room temperature. Transfer to an airtight container and store in the fridge. (It will keep for about a month before it starts getting soft.)

MAKE THE RENDERED BEEF FAT: Preheat the oven to 400°F (205°C). Cut the brisket into a 1-inch (2.5 cm) dice, then place in an ovenproof skillet and roast for about 30 minutes, until golden brown and toasty. Strain the fat from the skillet (discard the brisket as it will be quite tough) through a fine-mesh sieve and allow to cool, then cover and pack away in the fridge. (The rendered beef fat will keep for about a month.)

MAKE THE TARTARE: Chill four plates for serving. Pull the rendered beef fat from the fridge and allow to come to room temperature.

Cut the beef into ⅓-inch-thick (8 mm) sheets, then into long rectangles, and finally into small (about ⅓-inch / 8 mm) squares. It's easiest to do this when the beef is still semi-frozen, but has a little give. Place the beef in a mixing bowl, then add the sunflower and pumpkin seeds, Maldon salt, 2 tablespoons of the pickled cabbage, the chile oil, and 2 tablespoons of the rendered beef fat. Stir to combine, then taste and adjust if need be.

Buzz up the thickened buttermilk with an immersion blender to ensure smoothness, then spoon 1½ teaspoons onto each of the chilled plates. Divide the tartare among the plates, covering the buttermilk. Break the sesame crackers carefully into 3-inch (7.5 cm) square pieces and tuck a few into the tartare. Serve chilled.

beef short ribs with long-cooked romano beans and horseradish

SERVES 4

These flanken-style ribs are ideally suited for flash-grilling, and are a go-to for all my backyard get-togethers in the summer months. Because they are less thick, any marinade you apply to them will more easily penetrate the meat, adding a ton of flavor. In this case, I like to use creamy-sweet shio koji, a ferment made with the same inoculated rice grain that's used in the production of soy sauce and miso. In addition to providing sweetness and umami, it tenderizes the beef.

The charred ribs pair really well with romano beans cooked until they're meltingly tender in a stewy stovetop braise of tomatoes, onions, and garlic. This, to me, is the true star of the show, and is an homage to a technique I learned from Russ at Camino over a decade ago. You almost can't overcook them, so don't be afraid to really push it here. It can be unexpected fun to obliterate such a beautiful summer vegetable using a method more often deployed for winter produce, but the transformation is magical and well worth the (minimal) effort.

FOR THE BEANS:

¼ cup (60 ml) extra-virgin olive oil

3½ cups (380 g) thinly sliced Spanish onion (¼-inch-thick / 6 mm slices; about 1 onion)

⅓ cup (54 g) garlic cloves (about 10 cloves), crushed with the side of a chef's knife

1½ pounds (680 g) fresh romano beans, stem ends trimmed

1½ pounds (680 g) heirloom tomatoes

1 tablespoon kosher salt

FOR THE MARINATED SHORT RIBS:

1¼ pounds (570 g) flanken-style beef short ribs, cut ½ inch (12 mm) thick

¼ cup (60 ml) shio koji

1 tablespoon white miso paste

2 tablespoons soy sauce

¼ cup (25 g) thinly sliced peeled fresh ginger

4 thyme sprigs

1 cup (30 g) chopped fresh oregano (leaves and stems)

1 cup (30 g) fresh basil leaves

¼ cup (45 g) thinly sliced shallot (about 1)

1 (2-inch / 5 cm) piece fresh horseradish, peeled, for serving

MEAT

CONTINUED

MAKE THE BEANS: In a wide, heavy-bottomed pot, heat the olive oil over medium heat. Add the onion and sauté for a few minutes, until softened. Add the garlic, romano beans, tomatoes, and salt. Stir to combine, then cover and reduce the heat to low. Cook for about 45 minutes, stirring every 10 minutes or so, until the beans are very soft and the tomatoes and onions have melted into the sauce together. Let cool and then transfer the cooked beans and their liquid to an airtight container and store in the fridge until ready to use. (They can be cooked up to 2 days in advance.)

MAKE THE MARINATED SHORT RIBS: In a mixing bowl, combine the short ribs, shio koji, miso, soy sauce, ginger, thyme, oregano, basil, and shallot and toss to combine. (I like to do this with gloved hands at the restaurant to really massage the marinade into the meat.) Transfer the meat and marinade to a covered container and allow to marinate in the fridge for at least a few hours, but preferably overnight.

TO FINISH: Prepare a charcoal grill. Set a wire rack on a sheet tray and have it nearby.

Remove the short ribs from the marinade and slide off any herbs or other bits stuck to the meat. Discard the marinade. Place the short ribs on the grill over medium heat and cook, flipping often, until the exterior is caramelized and a thermometer inserted into the meat reaches an internal temperature of about 120°F (49°C). Do not to step away during this process. The sugars in the shio koji can cause the meat to char quite quickly. Transfer the short ribs to the rack-lined tray and let rest for about 5 minutes.

Meanwhile, warm the beans in a pot.

Remove the bones, then slice the short ribs into ½-inch-thick (12 mm) pieces, working against the grain (the natural lines in the beef that tell you which way the muscle fibers go), when possible. Transfer the beef to a serving dish, top with the warm beans, and grate the horseradish over top, and serve.

roasting and resting meats

I like to think of most dry-heat meat cookery—everything but braises and stews—as a form of rotisserie cooking. This was something I learned from reading Heston Blumenthal of England's Fat Duck and Magnus Nilsson, chef-owner of Fäviken in Sweden (until it sadly closed in 2019). In their books, both chefs stress the importance of moving meat around as you cook it. Most of us were brought up chasing those deep crosshatch grill marks on a steak. Leave it on the fire for a long time, move it a quarter turn, flip, and repeat. But Heston and Magnus completely ignore this practice, going so far as to completely remove meat from a hot surface, returning it minutes later to avoid cooking solely with that focused direct heat. High-heat searing, while an important piece of the puzzle, should only account for about one-quarter of the cooking process. The rest should be gentle and even heat.

The goal of this process is to avoid winding up with a large outer layer of overcooked meat with a too-rare center. If you're pan-searing, move the meat to different spots in the pan while flipping every 30 seconds or so, as both the pan and your stove will have different hot spots. Also, the meat you are cooking is probably hitting that pan cold—or at least cool. Wherever it sits still, it will lower the temperature in that particular spot. Moving the meat around the pan ensures a quicker sear that simultaneously properly cooks through the protein.

Resting a piece of meat after it cooks is as important as the cooking itself. All the care and attention that goes into roasting a beautiful bone-in rib eye can get thrown out the window if it's left sitting on the hot roasting pan. After it's cooked, we always rest meat on a room-temperature wire rack placed on top of a room-temperature sheet pan. Doesn't matter if it's grilled, pan-seared, or baked. Don't worry about your hard work getting cold. Most cuts of meat are dense and, once removed from the heat, can even continue cooking for a while before they even begin to cool (it's called "carryover cooking"). If you slice into a cut of meat too early in the carryover process, all the juices will come pouring out. Think of this as the period when the cooked meat has a second to relax and the juices inside have a chance to reintegrate and settle. Don't rush it.

A good general rule of thumb: The bigger the item being cooked, the longer the rest. Common wisdom is that the rest time should equal roughly half the cooking time. I like to follow that advice. During the rest time, I like to flip the meat a few times, in line with the rotisserie notion. This is because the side closer to the resting tray will be hotter than the side exposed to the surrounding air. If you just leave it, even if it's on a resting rack, you could end up with one side of the meat being more done than the other. So move the meat around.

Note that there are exceptions, such as the preparation of duck and certain cuts of pork, in which most of the care and attention is placed on rendering out a good portion of the fat before quickly kissing the other bits over low heat to help carry the meat to the desired temperature.

a perfect steak au poivre

SERVES 4

There's no better way to prepare steak than pan-roasted with a tremendous au poivre. A close second would be chargrilled over a wood fire with good olive oil and salt, or maybe even compound butter. But generally speaking, I keep it simple.

To be honest, I don't eat beef often at home. We don't even serve it that often at the restaurant. Beef keeps getting more and more expensive, so when I do feature it, it's mostly the underutilized cuts: tongue, tripe, zabuton, chuck flap, sweetbreads, bavette, and so on. But sometimes we go classic for a special occasion. In those instances, we spring for a New York strip (though rib eye would be just as indulgent). This is the time to grab some beautiful, sustainably raised Wagyu from a specialty butcher or a local prime cut at your farmers' market. Nothing factory farmed.

FOR THE AU POIVRE BASE:

5 tablespoons plus 2 teaspoons (80 g) unsalted butter

1 cup (100 g) small-diced Spanish onion (about ½ large)

1 teaspoon kosher salt

2 tablespoons finely chopped garlic

⅓ cup (75 ml) Cognac

2 cups (16 ounces / 480 ml) beef or chicken demi-glace

FOR THE STEAKS:

2 (1-inch-thick / 2.5 cm) boneless beef strip (shell) steaks

Kosher salt and freshly ground black pepper

1 tablespoon canola oil

2 tablespoons (30 g) unsalted butter

2 cloves garlic, crushed with the side of a chef's knife

1 bay leaf

4 or 5 thyme sprigs

TO FINISH:

2 tablespoons heavy whipping cream

2 tablespoons whole green peppercorns drained from their brine

1 teaspoon sherry vinegar

Kosher salt and freshly ground black pepper

MAKE THE AU POIVRE BASE: In a saucepan, melt the butter over medium heat. Add the onion and the salt and sauté until translucent (some color is okay), 5 to 7 minutes. Add the garlic and cook for another minute or so. Turn off the heat, add the Cognac, then turn the heat back on and cook until the smell of alcohol burns off. (Alternatively, you could flambé the alcohol by tilting the pan to expose the vapors to the flame of the stove or

CONTINUED

igniting it with a long lighter, but do this carefully.) You should still smell the Cognac, but it will be less sharp and alcoholic.

Add the demi-glace and cook for about 15 minutes, until the mixture has reduced by half. Set the au poivre base aside. (This can be prepared up to 5 days in advance. Store covered in the refrigerator until ready to use.)

MAKE THE STEAKS: Preheat the oven to 275°F (135°C). Set a wire rack on a sheet tray.

Season the steaks generously with salt and lots of black pepper. With all your windows open, your hood fan on turbo, and your fire alarms disassembled (don't actually do that!), heat the oil in a steel or cast-iron skillet over high heat until shimmering. Add the steaks and sear on one side for about 2 minutes. Carefully flip the steaks, lower the heat to medium-low, and add the butter and garlic. Tilt the pan and baste the steaks with the foamy butter. Slide the pan on and off the heat to maintain the foam and to ensure the butter doesn't burn. Flip the steaks carefully every so often to create a rotisserie effect (see also page 258). The best way to do this is to tilt the pan away from your body, then flip the steak up toward you so it doesn't splash in the fat. (The brown butter burn is something every line cook endures. Avoid it at all costs.) When the steak is quite brown, add the bay leaf and the thyme. Be careful, as the thyme will splatter a bit. This whole process should only take about 4 minutes.

Remove the steaks from the pan and transfer them to the rack-lined tray. Take their temp with an instant-read thermometer (hopefully it's around 80° to 90°F [30°C]), then place the garlic and herbs from the skillet on top and slide the tray into the oven. Cook for about 2 minutes, then flip the steaks and cook to an internal temp of about 115°F (46°C) for medium-rare and 120° to 125°F (49° to 52°C) for a nice medium, about 5 to 8 minutes. Transfer the steaks to a second rack to rest for about 8 minutes, flipping them halfway through to avoid the dreaded "ring of death" (the overcooked ring of meat surrounding an otherwise perfectly cooked steak).

TO FINISH: While the steaks are resting, in a skillet, heat the au poivre base over medium heat. Add the cream and the peppercorns and reduce down gently until you have a nice thick sauce. Be careful not to overreduce it or it could separate and become oily. Add the vinegar, taste, and adjust with salt, if need be.

Spoon the au poivre sauce over the rested steaks and serve immediately with those nice steak knives you got as a wedding gift years ago. This is their time to shine! Crack over more black pepper to really drive home the poivre factor.

cider-glazed pork chops with parsley salad

SERVES 4

I've always had a soft spot for the parsley salads served at St. John in London. I remember watching Anthony Bourdain visit Fergus Henderson on *A Cook's Tour* in the early 2000s. I was fascinated and inspired by Henderson's simple and straightforward cooking. It was honest and, at the same time, thoughtful and precisely British. I finally found a home for a pile of dressed parsley when we put a cider-glazed pork chop on the menu one winter. The chop was first brined, then charred on a grill and brushed with a vinegar-based glaze. The sweetness from the glaze and the smoky fat didn't need much. I ended up bringing out the great parsley salad.

Note: For a cleaner, less spicy onion flavor, you can shock your onions in an ice bath for about 3 minutes, then transfer them to a sheet tray lined with a towel to dry.

FOR THE PORK CHOP:

3 bone-in pork chops, (around 10 ounces / 280 g each)

1 batch A Simple Brine for Meat and Fish (page 317)

FOR THE CIDER GLAZE:

1¾ cups packed (400 g) dark brown sugar

1 cup (240 ml) cider vinegar

2 tablespoons fish sauce

1 teaspoon ground cinnamon

1 tablespoon smoked paprika

FOR THE PARSLEY SALAD:

4 cups (40 g) loosely packed fresh parsley leaves (leave on the small and tender stems)

½ cup (30 g) sliced red onion (see Note)

2 teaspoons red wine vinegar

1 teaspoon extra-virgin olive oil

Pinch Maldon salt, plus more to finish the dish

BRINE THE PORK: Put the pork chops in a deep container and pour the brine over the chops, making sure they are completely submerged. Let the pork chops brine for 3 hours in the fridge.

MAKE THE CIDER GLAZE: In a wide-bottomed saucepot, combine the brown sugar, vinegar, fish sauce, cinnamon, and paprika and bring to a boil. Reduce the heat to low and simmer for 30 minutes. Let cool.

CONTINUED

MEAT

GRILL THE PORK: Remove the pork from the brine and rinse well with cold water. Blot dry with a towel, then leave the pork chops out to continue drying. (You want the pork to be at room temperature before grilling.)

Meanwhile, prepare a charcoal grill for medium heat and have a sheet pan with a resting rack on top of it right near the grill. Warm 1 cup (240 ml) of the cider glaze in small pot. (You will have extra that can be reserved for another use.)

Once your grill is going, start your pork chops with the fat side down so you can begin to render the fat. I like to lean them against one another and use long tongs to keep them upright. If they flare up, don't panic. Simply remove them to the tray and let the grill calm down a bit, then proceed. Once you have some color on the fat, flip them onto their sides and grill them, flipping every minute or so until you get a nice golden color on both sides, about 8 to 10 minutes.

Using a pastry brush, begin to glaze the pork, flipping frequently during the process. Be mindful that the sugar in the cider glaze will cause the pork to burn very quickly. The pork will be done when it has a deep caramelized color and the internal temperature reaches about 145°F (63°C). This should only take about 8 to 10 minutes. If the chops are getting dark and the temperature isn't quite there, you can finish them in a 300°F (150°C) oven. You can always remove the chops to your rack throughout the grilling process to take their temperature if that's easier than hovering your hand (and the thermometer) over a hot grill.

MAKE THE PARSLEY SALAD: In a mixing bowl, combine the parsley and onion. Dress your salad with the vinegar, olive oil, and Maldon salt. Taste and adjust.

TO FINISH: Slice the pork off the bone and cut the meat against the grain into ½-inch-thick (12 mm) slices. Season the pork with Maldon salt and divide among plates. Plate your salad next to the pork and serve.

pull-apart pork shoulder with "baked beans," sweet rolls, and salty butter (*or: how to be a hero at your next neighborhood barbecue*)

SERVES 4 TO 6

My wife and I went through a phase where pretty much all we ate were baked beans. There's a shop here in the West Village called Myers of Keswick where she buys all her British and Irish essentials whenever pangs of homesickness hit. After one of her shopping trips, she introduced me to Heinz baked beans, which I only knew from the famous album cover for *The Who Sell Out*. I swear I ate them on buttered toast with a fried egg for six months straight. Still one of my all-time favorite breakfasts.

For this recipe, take chunks of fatty, marbled pork shoulder and bake them in a glaze with the flavor of those baked beans: ketchup, brown sugar, Worcestershire sauce, vinegar, and HP Sauce. HP is another British obsession of mine, basically a classier version of A.1. sauce.

The beans are added near the end of the cooking process, so they'll absorb some of the delicious juices, but don't overcook them. I serve the whole pot on the table with a pair of tongs, a spoon, and lots of sweet rolls with salted butter.

FOR THE SAUCE:

1 cup (240 ml) ketchup

½ cup packed (120 g) light brown sugar

1 tablespoon Worcestershire sauce

¼ cup (60 ml) cider vinegar

½ cup (120 ml) HP Sauce

FOR THE PORK:

¼ cup (60 ml) canola oil

2 pounds 4 ounces (1.1 kg) boneless pork shoulder, cut into 2-inch-thick (5 cm) steaks

2 tablespoons kosher salt

1½ cups (220 g) chopped bacon (½-inch / 12 mm chunks)

2 cups (300 g) small-diced carrots (about 3 medium)

2 cups (300 g) small-diced Spanish onion (1 medium)

3 bay leaves

2½ cups (500 g) drained canned great northern beans

1 cup (240 ml) Roasted Chicken Stock (page 324)

TO FINISH:

12 sweet rolls (King's Hawaiian, if possible)

½ cup (1 stick / 115 g) salted butter, at room temperature

MEAT

STAUB

MAKE THE SAUCE: In a medium bowl, whisk together the ketchup, brown sugar, Worcestershire, vinegar, and HP Sauce to combine.

MAKE THE PORK: Preheat the oven to 350°F (175°C).

In a Dutch oven or deep sauté pan, heat the canola oil over medium heat until it shimmers. Season the pork shoulder pieces with half the salt and then sear them in the oil, turning every now and then, until golden brown. You may need to adjust the heat to prevent burning. Remove the pork and set it aside on a sheet tray.

Add the bacon to the pot and cook until lightly browned, about 2 minutes. Remove the bacon with a slotted spoon and set aside on a plate, then discard ½ cup (120 ml) of the rendered fat from the pot. Add the carrots, onion, and remaining 1 tablespoon salt to the fat in the pot and sauté over low heat until slightly caramelized.

Return the pork and bacon to the pot. Add the sauce and bay leaves. Cover and bring to a simmer over low heat, then transfer the pot to the oven and cook for about an hour. Flip the pork pieces, add the beans, and stir, then return the pot to the oven, uncovered. Cook until the shoulder begins to pull apart very easily, about 1 hour more. Add the stock and cook for about 30 minutes more, then remove the pot from the oven.

Taste the sauce and adjust for salt if need be. (If you want a thicker sauce, return the pot to the oven to cook a bit longer to allow the sauce to reduce.)

TO FINISH: Put the pork on a platter with tongs for pulling the meat apart. (Alternatively, use a fork to pull it into chunks and mix it with the beans and sauce.) Serve with the beans, with the sweet rolls and salted butter alongside.

pork chop milanese with arugula and parmigiano-reggiano

SERVES 4

Whether you call it katsu, cutlets, or Milanese, fried pork chops are always going to be pretty incredible. Add some bright greens to cut through the crunch and oil, and they're even better. If I can offer a small word of advice, it's this: The better you "seal" the cutlets with the breading before frying, the better the result.

FOR THE PORK:

Canola oil, for frying

2 cups (240 g) all-purpose flour

4 large eggs, lightly beaten

2 cups (120 g) panko bread crumbs

4 (4-ounce / 115 g) boneless pork chops

Kosher salt

Maldon salt

FOR THE SALAD:

7 cups (5 ounces / 142 g) arugula

2 tablespoons red wine vinegar

¼ cup (60 ml) extra-virgin olive oil

Maldon salt

TO FINISH:

Freshly ground black pepper

1 (4-ounce / 115 g) block Parmigiano-Reggiano cheese

1 lemon, cut into 4 wedges

MAKE THE PORK: In a heavy Dutch oven or deep stockpot, pour about 3 inches (8 cm) canola oil and heat the oil over medium-low heat until the temperature reaches 350°F (175°C). Adjust your burner as needed to maintain that temperature as you proceed with the recipe. Have a pair of tongs handy and set a sheet tray topped with a rack nearby.

Line a sheet tray with parchment paper. Set up three shallow baking dishes. Put the flour in the first one, the eggs in the second, and the panko in the third.

Season all the pork chops with kosher salt, then, working one at a time, add a chop to the flour and immerse it, flipping it over to fully coat it. Pull it out of the flour and shake it slightly to remove any excess (extra flour will cause clumping and an uneven crust). Dip the chop in the eggs and flip it to coat. You really want to make sure the egg is fully coating the chop and that there are no dry spots. Lift out the chop and let the excess egg drain off, then place it in the bread crumbs. Press the chop firmly into the crumbs and then flip it and press again to fully coat all sides. Press breading firmly in to seal. Transfer the breaded chop to the parchment-lined tray and repeat the process with the rest of the pork chops.

When the oil is hot, fry the pork chops one at a time, turning once, until golden brown on both sides, about 3 minutes. Carefully remove with tongs and place on the prepared rack. Season with a good pinch of Maldon salt while they're still warm.

MAKE THE SALAD: In a mixing bowl, toss the arugula with the vinegar, olive oil, and a pinch of Maldon salt.

TO FINISH: Transfer the pork chops to warm plates and crack on some black pepper. Top with the arugula salad, then shave on some cheese to your liking with either a wide-ribbon Microplane or a peeler. Serve each chop with a wedge of lemon.

"pjs"

I think my cooks would call this entire undertaking into question if I didn't tell you about precious juices, or "PJs," as they're affectionately known in our kitchen. I wax poetic about them constantly. New hires sometimes give me a bemused look the first time they hear it. What are precious juices? Nothing more than the excess liquid you would be foolish to discard after making certain recipes. Here's what I am referring to: If you marinate a salad of cucumbers, squid, onions, and coriander berries, they exude liquid as they sit together, and all those flavors mingle at the bottom of the bowl to form PJs—don't leave a drop behind. The golden drippings in the pan below the rack that gorgeous chicken was just roasted on? Get that into a pot of simmering beans, or even back onto the chicken once you've carved it. Same goes for the macerated goodness you get from roasting stone fruits, berries, and grapes; the excess liquid left in bones slowly simmered in a stock, which you can extract with one last nudge through the colander; and the collagen from roasting Dover sole or turbot, just waiting for someone to help it emulsify with the fish's own juices to create an extraordinarily elegant sauce. So, as you braise, marinate, stew, broil, poach, and sauté, please don't forget to give those PJs a taste before tossing them aside.

fried chicken with cipollini onions, maitake mushrooms, and marsala

SERVES 4

Truth be told, this recipe started at The Four Horsemen as a veal sweetbread dish. As much as I love sweetbreads, though, I can't imagine many home cooks procuring them without running into a slew of frustrations along the way. Replacing the sweetbreads with chicken and pairing the crunchy, crispy thigh with a rich, luxurious, Italian-American-joint-inspired Marsala sauce might be even more delicious.

FOR THE BRINE:

4 cups (1 L) warm water

5 tablespoons plus 2 teaspoons (80 g) light brown sugar

¼ cup (80 g) kosher salt

4 (5½- to 6-ounce / 155 to 170 g) boneless, skinless chicken thighs

FOR THE MUSHROOMS AND ONIONS:

2 (8-inch / 20 cm) clusters maitake mushrooms

Extra-virgin olive oil

Kosher salt

14 cipollini onions, peeled and cut into ¼-inch-thick (6 mm) slices

FOR THE BREADING:

2¼ cups (500 g) egg whites (from about 14 large eggs)

1¾ cups (350 g) cornstarch

2 cups (250 g) all-purpose flour

1 tablespoon kosher salt

3 cups (225 g) panko bread crumbs

Canola oil, for frying

FOR THE SAUCE:

6 cloves garlic, thinly sliced

1 cup (2 sticks / 225 g) unsalted butter

1 cup (240 ml) Marsala wine

1½ cups (12 ounces / 360 ml) chicken demi-glace

1 tablespoon fresh lemon juice

Kosher salt

Maldon salt

Freshly ground black pepper

MAKE THE BRINE: In a mixing bowl, stir together the warm water, brown sugar, and kosher salt. Allow to cool to room temperature, then add the chicken thighs, cover, and refrigerate for 3 hours.

MAKE THE MUSHROOMS AND ONIONS: Preheat the oven to 375°F (190°C). Break up the maitake mushrooms into little golf ball–size clusters by hand or with a knife. Toss them with olive oil and a good pinch of kosher salt, then roast on a sheet tray for about 20 minutes, until they're golden

CONTINUED

with some crispy edges. Toss the cipollini onions with olive oil and a pinch of kosher salt and roast on a separate sheet tray until golden, about 25 minutes. Set both aside until cool, then combine in an airtight container and store in the fridge until ready to use.

BREAD THE CHICKEN: Remove the chicken thighs from the brine and discard the brine, then rinse the thighs with cool water and pat dry. Lay out a sheet of plastic wrap on a work surface and place the thighs on the plastic, a few inches apart. Place another layer of plastic wrap on top, then use a meat mallet or a heavy-bottomed pot to carefully pound the chicken to an even thickness of about ½ inch (13 mm). Remove the plastic, then place the pounded chicken thighs on a plate and set aside.

In a blender, combine the egg whites and cornstarch and blend on high until smooth. Transfer to a shallow baking dish. Put the flour and kosher salt in a second baking dish and stir with a fork to combine. Put the panko in a third baking dish.

Working with one piece at a time, dredge the chicken in the flour, then dip it in the egg white mixture, followed by the panko. Make sure the chicken is coated by each of these before moving on to the next stage. For the bread crumb stage, really press in the crumbs and kind of bury the chicken in the panko while pressing down firmly to ensure even coating. Set the breaded chicken on a parchment-lined sheet tray, then wrap tightly in plastic wrap and store in the refrigerator.

In a heavy Dutch oven or deep stockpot, pour about 3 inches (8 cm) canola oil, and heat the oil over medium-low heat until the temperature reaches 350°F (170°C). Adjust your burner as needed to maintain that temperature as you proceed with the recipe.

MAKE THE SAUCE: While the oil is heating up, in a skillet, sweat the garlic with half the butter over medium heat until softened and fragrant, about 2 minutes. Add the Marsala and cook until the smell of alcohol burns off, about 3 minutes. Add the demi-glace and bring to a simmer. Reduce until the sauce has thickened slightly and coats the back of a spoon, about 10 minutes. Remove from the heat and set aside. Don't worry if a thin skin forms on the surface; when you reheat the sauce, it will disappear.

FRY THE CHICKEN: Have a spider handy and set a sheet tray topped with a rack nearby. Work in batches to avoid crowding and lowering the oil temperature too severely. Carefully add 2 pieces of chicken to the hot oil and fry until golden brown and a thermometer inserted into the thickest

part reaches 175°F (80°C), about 5 minutes. Gently cradle out the chicken with a spider or tongs and place on the prepared rack. Season with salt on both sides. Repeat with the remaining chicken.

FINISH THE SAUCE: Add the mushrooms and onions to the sauce and warm it over low heat. Add the remaining butter and swirl the pan to incorporate it, then finish with the lemon juice. Taste and adjust for slight acidity and salt.

To serve, plate the chicken and spoon the mushroom and onion sauce over the top. Finish with a pinch of Maldon salt and lots of black pepper, then serve.

AFTER-DINNERS

Since we don't serve cocktails at the restaurant (our bar is just too small), we've gone a little hard on the after-dinner selection. We offer around fifty different eau de vie, vintage amari, brandy, grappa, dessert wines, macvin, mezcal, ratafia, and the like. Sweet wines have fallen out of fashion in many circles, but that means that so many of our sources for wine are sitting on cases upon cases of the stuff. Wine companies are often shocked when I call and clean them out of fifty bottles of vintage Sauternes that they've had in their warehouse for the past five years and thought they'd never sell. These wines have found a home on our list and in the guests' glasses, and something about them just works here, especially because their stodgy reputation and uncoolness completely play against expectations. This will also work for you at home because sweet wine is just sitting in your local shop, often discounted, aged, and waiting for you.

Sometimes, after a long meal, I prefer to have a complex sweet wine or eau de vie instead of dessert. I love a nightcap—a moment to splurge slightly and just relax. What's not fun about drinking a 1950s fernet, 1970s pastis, or a perfect glass of chartreuse while you linger at the table and stretch out the moment for all it's worth? It's just as important to think about the way the dinner ends as much as how it starts, and twenty more minutes at the table with a glass of Cyril Zangs's cider eau de vie or a vintage Rivesaltes or Banyuls is a perfect wrap.

If you do want something to drink with dessert, this is yet another great moment for that bottle of Champagne you opened early in the evening that's still sitting in the ice bucket. Bookending your meal with the same wine is a great lesson showing how the same bottle can taste completely different depending on the course. I also like fruit brandies like Calvados or Vieille Prune with sweets. The sugar in the dessert balances really wonderfully with the ripeness of the fruit in the brandy.

DESSERT

DESSERT

We don't have a pastry chef at The Four Horsemen. We never have. Honestly, we don't have the space in our tiny kitchen for a dedicated section. But I like how that forces the team and I to consider and appreciate the sweet side of the menu. And, partly as a result of these limitations, the desserts in the following pages should translate really well to cooking at home.

When creating sweet things (as with our savory food), we look at what's in season and see what feels right for the moment. We leave the strawberry and cherry desserts for those long summer days and save the figs and quince for times when you wish you could end your meal by the fireplace with a blanket over your lap and a glass of brandy; bright in spring to celebrate surviving another dull winter, and warm and nurturing around the holidays.

Here are a few of our favorites.

COMTÉ AND SOME PERFECTLY ROASTED NUTS

Comté, elegant and compelling while complementing so many flavors, is the ultimate cheese to have up your sleeve. Made in the Franche-Comté region in eastern France, this Alpine-style cow's-milk cheese is the perfect match for the oxidized, nutty vin jaune wines of the Jura. At the restaurant, we've long championed the grapes and producers of this region, and not a winemaker dinner goes by that Justin doesn't ask me if it might be possible to sneak a little Comté into the dining room for our guests at the end of their meal. Comté never fails, needing little more than a few toasted nuts to heighten its sweet and grassy notes. Walnuts are the classic choice, but I also really love a scattered handful of hazelnuts.

We keep the slices rustic and misshapen, as a wine grower might have it after a day in the fields picking clusters of savagnin and poulsard grapes. This is a very low-lift crowd-pleaser that can beautifully extend those leisurely after-dinner sessions when you could linger at the table forever.

two frangipane tarts

Sit down for a meal at The Four Horsemen at any time of year, and there's a good chance you'll find a frangipane tart on the menu. Rhubarb, pear, quince, strawberry, huckleberry: These are just a few of the ingredients that have worked perfectly with frangipane as the base. The rich and sweet almond paste combines with seasonal fruit to make a sort of sophisticated Pop-Tart of the gods. The techniques for pulling off one of these are super easy, but they're so delicious and elegant, guests still scratch their heads, wondering how something so simple can give so much joy.

I'm including two of my favorite versions here to give you some idea of the recipe's versatility. Cherries (like Rainier or Bing) make for a great spring treat, while in winter, using fresh apples provides an excellent pie alternative that, while feeling elevated, is arguably easier to execute. In both, the fruit flavors are amplified by a layer of jam or apple butter, respectively. The jam can be a store-bought preserve you enjoy—cherry and strawberry both work really well. You can purchase apple butter or make your own (see page 323).

sweet tart crust

MAKES ONE 9-INCH (23 CM) TART SHELL

- 3 cups plus 2 tablespoons (390 g) all-purpose flour, plus more for dusting
- ⅓ teaspoon kosher salt
- ¼ teaspoon baking powder
- 1 large egg yolk
- 1 large egg
- ⅓ teaspoon pure vanilla extract
- ¼ cup (60 ml) heavy whipping cream
- ¾ cup (1½ sticks / 175 g) unsalted butter, chilled and cut into cubes, then softened to room temperature
- ⅓ cup (68 g) sugar

In a mixing bowl, combine the flour, salt, and baking powder. In a separate bowl, combine the egg yolk, egg, vanilla, and cream.

Pulse the butter and sugar in a food processor until the butter is pale and fluffy. Pulse the flour mixture into the butter, followed by the egg mixture. Continue to pulse until both are incorporated and a dough forms. It will be a bit shaggy but should form into a ball.

Transfer the dough to the counter and flatten it out into a 1-inch-thick (2.5 cm) disc, then wrap in plastic wrap and refrigerate until ready to use, up to 5 days. (You can also freeze the dough for up to a month.)

BLIND-BAKE THE TART SHELL: Remove the dough from the fridge and leave it on the counter for 30 minutes.

Scatter a bit of all-purpose flour on a work surface, then use a rolling pin to roll out the dough, rotating it a quarter turn after each roll and only adding more flour if it sticks. Roll in this manner until the round is about an inch or two (2.5 to 5 cm) wider than the tart pan.

Place a 9-inch (23 cm) tart pan on the work surface. Place the rolling pin at the top of the dough round, the point farthest from you. Pull the dough up over the pin and then roll the pin toward you, lightly wrapping the dough around it. Hold the rolling pin over the tart pan and, starting at the edge of the pan closest to you, unroll the dough away from your body, draping it over the pan. The dough will hang over the edge by a few inches, but leave that for now. Press the dough into the bottom and sides of the pan with your fingertips, then poke the bottom of the dough all over with a fork. Place the tart shell in the freezer for 30 minutes.

Preheat the oven to 350°F (175°C).

Line the tart shell with aluminum foil and then fill with dried beans or pie weights. Place on a sheet tray and bake for 25 minutes. Remove the beans or pie weights and foil, then bake for another 10 minutes, or until golden brown. Remove from the oven and let cool slightly. Using a Microplane or a serrated knife, carefully file off the excess tart shell hanging over the edge of the pan, making the top of the shell even with the top of the pan. This will give your tart shell a nice crisp edge.

If not using the tart shell right away, wrap it in plastic wrap (leaving it in the pan) and store in the fridge for up to 3 days.

frangipane filling

MAKES ENOUGH FILLING FOR ONE 9-INCH (23 CM) TART

½ cup (115 g) unsalted butter, at room temperature

½ cup (100 g) sugar

2 large eggs, at room temperature

1⅓ cups (130 g) almond flour

1¾ teaspoons pure vanilla extract

⅛ teaspoon pure almond extract

Pinch kosher salt

In the bowl of a stand mixer fitted with the paddle attachment, beat the butter and sugar on medium speed for 4 to 5 minutes, until the mixture is a little fluffy. Scrape down the bowl and beat the eggs in one at a time. Remove the mixer bowl and, by hand, mix in the flour, vanilla, almond extract, and salt until combined. The texture will be a bit grainy and rough, but don't be alarmed.

Transfer the frangipane filling to a deli container or other sealable container and store it in the fridge for up to a week. About an hour before using, pull it out and let it come to room temperature. (The butter will firm up and make it harder to spread into the tarts if it's used straight out of the fridge.)

frangipane tart with baked apples

MAKES ONE 9-INCH (23 CM) TART

- **3 apples, such as Honeycrisp, Fuji, or Gala, peeled, cored, and cut into 1-inch (2.5 cm) chunks**
- **3 tablespoons sugar**
- **2 tablespoons Apple Butter (page 323)**
- **1 blind-baked Sweet Tart Crust (page 282)**
- **1 batch Frangipane Filling (page 284), at room temperature**

Preheat the oven to 350°F (175°F).

In a mixing bowl, toss the apples with 2 tablespoons of the sugar until the sugar has mostly dissolved and the fruit looks glazed.

Spoon the apple butter into the base of the tart shell and spread it to evenly coat the bottom. Carefully spoon the frangipane over the butter in large dollops, then use an offset spatula or the back of a spoon to smooth it out. Add the apple pieces one at a time, pressing them into the frangipane as you go; they should be almost three-quarters of the way submerged in the frangipane.

Sprinkle on the remaining 1 tablespoon sugar and bake until golden brown, about 30 minutes. Remove from the oven and allow the tart to cool slightly in the pan, then remove from the pan.

Slice and serve while still warm. The tart can also be made a day or two in advance and stored, covered, in the fridge, then warmed in a low-temperature oven before serving.

frangipane tart with sweet cherries

MAKES ONE 9-INCH (23 CM) TART

- **2 cups (304 g) sweet cherries, pitted**
- **3 tablespoons sugar**
- **2 tablespoons cherry or strawberry jam**
- **1 blind-baked Sweet Tart Crust (page 282)**
- **1 batch Frangipane Filling (page 284), at room temperature**

Preheat the oven to 350°F (175°F).

In a mixing bowl, toss the cherries with 2 tablespoons of the sugar until the sugar has mostly dissolved and the fruit looks glazed.

Spoon the jam into the tart shell and spread it to evenly coat the bottom. Carefully spoon the frangipane over the jam in large dollops, then use an offset spatula or the back of a spoon to smooth it out. Add the cherries one at a time, placing them cut side down and pressing them into the frangipane as you go; they should be almost three-quarters of the way submerged in the frangipane. Sprinkle evenly with the remaining 1 tablespoon sugar and then bake until golden brown, about 30 minutes. Remove from the oven and allow the tart to cool slightly in the pan, then remove from the pan.

Slice and serve while still warm. The tart can also be made a day or two in advance and stored, covered, in the fridge, then rewarmed in a low-temperature oven before serving.

flourless chocolate cake with zabaglione

MAKES ONE 9-INCH (23 CM) CAKE

Flourless chocolate cake really had a moment in the early aughts. Between 2002 and 2008, it was on basically every menu in the country. (Don't bother looking that up. It's just a fact, OK? Just go with me here.) That being said, its widespread popularity will make total sense after you've tasted this recipe.

The cake is intensely chocolaty and incredibly rich, and its texture is like a smooth and fudgy brownie that melts in your mouth. When served warm (which I recommend), the barely set center allows the top of the crust to sag a bit due to the soft foundation below.

To keep it simple, ice-cold soft-whipped cream would be a very fine accompaniment. But to turn it into a true pièce de résistance, whip up some Marsala-infused zabaglione. This light and airy Italian custard, whisked over a hot water bath, is composed of egg yolks, sugar, and a liqueur. Just excellent.

FOR THE CAKE:

Nonstick cooking spray

12¼ ounces (350 g) 70% dark chocolate

12¼ ounces (350 g) unsalted butter

1½ cups (150 g) almond flour

1 cup (100 g) unsweetened cocoa powder

1½ (250 g) sugar

6 large eggs

½ teaspoon pure vanilla extract

1 teaspoon kosher salt

FOR THE ZABAGLIONE:

6 large egg yolks

4 ounces (115 g) sugar

¾ cup plus 2 tablespoons (210 ml) Marsala wine

Pinch kosher salt

MAKE THE CAKE: Preheat the oven to 350°F (175°C). Generously spray the bottom and sides of a 9-inch (23 cm) springform pan with cooking spray.

In a 2-quart (2 L) saucepan, melt the chocolate and butter together over low heat, stirring frequently to prevent the chocolate from scorching, until fully melted and combined. Remove from the heat and set aside to cool slightly.

Sift together the almond flour and cocoa powder into a bowl and set aside.

In the bowl of a stand mixer fitted with the whisk attachment, combine the sugar and eggs and whisk on low speed for 1 minute, then increase the speed to medium-high and whisk until light and fluffy.

CONTINUED

DESSERT

Switch to the paddle attachment. With the mixer running on low speed, stream the warm chocolate mixture into the eggs (be sure it has cooled enough that it won't cook the egg). Add the vanilla and salt, then add the sifted flour and cocoa powder. Mix for an additional 4 to 5 minutes, scraping down the bowl every now and then.

Pour the batter into the prepared pan and smooth out the top with a wet offset spatula. Bake for 35 minutes, then remove from the oven. The cake will still appear soft and jiggly. Let cool in the pan for 2 to 3 hours, then remove the springform ring, invert the cake onto a plate, and remove the pan bottom. (The cake can be baked 3 to 4 days ahead; allow it to cool, then wrap tightly in plastic wrap and store at room temperature.)

MAKE THE ZABAGLIONE: Fill a 6- to 8-inch (15 to 20 cm) pot with an inch or two (2.5 to 5 cm) of water, then wrap a damp tea towel around the rim of the pot. Bring the water to a boil, then reduce the heat to maintain a simmer.

Find a metal bowl that will fit over the pot; the bottom of the bowl should not touch the water. In the bowl, combine the egg yolks, sugar, Marsala, and salt, then set the bowl over the pot (the towel will provide stability). Cook, whisking continuously, until the mixture is super light and airy, about 8 minutes. Be careful to maintain a low simmer and not allow the water to boil, as this will cook the eggs too quickly. Remove the bowl from the pot. (The zabaglione can be made ahead. Chill and then store in an airtight container for up to 3 days. Just give it a stir before serving. It won't be as airy but will taste great and be a nice contrast to the warm cake.)

To serve, slice the cake and then rewarm the slices on a baking tray in a 275°F (135°C) oven for 8 minutes. Spoon the zabaglione over the warm cake.

grape-nuts semifreddo with miso caramel

SERVES 4

The idea for this recipe comes straight from my mom. She was born and raised in Maine and used to eat Grape-Nuts ice cream in the summer with her friends. Apparently, that's a thing. When my brother and I were growing up, she passed along this weird tradition on to us, complete with happy memories of churning ice cream in the garage, waiting impatiently for the tiny ice crystals to form. Writing this book, I've been struggling to think of anything better as a kid than eating freshly spun ice cream. Nothing comes to mind.

At the restaurant, we opted to make a semifreddo instead, which requires no churning. The light airiness results from gently folding a few whisked ingredients together so that their air bubbles remain suspended throughout the freezing process—a semifreddo is, essentially, frozen mousse. We finish it with a little miso caramel. The toasty, salty flavor of the sauce works wonders with the crunchy little bits of wheat and barley.

FOR THE SEMIFREDDO:

6 large eggs

⅔ cup plus 2 tablespoons (180 g) sugar

½ teaspoon kosher salt

1¼ cups (300 ml) heavy whipping cream

1 teaspoon pure vanilla extract

1 cup (115 g) Grape-Nuts cereal

FOR THE MISO CARAMEL:

2 cups (350 g) sugar

¾ cup (180 ml) heavy whipping cream

2½ tablespoons white miso paste

MAKE THE SEMIFREDDO: Place the eggs, sugar, and salt in the bowl of a stand mixer.

Fill a 6- to 8-inch-wide (15 to 20 cm) pot with an inch or two (2.5 to 5 cm) of water, then wrap a damp tea towel around the rim of the pot. Bring the water to a boil, reduce the heat to maintain a simmer, then place the bowl of the stand mixer on top of the water bath (the towel will help keep it secure). Cook the egg mixture over the water bath, whisking continuously, until a thermometer gets to within a few degrees of 168°F (75°C). Transfer the bowl to the mixer and, using the whisk attachment, whip the egg mixture on high speed until tripled in size and cooled to room temperature, 6 to 7 minutes.

CONTINUED

Meanwhile, pour the cream into a mixing bowl and whisk by hand until soft peaks have formed. Add the vanilla, whisk a bit more, then set aside.

When the egg mixture is pale, fluffy, and voluminous, gently fold in one-third of the whipped cream. When it's fully incorporated, gently fold in the remaining whipped cream until no streaks of white remain.

Pour one-quarter of the semifreddo base into a 9 by 6-inch (23 by 15 cm) baking dish. Sprinkle on one-quarter of the Grape-Nuts, then spoon over more semifreddo. Continue doing this with the remaining semifreddo and Grape-Nuts, then give the whole thing a stir or two to evenly distribute the Grape-Nuts.

Cover and freeze the semifreddo overnight. (It will keep for 2 to 3 weeks in the freezer. If it gets quite hard, pull it out of the freezer 30 minutes or so before serving to allow it to soften slightly at room temperature.)

MAKE THE MISO CARAMEL: Put the sugar in a heavy-bottomed pot and place over medium heat. Cook, without stirring, until you see little pockets of dark caramel popping up here and there. At this point, start to gently stir the sugar with a spatula and cook until it's just past a light amber color and giving off wisps of smoke. Remove the pot and carefully add the cream in one quick and steady stream. Return the pot to low heat and stir until all the sugar has melted and the caramel is smooth. Add the miso and stir to combine, then strain the caramel through a fine-mesh strainer into a metal bowl and let cool to room temperature. (Cover and store in the fridge if you're not using immediately. Gently rewarm it in a small pot until it reaches room temperature before using.)

When ready to serve, chill four bowls in the freezer for 15 minutes. Remove the bowls and scoop a bit of semifreddo into each one (note that this recipe will leave you with a bit of extra semifreddo), then drizzle over a good spoonful of the caramel and serve.

DESSERT

butterscotch budino with whipped cream and hazelnuts

SERVES ABOUT 8

This dessert taps into one of my oldest flavor memories. As a kid, my mom would take my brother and me to Fentons Creamery in Oakland, California. It was an old-timey soda fountain sort of place that made our family's favorite sundaes. I always ordered their signature item, the black and tan, made with toasted almond ice cream, vanilla ice cream, hot fudge, whipped cream, and their very own "handmade caramel sauce."

I loved that caramel sauce so much and have thought about it for years. This, I think, is the power of food. To this day, I remember the experience of eating that sauce, and I've wanted to make a dessert that incorporated it ever since I was a kid. A silky Italian custard called budino finally felt like the ideal vessel.

We like to set the budino in a baking dish and then scoop it out into individual bowls to top with the whipped cream, salted caramel, and hazelnuts. To re-create the original version of this dish, we added feuilletine flakes on top; these are sweet and crunchy pastry shards with a caramel-like flavor. Chocolate shavings are fun, too.

FOR THE BUDINO:

4 tablespoons (55 g) unsalted butter

1¼ cups packed (275 g) dark brown sugar

4 cups (1 L) heavy whipping cream

10 large egg yolks (154 g)

1 teaspoon kosher salt

1 teaspoon pure vanilla extract

2½ (8 g) sheets unflavored silver-strength gelatin

FOR THE TOPPING:

1 cup (150 g) hazelnuts

1¼ cups (300 ml) heavy whipping cream

1 teaspoon pure vanilla extract

Maldon salt

⅔ cup (75 g) feuilletine flakes (see headnote; optional)

⅔ cup (75 g) chocolate shavings (optional)

MAKE THE BUDINO: In a heavy-bottomed pot, preferably a Dutch oven, melt the butter over medium heat, then add the brown sugar. Cook, stirring often with a rubber spatula, until the sugar smells toasty and gives off tiny wisps of smoke. Switch to a whisk and, while whisking gently, carefully add the cream. Some of the caramel will seize up a bit, but that's okay. Increase the heat to medium and whisk until all the sugar has dissolved and the mixture looks nice and smooth. You may have to really get the whisk into those corners as it's bubbling to dislodge some stuck sugar.

CONTINUED

While the caramel is melting in the cream, put the egg yolks in the bowl of a stand mixer fitted with the whisk attachment and whisk on medium-high until thickened and pale yellow, about 2 minutes. Once the yolks have thickened, turn the mixer to low speed and slowly stream in 2 cups (480 ml) of the hot caramel mixture, ¼ cup (60 ml) at a time, to temper the egg. Be careful not to add the caramel mixture too quickly or it will cook the egg.

Use a rubber spatula to scrape the tempered egg mixture into the pot with the remaining caramel mixture, then add the salt and vanilla and stir over low heat with the spatula.

While the custard is cooking, soak the gelatin sheets in ice water for about 10 minutes (no more than that).

Continue stirring the budino until it is thick and an instant-read thermometer reaches 180°F (82°C), 4 to 5 minutes. When it hits this temperature, immediately remove it from the heat, squeeze any excess water out of the gelatin sheets, and add them to the budino. Whisk to incorporate the gelatin, then strain the budino through a conical sieve into a 9 by 13-inch (22 by 33 cm) baking pan or into a container from which you can pour the budino into individual ½ cup (3¼-ounce / 95 ml) molds.

Cover the top of the warm custard with parchment paper, pressing it against the surface to prevent a skin from forming, and refrigerate for at least 6 hours, though overnight will yield ideal results. (The budino can be made a few days in advance.)

MAKE THE TOPPING: Preheat the oven to 350°F (175°C). Arrange the hazelnuts in a single layer on a sheet tray and toast in the oven, shaking the pan and swirling the nuts with a spoon every few minutes, until lightly browned, 12 to 15 minutes. Once toasted, transfer the nuts to a plate and allow them to cool, then crush them with the bottom of a pot. Try to keep the pieces on the larger side. If a few whole nuts sneak in, that's fine.

MAKE THE WHIPPED CREAM: Pour the heavy cream into a mixing bowl and whisk by hand until soft peaks have formed. Add the vanilla, whisk a bit more, then set aside.

TOP THE BUDINO: Discard the parchment covering the budino and scoop out a few spoonfuls of budino into individual bowls (skip this if you've made individual portions). Top with the whipped cream, hazelnuts, and Maldon salt. Finish with the feuilletine and/or chocolate shavings, if desired, and serve.

burnt cheesecake with amontillado vinegar

MAKES ONE 9-INCH (23 CM) CHEESECAKE

Burnt cheesecake, or Basque cheesecake, as it is sometimes called, is a great dessert to have in your arsenal. Unlike a traditional American cheesecake, the Spanish counterpart isn't baked in a water bath. That alone gives it some bonus points for ease of execution. This tarta de queso is the brainchild of Santiago Rivera of La Viña in San Sebastián, Spain. His masterpiece is just barely set in the center, which provides a very custardy texture. Our version is cooked a bit longer and falls somewhere between his and a classic American version. The results are subtle, deep, and unquestionably silky.

Note that every oven is different, so you may need to adjust cooking time and temperature accordingly. You're looking for a nice dark top and a slightly jiggly center when the cake is done. It may smoke a bit and look charred, but trust the process!

I prefer a local wildflower honey for this, but feel free to use your favorite.

FOR THE CAKE:

1½ pounds (680 g) cream cheese

Unsalted butter, for the pan

1¼ cups (225 g) sugar

4 large eggs

1 large egg yolk

1½ cups (360 ml) heavy whipping cream

1 teaspoon kosher salt

1 teaspoon pure vanilla extract

¾ teaspoon amontillado vinegar (regular sherry vinegar and Pedro Ximénez are both good substitutes)

¼ cup (31 g) all-purpose flour

FOR FINISHING:

1½ teaspoons amontillado vinegar

6½ tablespoons (105 g) honey (see Note), at room temperature

Maldon salt

MAKE THE CAKE: Remove the cream cheese from the fridge 1 hour before making the batter. Preheat the oven to 450°F (230°C). Generously grease two 8 by 12-inch (20 by 30.5 cm) sheets of parchment paper with butter. Overlap the two pieces of parchment and place them buttered side up in a 9-inch (23 cm) springform pan so the parchment covers all parts of the pan and rises a few inches above the rim.

CONTINUED

In the bowl of a stand mixer fitted with the paddle attachment, beat the cream cheese until smooth, scraping down the sides every now and then with a rubber spatula. With the mixer on medium speed, stream in the sugar and mix to incorporate, then scrape down the sides.

With the mixer running on low speed, add the eggs one at a time, mixing each until fully incorporated before adding the next. Add the egg yolk and mix until incorporated, then scrape down the sides and mix on medium speed for 1 minute.

Reduce the mixer speed to low and add the cream in a steady stream. Add the kosher salt, vanilla, and vinegar and mix until incorporated. Turn off the mixer and sift in the flour, then mix on medium speed for 2 to 3 minutes, until all the flour is incorporated.

Pour the batter into the prepared pan and place on a sheet tray. Bake for about 40 minutes, until the top of the cake has risen above the edge of the pan and has a nice char with about an ⅛-inch (3 mm) crust. When you shake the sheet tray, the cake should still be very jiggly. Every oven is a little different, so start checking the cake after 30 minutes. Remove from the oven and allow to cool for 3 hours.

Remove the ring from the springform pan and pull back the parchment slightly. Place a large plate on top of the cake and flip the cake and plate over together. Remove the bottom of the pan and the parchment, then place a serving tray on top of the cheesecake and flip the tray and plate carefully to invert the cake so the blackened side is facing up. (The cheesecake can be wrapped in plastic and stored for up to 3 days in the fridge. Let it sit on the counter for 2 to 3 hours to come to room temperature before serving.)

TO FINISH: In a small bowl, whisk the vinegar into the honey.

Slice the cake and spoon over the vinegar honey. Sprinkle on some crunchy Maldon salt and serve.

THE WINE PANTRY

In the same way that you would build a kitchen pantry or a home bar, I like to tell friends that it's just as important to build a wine pantry. I don't mean a wine collection or cellar. I mean looking at wine the same way a chef looks at their mise en place. It doesn't take a lot of time or money to have the right bottles within reach at all times, whether you're relaxing after a tough Monday with some takeout and a glass, or you've made a perfect au poivre for friends on a Saturday night. Just a little planning in advance–and a willingness to occasionally buy an extra bottle here and there–will improve your home drinking exponentially.

Take it from me: It's the kind of Swiss Army knife that saves you the rushed trip to the wine shop after waiting 30 minutes in line at the grocery store with your impatient kid. This method will pay off every time, and I've found that when I have a solid selection at home–which requires only a little forethought–I'm drinking better bottles without shelling out more money.

Depending on where you live, the process starts with finding a local wine shop or an online wine seller that you trust. Many shops offer discounts if you are buying six or twelve bottles together, and online retailers often offer free shipping or discounts for first-time buyers. This is a great opportunity to buy a mixed case and get yourself set up. Subscription clubs are also a good move. Find one that you really believe in, that sells wine you've enjoyed before. Again, you may end up with more wine than you think you need, but before you know it, you'll have a little library of bottles to fit a variety of situations. To get started, I'd recommend a mixed case of twelve bottles: two entry-level sparkling wines and a Champagne; three white wines; three orange wines; and three reds.

I don't want to beat you over the head too intensely with specific winemakers, so I'll limit the namechecks. It's about what you like (and what's within reach). So, when you're figuring out *your* selection, think about the way you eat or the way you like to drink. It's that easy. Are you a one-glass-every-couple-of-days kind of person? Then maybe avoid wines with zero sulfur, because sometimes they might only have a couple of days in the fridge before they oxidize. Pescatarian? The apple-like acidity and concentrated fruit of a chenin blanc from Thierry Germain in Saumur or a skin contact godello from Nacho Gonzalez in Galicia would work wonderfully. Is it steak or burger night? Grenache from the Southern Rhône like Poignée de Raisins from Domaine Gramenon, or Ascona Vineyard syrah in the Santa Cruz Mountains from Madson Wines, are a guaranteed great time.

Again, though, it goes beyond pairings. If something really moves you, look at the label on the bottle. That'll tell you what part of the world it's from and what year it was made. This is a great next step beyond, "I like pinot noir." There are so many ways to go here overall, and my most repeated advice is to just keep opening bottles. For me, it's about experience over academics.

When I first started out as a retail wine buyer, I asked many of my peers for advice, but the one phrase that has stuck with me after all these years came from wine importer David Bowler. He told me, "Remember, there's no such thing as a wine emergency." He was giving me permission to relax; it's just wine, it's not a big deal. Just taste, enjoy, and learn. Here are the nine styles of wine that I keep in my wine fridge that will keep you ready for whatever you're putting on the table tonight.

SPARKLING

Most wine regions have a sparkling wine culture, so it doesn't just have to be Champagne. Plus, the wines come in every color of the rainbow. Look outside of classical pairings like oysters or appetizers. Fizzy wine and fried food is always a win, or try pink-fleshed fish like sockeye salmon with rosé sparklers. Think Champagne, pét-nat, Lambrusco.

LIGHT WHITE

Fresh, bright whites are well-known knockouts with flaky fish or roast chicken, and they can become more complex and compelling as they warm up in the glass from the frigid temps of your ice bucket. These are also the best move for dishes with lots of fresh herbs like tarragon and sage, or spices like turmeric. Think Loire Valley, Canary Islands, Savoie.

FULL-BODIED WHITE

Here's the moment for those cream sauces, dishes with just a little more butter than you're comfortable with, or the pre-dessert cheese course. Bigger wines from riper years can work where you might've been told only red wine works. Think white Burgundy, Anjou, Styria.

ORANGE

As I've said before, skin-macerated wines can work with savory foods in a way that can convince even the most anti-orange friends you have. Keep an open mind as the amount of skin contact in these wines varies wildly; some will be deep yellow and some an intense amber, so play it by ear and embrace the surprise. Think Friuli, Slovakia, Croatia.

LIGHT RED

I don't mean rosé. There's a whole world of red wine out there that I love to drink chilled with salads, anything on the grill, and toasts. They often have lower alcohol and seem to disappear quickly enough that you might want to have a second bottle waiting in the fridge. Think Tavel, Touraine, Roussillon.

MEDIUM RED

Another category that I like with a light chill, these are great weeknight wines when you want a glass but don't want to feel it tomorrow, and they are food friendly no matter what you are eating. Think Beaujolais, Burgenland, Catalonia.

FULL RED

Contrary to popular belief, not all natural red wine is glou-glou fruit juice. While it does seem like many young drinkers are looking for the fresher, brighter side of things, roasted dishes and even apéro courses like chicken liver mousse are great with deep, full reds. I mean, when was the last time you had some tannin? Think Côte-Rôtie, Barolo, Ribera del Duero.

OXIDATIVE

We love having multiple oxidative wines on the menu by the glass. They often surprise us as much as the guest. Of course, there are few things better than a glass of vin jaune from the Jura and a chunk of aged Comté, but these wines work as well with raw fish and even artichokes. Think Jerez, Jura, Sicily.

DESSERT

The name of the wine says what it does best. And as they've fallen out of fashion, they're often a bargain at the wine shop. Try them with chocolate, fruit and nut tarts, or cheesecake. Think Banyuls, Rivesaltes, Tuscany.

SPARKLING
CHAMPAGNE
LIGHT WHITE
MUSCADET
FULL-BODIED WHITE
CHABLIS
ORANGE
FRIULI
LIGHT RED
TAVEL
MEDIUM RED
BEAUJOLAIS
FULL RED
CÔTE-RÔTIE
OXIDATIVE
JEREZ
DESSERT
BANYULS

a good pantry

Great cooking starts with a well-stocked pantry. Over the years, professional chefs and cooks build a catalog of taste memories; each is mirrored by different go-tos in their larder. Honestly, I'm lucky to work in New York City. One minute I'm stopping at the Japanese shop called Sunrise Mart to grab some curries, preserved plums, and sesame pastes loaded with umami. The next, I can hop on the subway to Kalustyan's, one of the greatest spice-and-condiment markets outside New Delhi, to load up a cart full of grape leaves, black limes, and the most aromatic cardamom you've ever smelled. From there, I'm minutes from one of the city's many different Chinatowns, the Manhattan version of which bumps up against a Little Italy. I have to admit, I'm a bit spoiled, but this is one of the main reasons so many of us choose to endure the more punishing aspects of New York life.

But no matter where you call home, you can, with a little effort, build a formidable pantry of your own. When you want to cook excellent food, especially excellent *simple* food, the quality of your building blocks is more than half the battle.

If you're open to the world and all the care that different communities devote to their foodways, you never know what amazing pantry treasures you'll find. At the very least, you're guaranteed to come across some great new snacks on your search.

These days, the internet is also a great way to find pantry items that may be out of your geographical reach; the great chefs of the world use it as a tool, and you might as well, too. But don't beat yourself up too much if you still can't find everything you're looking for, or if buying some particular ingredient doesn't make sense with your budget. Throughout this book, I've tried my very best to point out substitutions—omissions, even—for harder-to-source ingredients.

Because, ultimately, a recipe should be a guide, not a rigid structure designed to restrain you. Don't ignore your personal taste, or your own ideas. Learn to go with your instincts, trying something just because you feel like it. If you don't like cilantro, don't use it; throw in a handful of basil instead. No crème fraîche? That's totally fine: Yogurt or sour cream can work in a pinch. My hope is that as you build up your pantry, you'll reach the point where these substitutions are almost effortless and part of the fun, helping you grow into a stronger and more confident cook along the way.

MAKING ESSENTIALS AT HOME

Grocery store shelves are cluttered with packaged condiments that claim to make your life easier. Unfortunately, most of this stuff is packed with preservatives, sugars, and weird flavorings. I'd like instead to share with you a few little things I make myself and can stand by. Keep them up your sleeve. All of these play small but important roles in a bunch of the recipes strewn throughout this book, but I also think they can be useful in their own right, as they can make your food more interesting without requiring additional effort beyond what it takes to master them once. Sure, it may not be as convenient as picking up a jar of something at the supermarket, but it can be a surprising pleasure to prepare these condiments from scratch. Throw on some music while you work, and enjoy the knowledge that you're setting yourself up for days, even weeks, of really great meals.

YOUR ESSENTIALS: CONDIMENTS, DRESSINGS, PICKLES + MORE

mayonnaise

MAKES 2 CUPS (480 ML)

Emulsifying a sauce can be a bit tricky at first, but I've found a few ways to make the process go smoothly. A key factor is keeping everything quite cold: Higher temperatures mean there's a greater chance of separating, so we refrigerate everything but the salt about an hour ahead of time. Another helpful move is using a food processor—and keeping the machine cold, too, by buzzing up some ice before you begin. Of course, you can also make the mayonnaise by hand with a whisk. Just make sure to chill your bowl in the fridge at the outset. And that you have a strong arm.

5 large egg yolks (70 g)

2 teaspoons red wine vinegar

1 teaspoon kosher salt

1⅔ cups (405 ml) canola oil

In a food processor, combine 1 tablespoon water, the egg yolks, vinegar, and salt and buzz until smooth.

With the food processor running, in a slow and steady stream, begin adding the oil to the egg yolk mix. Once the emulsion starts to thicken, you can begin to incorporate the oil a bit faster.

When all the oil is incorporated, pack up the mayo into an airtight container and store it in the fridge. It should keep for about a week.

spicy cilantro mayo

MAKES 2 CUPS (480 ML)

This sauce is heavily inspired by the North African sauce chermoula, an accompaniment to lamb and other grilled meats that is quite oily and driven by warm spices. I went back and forth on whether to actually call this a chermoula, though, since anyone familiar with the sauce will be taken aback by the fact that there's mayo in mine. In the end, I decided not to offend the traditionalists. For this recipe, toasting the cumin and coriander properly is crucial, as the toasted spices lend the sauce a depth of flavor that elevates little fried snacks or vegetable crudités. It's forever on the menu at The Four Horsemen in some way, shape, or form. Note that keeping some stems on the parsley and cilantro is A-OK, even advisable.

1½ cups (360 ml) Mayonnaise (previous recipe)

2 cups (80 g) loosely packed fresh parsley, coarsely chopped

2 cups (80 g) loosely packed fresh cilantro, coarsely chopped

6 green onions (110 g), coarsely chopped

2 jalapeños (70 g), stemmed, split lengthwise, and seeded

1 tablespoon cumin seeds, toasted

4 teaspoons coriander seeds, toasted

2½ teaspoons champagne vinegar

2 teaspoons kosher salt

Combine all the ingredients in a blender and purée on high speed until smooth. Taste and adjust to your liking. Transfer to an airtight container and store in the fridge until ready to use, up to 1 week.

aioli

MAKES 2 CUPS (480 ML)

Any of our cooks will tell you that I'm adamant about the freshness of the garlic in an aioli. It's just so important: It should be added the day of use. If not, it tends to become unpleasantly astringent at an exponential rate. We grate the garlic with a fine Microplane to disperse it evenly. Beyond that, we add water, a few drops at a time, to gain the desired consistency. You generally want to avoid a "bouncy" aioli, meaning one that's so firm it has difficulty coating whatever is dipped into it (like our Patatas Bravas, page 87). I like it a little tighter if it's going in something brothy and a little looser if it's going to be a dip.

2 cups (480 ml) Mayonnaise (page 304)

1 large clove garlic, plus more if needed

Put the mayonnaise in a mixing bowl. Using a Microplane, grate the garlic (you should have around 1½ teaspoons) and then stir into the mayo to combine.

Taste and adjust to your liking, then add a few drops of water to thin out the aioli to your desired consistency. Make sure to serve it the same day it is made.

yuzu kosho aioli

MAKES 2 CUPS (480 ML)

Yuzu kosho, a citrusy, spicy Japanese fermented chile condiment, sings with the richness of aioli. This makes a great dip for the Chicken Karaage on page 93, but it's also so fun on sandwiches, grilled fish, and vegetables such as asparagus, cucumbers, and wax beans. It is a stalwart of Four Horsemen family meals for this reason.

2 cups (480 ml) Aioli (previous recipe)

1¼ tablespoons yuzu kosho, plus more if needed

Add the aioli to a mixing bowl and, using a rubber spatula, stir in the yuzu kosho.

Taste and adjust to your liking, then add a few drops of water, if needed, to achieve your desired consistency. Make sure to serve the same day it is made.

garlic chile oil

MAKES 1½ CUPS (360 ML)

It feels like any chef worth their weight in salt has a chile oil condiment in their arsenal. This is the one we use at the restaurant. We've had it on the menu since day one, and during the height of the COVID-19 pandemic in 2020, we even jarred it up and sold it. My sous chef Ben and I couldn't produce enough of it. But Ben certainly tried, bubbling vats of the stuff and perfecting it over time. We like to make a little sachet of the spices so they're easy to remove after they've infused their flavors into the oil, yielding a pleasantly spicy, mild, and versatile topping with myriad applications. Garlic chile oil is an obvious go-to for rice and brothy soups, but is equally satisfying spooned over some fried eggs with chunks of ripe avocado as a quick breakfast that will wake up your senses even before your coffee. It's really shelf-stable, so feel free to make it in advance just to have on hand. It's definitely one of those "gets better with time" condiments.

FOR THE SACHET:

1 teaspoon whole Sichuan peppercorns

3 star anise pods

2 teaspoons chopped peeled fresh ginger

½ cinnamon stick

FOR THE OIL:

2 tablespoons minced garlic

½ cup (67 g) New Mexico chile flakes

1¼ cups (300 ml) canola oil

1 teaspoon kosher salt

MAKE THE SACHET: Spread out a double layer of cheesecloth on the counter. Place the peppercorns, star anise, ginger, and cinnamon in the center. Pull up the sides and tie the top tightly with kitchen twine to close.

MAKE THE OIL: In a 1-quart (1 L) pot, combine the garlic, chile flakes, oil, salt, and the sachet. Heat over medium heat until the mixture bubbles, then reduce the heat to low and cook for about an hour, stirring every 5 minutes or so.

Remove from the heat and allow to cool. Transfer the chile oil to a Mason jar or another container with a lid (include the sachet, as it will continue to infuse the oil over time) and cover. Let sit overnight to let the flavors marry before using. Store in the refrigerator for up to 3 months.

garlic confit and garlic confit oil

MAKES 1 CUP (50 G) GARLIC CLOVES AND 1 CUP (240 ML) OIL

There's not much to it, but garlic confit is really quite special. Sneak this into sauces, fold it into marinades, spread it on vegetables, or mash it onto slices of meat. I suggest keeping a batch in your refrigerator at all times. If you're anything like me, you'll find yourself putting the cloves into action often. Just make sure they're fully submerged in the oil so they cook evenly. And if you're making this garlic confit, you should definitely make the Garlic Yogurt (recipe follows), too.

1 cup (150 g) peeled garlic cloves (about 2 heads)

Scant 1 cup (225 ml) extra-virgin olive oil

Combine the garlic and the olive oil in a small pot. The pot should be small enough and with high enough sides that all the cloves of garlic are submerged in the oil. Heat the oil over medium heat until it begins to bubble, about 3 minutes. Reduce the heat to low and cook the garlic gently until quite soft and lightly golden, about 20 minutes. Remove from the heat and allow to cool to room temperature.

Transfer the garlic confit and its oil to an airtight container—use one of a size that ensures the garlic cloves are fully submerged in the oil—and cover. Store in the fridge for up to about a month. As you remove cloves from the jar, be sure the rest remain submerged with oil, topping it off as needed.

garlic yogurt

MAKES ABOUT 2 CUPS (480 ML)

So many recipes influenced by the the Mediterranean or the Middle East will benefit from the addition of garlic yogurt. A few fast friends include oven-roasted cauliflower, grilled flatbreads, flaky fish over jasmine rice, and butter beans loaded with cucumbers and handfuls of cilantro. Full-fat yogurt is kind of a requirement here.

2 cups plus 3 tablespoons (525 ml) plain full-fat yogurt

4 teaspoons Garlic Confit Oil (previous recipe)

Zest of 2 lemons (about 2 tablespoons)

1 tablespoon fresh lemon juice

1½ teaspoons Maldon salt, plus more if needed

In a mixing bowl, combine the yogurt, oil, lemon zest, lemon juice, and salt and stir with a rubber spatula until well combined. Taste and adjust the salt to your liking.

Transfer the yogurt to an airtight container. Store in the fridge for about 1 week.

salmoriglio

MAKES 2 CUPS (480 ML)

This Southern Italian salsa verde enhances meat, fish, and roasted potatoes, and I like using it in chunky tuna fish sandwiches. I also love it in the Butter Beans on page 195. Calabrian chiles bring heat, anchovies depth. For maximum freshness, the macerated shallots should be incorporated at the very end of the process, so the vinegar doesn't "cook" the herbs. Go ahead and add basil or capers or nasturtiums if you're feeling inspired.

For ease, you can mix everything up except the shallots and vinegar and store it in the fridge for a week or so, then incorporate the shallots and vinegar the day you plan to use it.

½ cup (50 g) minced shallots

½ cup (120 ml) red wine vinegar

1¾ cups (53 g) fresh oregano leaves, finely chopped

2 cups (45 g) fresh parsley leaves, finely chopped

1 cup (240 ml) extra-virgin olive oil, plus more to cover

1 tablespoon finely chopped seeded Calabrian chiles

9 anchovies (30 g total), finely chopped

Zest of 1 lemon

2 teaspoons grated garlic (use a Microplane)

In a small bowl, combine the shallots and vinegar and set aside to macerate for 30 minutes or so.

In a separate bowl, toss the oregano, parsley, olive oil, chiles, and anchovies to combine.

Spoon the shallots out of the vinegar and add them to the herb mixture. Spoon in 3 tablespoons of the vinegar left over from macerating the shallots. Add the lemon zest and the garlic and stir to combine. Taste and adjust to your liking.

Pack the salmoriglio into an airtight container and cover the surface with a thin layer of olive oil to prevent oxidation, then cover with the lid. Use the sauce within 8 hours to preserve its color, or store in the fridge if not using within an hour or two.

thai chile and herb sauce

MAKES 2 CUPS (480 ML)

This sauce came about during a set lunch paying homage to the thrilling use of heat, acid, fresh herbs, and vegetables in Thai cuisine. In Thai, it's known as *nam chim*, which means "dipping sauce," but you can just as easily spoon it over baked fish or grilled pork as well. I like to leave the nam chim a little chunky, and I'm fairly generous with the cilantro. You can adjust the ratios to your liking.

- Zest of 2 limes (1 tablespoon)
- ½ cup (120 ml) fresh lime juice (from 4 to 5 limes)
- 6 tablespoons (90 ml) fish sauce
- 4 medium shallots (100 g), coarsely chopped
- 1 medium clove garlic, crushed with the side of a chef's knife
- 4 Thai (bird's-eye) chiles, stemmed
- 4 cups (70 g) loosely packed fresh cilantro
- 4 cups (70 g) loosely packed fresh parsley leaves (soft stems are okay)

Combine the lime zest, lime juice, fish sauce, shallots, garlic, and chiles in a blender. Blend on medium speed until a vortex forms in the blender jar, then increase the speed to high.

Add the cilantro and blend for about 10 seconds before adding the parsley, then blend for 1 to 2 minutes more, until mostly smooth. Some finer bits of pulpy herbs and stems will remain—we like it with these little bits, but feel free to go as smooth or as coarse as you like. Taste and adjust to your liking. Store covered in the fridge for up to 3 days.

chipotle-tomato jam

MAKES 2 CUPS (480 ML)

One of my favorite things to eat while traveling through Spain is patatas bravas, a humble dish of crispy potatoes served with aioli and a spicy-sweet tomato sauce. I particularly like it when the bravas sauce has body to it and really celebrates the tomato. Hence this "jam," a concentrated tomato sauce that's steeped with smoky chipotle peppers and two of my favorite spices, coriander seed and fennel seed. It's cooked low and slow, then blended or passed through a food mill. Naturally, we serve it with fried potato chunks (see page 87). This jam can play a versatile role in your pantry: Dip chips into it, use it as a base for stews, or spread it onto a hero roll and top with cold leftover fried chicken, shredded lettuce, and aioli.

- 1 teaspoon fennel seeds
- 2 teaspoons coriander seeds
- 3 tablespoons plus 1 teaspoon (50 ml) extra-virgin olive oil
- ½ Spanish onion, cut into roughly ¼-inch (6 mm) dice
- 1 teaspoon kosher salt
- 3 chipotle chiles, split and seeded
- 2 large dried pasilla or New Mexico chiles, split and seeded
- ¾ teaspoon minced garlic
- 4 (16-ounce / 480 ml) cans whole peeled San Marzano tomatoes

Preheat the oven to 350°F (175°C).

Using a spice grinder or a mortar and pestle, grind the fennel and coriander to a coarse consistency. Set aside.

In a large Dutch oven, heat the olive oil over medium heat. Add the onion and salt. Cook, stirring often, until golden and soft, 8 to 10 minutes. Add the chiles and garlic and stir. Cook for an additional minute or two and avoid browning the garlic, as this can make it bitter. Reduce the heat, if necessary, to keep everything nice and light and toasty. Add the tomatoes, crushing them by hand as you drop them into the pot, and their juices. Bring the mixture to a simmer and cook, stirring often, for about an hour. Transfer the pot to the oven and cook, uncovered, for about an hour, stirring the jam every 15 minutes and making sure the chiles stay submerged. When the jam is nice and thick and brick red, let it cool, then remove the chiles.

Transfer the cooled jam to a food processor and pulse until you have a chunky purée. Taste and adjust the salt to your liking. Store the jam in an airtight container in the refrigerator for up to a week. Bring to room temperature before serving.

green goddess dressing

MAKES 4 CUPS (1 L)

The first time I tried this creamy-tangy Bay Area staple was at Chez Panisse, and that preparation will always remain my gold standard. In full California fashion, I add ripe avocado to my recipe, which only makes it more decadent. As such, this dressing is best suited for sturdy greens like romaine hearts or Little Gems. It is also exceptional with raw vegetable snacks—think carrots, radishes, kohlrabi, fennel—and even cooked fish.

- 2 large cloves garlic, peeled
- 8 to 10 green onion tops (reserve the bottoms for another use, such as the Poached Chicken on page 173)
- 1 tablespoon plus 1 teaspoon colatura di alici or other fish sauce
- ½ cup (7 g) loosely packed fresh chervil (including stems), coarsely chopped
- 1 cup (13 g) loosely packed fresh tarragon leaves
- ¼ cup plus 2 tablespoons (60 ml) Mayonnaise (page 304)
- 1 avocado, pitted and flesh scooped from the skin
- 2 cups (480 ml) canola oil
- 1 teaspoon kosher salt
- 2 tablespoons fresh lemon juice

Combine the garlic, green onions, colatura, chervil, tarragon, and ¾ cup (180 ml) water in a blender and purée on medium speed until smooth.

Add the mayonnaise and avocado to the blender. With the motor running, drizzle in the canola oil. When all the oil has been added, turn the blender down to low speed and add the salt and lemon juice. Taste and adjust, if need be, then store in an airtight container in the fridge for up to 1 week.

pine nut vinaigrette

MAKES 2 CUPS (480 ML)

This is a graduate-level course on the importance of balance. Heat from the chile and a good pop of acid keep the intense richness of the pine nuts from overpowering the dressing. The addition of fish sauce heightens the umami. I love this dressing in the Sweet Corn Salad on page 125, but it can also bring simple snacks, such as a chicken salad sandwich or herb-marinated tomatoes, to life.

1½ cups (175 g) pine nuts

⅓ cup (80 ml) red wine vinegar

2 cloves garlic, peeled

2 Thai (bird's-eye) chiles

2 tablespoons plus 1 teaspoon fish sauce

¼ cup (60 ml) extra-virgin olive oil

½ teaspoon kosher salt

Preheat the oven to 325°F (165°C). Arrange the pine nuts in a single layer on a sheet tray and toast in the oven, shaking the pan and swirling the nuts with a spoon every few minutes, until lightly browned, about 10 minutes. Once toasted, transfer the nuts to a plate and allow them to cool.

Transfer the cooled pine nuts to a blender and add ¼ cup (60 ml) water, the vinegar, garlic, chiles, fish sauce, olive oil, and salt. Buzz it all up until smooth. Taste and adjust to your liking.

Store in an airtight container in the fridge for up to 1 week.

tahini vinaigrette

MAKES 1½ CUPS (360 ML)

Tahini is an earthy, centuries-old Middle Eastern ingredient made by pounding sesame seeds into a paste, and you've likely enjoyed it in such dishes as baba ghanoush, halvah, falafel, and shawarma. It's really shelf-stable and a nice go-to in the pantry. Tahini is generally available on grocery store shelves, but note that not all tahini is created equal, and cheaper brands tend to be a bit bitter, one-note. My suggestion is to do a little digging online to find a jar of organic, small-batch tahini worthy of your food.

Moscatel vinegar and vincotto (see page 136) are both on the sweeter side and really help balance out the depth of the tahini. If they prove too difficult to find, feel free to substitute champagne vinegar for the moscatel and saba or balsamic vinegar for the vincotto.

1 large egg yolk

1½ teaspoons Dijon mustard

¼ cup (60 ml / 125 g) tahini

2 tablespoons vincotto

1 tablespoon moscatel vinegar

2½ teaspoons red wine vinegar

½ teaspoon kosher salt

½ cup (120 ml) canola oil

Combine the egg yolk, mustard, tahini, vincotto, vinegars, salt, and ½ cup (120 ml) water in a blender and buzz until smooth. With the blender running, start slowly drizzling in the oil in a steady stream until all of it has been incorporated. The color should be an opaque tan, and it should coat the back of the spoon.

Store in an airtight container in the fridge for up to 1 week.

moscatel and vermouth vinaigrette

MAKES 2 CUPS (480 ML)

When working with winter greens and heartier vegetables, which can withstand a strong dose of dressing, this is one of my favorite choices. The idea is to simply balance the bitter, aromatic qualities of the vermouth vinegar with the sweetness of the moscatel and cider vinegars.

½ cup (120 ml) vermouth vinegar

¼ cup (60 ml) moscatel vinegar

¼ cup plus 3½ teaspoons (77.5 ml) cider vinegar

½ teaspoon kosher salt

1 cup (240 ml) extra-virgin olive oil

Combine the vinegars and salt in a blender. With the blender running, slowly incorporate the oil in a steady stream.

Store in an airtight container in the fridge or in a cool, dark cupboard for up to 2 months. The vinaigrette will separate easily, but a quick shake before using will re-emulsify it.

palm sugar vinaigrette

MAKES 2⅔ CUPS (630 ML)

I'm not about to pick a fight with maple syrup, but of all the delicious things that can be extracted from a tree, palm sugar is definitely up there. It plays really well with herbs, chiles, and fresh, juicy vegetables. If you dressed some shredded cabbage, cilantro, and jalapeños with this vinaigrette and spooned it over a piece of fried fish, you'd be in a pretty good spot.

I call for a blender, but for a more rustic interpretation that's closer to the typical Thai approach, you can definitely use a mortar and pestle. Follow the instructions for the palm sugar syrup as written. Then, in the mortar, pound the chiles and lime zest into a paste with the pestle. Finally, add the chile-lime paste, lime juice, vinegar, and fish sauce to the syrup and stir to combine.

⅔ cup (100 g) palm sugar

1 tablespoon lime zest

5 tablespoons (75 ml) fresh lime juice

½ cup (120 ml) fish sauce

2 Thai (bird's-eye) chiles

¾ cup (180 ml) rice vinegar

In a small pot, combine the palm sugar and 1 cup (240 ml) water and bring to a simmer. When the sugar has dissolved, set aside to cool to room temperature.

In a blender, combine the palm sugar syrup, lime zest, lime juice, fish sauce, chiles, and vinegar. Blend on high until smooth. Taste and adjust to your liking.

Store in an airtight container in the fridge for up to 5 days.

meyer lemon vinaigrette

MAKES 2 CUPS (480 ML)

It's easy to rattle off all the incredible ingredients that pop up during the spring and summer. Winter, not so much. That's why Meyer lemons are so special. In the colder months, they bring sunshine to bitter greens as the star of this vinaigrette. But this dressing would, without question, also be great with delicate spring greens.

- Zest of 2 Meyer lemons
- ¾ cup plus 2 tablespoons (210 ml) Meyer lemon juice (from about 6 lemons)
- 4 teaspoons Dijon mustard
- 2 tablespoons champagne vinegar
- 1 clove garlic, finely grated with a Microplane
- 2 teaspoons kosher salt
- 1 cup (240 ml) extra-virgin olive oil

In a mixing bowl, whisk together the lemon zest, lemon juice, mustard, vinegar, garlic, and salt. While whisking, slowly drizzle in the oil and whisk until emulsified.

Store in an airtight container in the fridge for up to 1 week.

our all-purpose dry rub

MAKES
1 CUP
(105 G)

This rub, or some form of it, has been a go-to of ours since the restaurant opened. A measured dose is fantastic on whole fish, and you could easily spread some olive oil over brined chicken legs and cover with the rub before grilling. Same goes for pork chops. One of my favorite things to do with it is to fold some into thick Greek yogurt for a dip to accompany Grilled Flatbreads (see page 99).

The only real key to making this is to keep the spices quite coarse. I like to think of most of them as just being "cracked." Pulse them in a spice grinder separately and in small batches so you can control the texture.

Aleppo pepper flakes can be found easily online. Ground from a sun-dried Turkish chile, they impart a raisin-like sweetness and mild heat. For the New Mexico chile, we shake the seeds out of whole dried chiles, then buzz the chiles into flakes in a spice grinder.

- 3 tablespoons cracked fennel seeds
- 3 tablespoons cracked coriander seeds
- 3 tablespoons cracked cumin seeds
- 2 teaspoons Aleppo pepper flakes
- 2 teaspoons New Mexico chile flakes
- 2 teaspoons fennel pollen

In an airtight container, combine all of the ingredients. Store the rub in your pantry and use within a month or two—when you open the container, the spices should still be nice and fragrant. When they're not, it's time to make a new batch.

a simple brine for meat and fish

MAKES 8 CUPS (2 L)

This is our universal brine. We use it for almost everything at the restaurant: chicken legs, pork chops, whole quail, fish, and much more. You can make a larger batch than called for here and store it in the fridge for a few months. Since you always want your brine to be cold when you're submerging meats and fish, it's helpful to have some on hand, chilled and ready to use, so you don't find yourself having to boil and cool a batch when you need it in a pinch.

Make sure whatever ingredient you're brining is fully submerged in the liquid. At home, I'll sometimes use a plate to weigh down larger ingredients like pork shoulder.

I don't really bother with aromatics in brine—I'm more concerned with seasoning. You can feel free to experiment, though, by adding spices, herbs, and vegetables to the liquid when it's coming up to a boil. (Just note that if you add any of these to the brine, they'll deteriorate, and the brine won't keep as long in the fridge.) Rosemary and garlic are great with pork; black peppercorns, parsley, and bay leaves are nice with chicken. Like I said, we use it for almost everything. It's a pretty flexible recipe.

For fish, a quick brine is sufficient: 3 to 5 minutes for fish in the ½-inch-thick (12 mm) range and 10 to 12 minutes for anything thicker. Meats can be brined longer: Pork chops, for example, can be brined for anywhere from 3 to 6 hours. Whole chickens, even longer. Recipes in this book that call for brining meat will usually indicate the brining time.

Note: Don't reuse brine—discard it after removing whatever you've used it for. It has animal proteins and can spoil.

⅔ cup packed (150 g) light brown sugar

⅔ cup (150 g) kosher salt

In a pot, combine 8 cups (2 L) water, the brown sugar, and the salt and bring to a boil. Turn off the heat and allow the brine to cool.

Store in an airtight container in the fridge for up to 2 months.

our house pickling liquid

MAKES 4 CUPS (1 L)

Do a quick Google search, and you'll find 63,800,007 results for pickling liquid (trust me, I just checked), so I'm not inventing the wheel here. Let's just say I'm not bringing anything new to the table. I do, however, really like this recipe for its simplicity and versatility. It allows whatever we're pickling at the restaurant to shine. It's bright, clean, and not too salty, which also allows us to incorporate any leftover brine into dressings and vinaigrettes without it being overpowering. Sometimes we even pickle items specifically for all the beautifully infused liquid we end up with. Such is the case with the summer "seasoning" peppers (page 321).

You should play around with this pickle brine, though. It's worked wonders in more situations than I can recall. You just need to keep in mind how you cut whatever it is you're pickling. If you want larger and crunchier cuts of vegetables—radishes, for example—you will have to heat up the pickling liquid and pour it over the vegetable while it's still hot. For thinner and more delicate specimens, like the green tomatoes, simply submerge them in the brine and wait a few days. It's a good idea to taste your pickles along the way to track their progress. Take mental notes of the texture, saltiness, acidity, etc. Learn what you like and don't like and adjust the next time.

1 cup (240 ml) champagne vinegar

¾ cup (150 g) sugar

3 tablespoons kosher salt

In a pot, combine 2 cups (480 ml) water, the vinegar, sugar, and salt and bring to a simmer over medium-high heat. Whisk to make sure the salt and sugar have dissolved and cook for 1 to 2 minutes. Transfer to an airtight container and set aside to cool to room temperature.

When the brine has cooled, place a lid on the container and store in the fridge; it will keep for months.

pickled green tomatoes

MAKES 1 QUART (895 G)

Green tomatoes are deeply associated with the American South, where they are often deep-fried to crispy perfection in antique cast-iron skillets. I love this tradition, and we definitely fry up our fair share of green tomatoes at the restaurant in early summer. But I also like to slice them really thin to make pickles that will carry us through fall. When treated this way, they lend an incredible crunch and splash of acidity to so many dishes.

2 cups (480 ml) Our House Pickling Liquid (page 318)

1 pound (455 g) green tomatoes (about 4), cored

In a pot, bring the pickling liquid to a simmer over medium-high heat. Turn off the heat and allow the liquid to cool slightly, about 5 minutes.

Meanwhile, use a mandoline or a sharp knife to cut the tomatoes horizontally into ⅛-inch-thick (3 mm) rounds. Place the sliced tomatoes in a heatproof container and pour over the pickling liquid, then let cool to room temperature.

Cover the container and pack the tomatoes away in the fridge for a couple of days before using them. They should keep in the fridge for a few months without too much textural breakdown.

pickled persian cucumbers

MAKES 2 QUARTS (1.5 KG)

This very handy pickle is a bright, crisp, slightly sweet alternative to whole-dill pickles and spears. We use them to bump up the acidity and crunchiness of my salads through the summer months and to top grilled dishes. Spoon some on a nice piece of grilled fish, and you're cooking in The Four Horsemen tradition. I generally like to work with Persian cucumbers because they aren't too seedy and tend to keep their texture after pickling.

2 to 3 Persian cucumbers (1¼ pounds / 575 g), halved lengthwise, sliced into ¼-inch-thick (6 mm) half-moons, and rinsed quickly with warm water (4 cups / 1 L)

4 cups (1 L) Our House Pickling Liquid (page 318)

1 tablespoon yellow mustard seeds

1 tablespoon whole black peppercorns

1 tablespoon coriander seeds

Put the cucumbers in a heatproof container.

In a pot, combine the pickling liquid, mustard seeds, peppercorns, and coriander and bring to a simmer over medium heat. Remove from the heat and allow the spices to steep for about 10 minutes, then pour the liquid over the cucumbers and let cool to room temperature.

Cover the container and pack away in the fridge for a couple of days before using. The pickles should store nicely in the fridge for about a month; after that, they may lose their fresh crispiness.

pickled long hot peppers

MAKES 1 PINT (600 G)

These pickles have become an annual favorite. We don't use our house brine for the recipe, but they're so good that I must share them with you. Credit here needs to be given to Nick and Massimo, our Williamsburg neighbors, who run one of the city's best slice shops—although calling L'industrie a "slice shop" doesn't do it justice. I just did a bit of reverse engineering of their spicy condiment, which is great on grilled fish, in salads, and, of course, on sandwiches.

About 4 long peppers, cut into 1⁄16-inch-thick (2mm) rounds (2 cups / 160 g)

4½ teaspoons extra-virgin olive oil

2 or 3 cloves garlic, crushed with the side of a chef's knife

1 cup (240 ml) rice vinegar

4½ teaspoons sugar

1 tablespoon kosher salt

Place the peppers in a heatproof container.

In a pot, heat the olive oil over low heat. Add the garlic and cook until it's sizzling around the edges and browning just slightly, about 2 minutes. Add ⅓ cup (75 ml) water, the vinegar, sugar, and salt, increase the heat to medium, and bring the liquid to a simmer. Simmer for 3 minutes, then pour the pickling liquid over the peppers and let cool to room temperature.

Cover the container and pack the pickles away in the fridge. Wait 2 to 3 days before using. They should keep for months.

pickled summer peppers

MAKES 1 PINT (438 G)

Every week in August and September, I buy summer peppers by the bushel for pickling. My favorite varieties are Caribbean "seasoning" peppers, such as ají dulce, Habanada, Grenada, and Trinidad Perfume, which often appear at the market during the season. Although some pack a fair amount of heat, most are mild, floral, and sweet. You can, of course, feature them fresh in salads and marinades for meats, as is common in the West Indies. I also think they shine when pickled and applied to vinaigrettes, stews, marinades, sauces, and more. The flavors they impart are vibrant and piquant. The aroma of the pickling liquid is itself intoxicating.

8 ounces (225 g) summer peppers

2 cups (480 ml) Our House Pickling Liquid (page 318)

Rinse the peppers in warm water and remove their stems. Split them in half lengthwise and tap out some of the seeds (the seeds generally remain tough after pickling and aren't particularly pleasant to eat, though a few here and there will be fine).

In a pot big enough to hold the peppers and the pickling liquid, bring the pickling liquid to a simmer over medium-high heat. Add the peppers and turn off the heat. Carefully place a plate on top of the peppers to keep them submerged (they love to float to the top) and let stand until the liquid cools to room temperature.

Transfer the peppers and their pickling liquid to an airtight container and cover tightly. The peppers should be submerged in the liquid; if they aren't, you may need to place something on top of them to keep them below the liquid before covering the container, such as a small bowl or plate. Pack them away in the fridge for about a week before you use them. They will keep in the fridge for months.

curry butter

MAKES 1 POUND (455 G)

This butter is stupidly amazing on grilled meats and vegetables as well as roasted fish. You could also stuff the butter under the skin of a whole chicken before baking, or just fold a knob of it into some steamy rice. Seriously.

1 pound (455 g) unsalted butter, softened

1 tablespoon S&B Oriental curry powder or curry powder of your choice

1 teaspoon Maldon salt

In the bowl of a stand mixer fitted with the paddle attachment, combine the butter and curry powder and beat on medium speed until fully incorporated and smooth. Stop the mixer and scrape down the bowl with a rubber spatula, then return the mixer to low speed. Add the Maldon salt and mix for a few seconds to incorporate.

Pack the butter into an airtight container and store in the fridge for up to a few weeks; it also freezes well.

herb butter

MAKES ABOUT 1 POUND (455 G)

This butter is a proper cheat code that instantly adds loads of flavor to anything. It's also highly adaptable. You can incorporate basil and shiso in the summer, for example. For subtle heat, add some chile flakes, or, in the spring, incorporate some tarragon and chervil and use the butter to finish a piece of slow-roasted fish. Just avoid using dried herbs.

1 pound (455 g) unsalted butter, softened

⅔ cup (35 g) finely chopped fresh parsley

¾ cup (25 g) finely chopped fresh oregano

6 cloves Garlic Confit (page 307), drained and finely chopped

3 tablespoons finely chopped fresh thyme leaves

Zest of 1 lemon

1 teaspoon Maldon salt

In the bowl of a stand mixer fitted with the paddle attachment, combine the butter, parsley, oregano, garlic, thyme, and lemon zest and beat on medium speed until fully incorporated and smooth. Stop the mixer and scrape down the bowl with a rubber spatula, then return the mixer to low speed. Add the Maldon salt and mix for a few seconds to incorporate.

Pack the butter into an airtight container and store in the fridge for up to a few weeks; it also freezes well.

apple butter

MAKES 3 CUPS (732 G)

This is a very silky and vibrant sauce made from apples that I like to have on hand in the wintertime. Contrary to the title, the sauce contains no dairy—"butter" is more of a nod to its smooth and rich consistency, à la "peanut butter." I prefer Honeycrisp apples for this, but I've also had good success with the Fuji and Gala varieties.

Use this apple butter where you would normally use applesauce. It's also great with salty and harder cheeses, such as clothbound Cheddars, as well as crispy grilled sausages or pork chops. I've even folded it into vanilla ice cream for a nice little post-service treat.

- 7 or 8 large apples (1.2 kg), peeled, quartered, and cored
- ½ cup plus 3 tablespoons (132 g) sugar

Preheat the oven to 375°F (190°C).

In a large bowl, toss together the apples and sugar. Massage them with your hands or stir them well with a wooden spoon. You want most of the sugar to dissolve and to create some juices in the bowl. It's okay to beat up the apples a bit during this process to yield more liquid to coat the apples.

Transfer the apples and any juices in the bowl to a baking dish (crowding is okay). Bake for about 90 minutes, stirring every 30 minutes or so, until the apples are dark golden in color. You may end up with some slightly charred corners here and there. That's okay. Remove from the oven and let cool slightly.

Transfer the apples and any juices from the baking dish to a blender and purée until very smooth. Spoon the purée into a container and allow to cool to room temperature.

Cover the container and store the apple butter in the fridge for up to a couple of months.

roasted chicken stock

MAKES 2 QUARTS (2 L)

Making stock should not be a fussy affair. The more straightforward the recipe, the more shelf-stable as well. Try to avoid onion and garlic, which can start to smell like hot compost when simmered all day long. I'm also not a fan of wine (in this context!) as it can occasionally create a cloying bitterness. All I want is a versatile liquid that I can plug into any scenario and embellish, on the spot, with whatever suits what I'm cooking at that particular moment.

This is a super straightforward, lovely, clean, and "roasty" chicken stock. I keep vegetables and herbs out of the mix: I'm looking for a warming, neutral broth that I can more precisely flavor *after* it has been cooked.

2 pounds (910 g) chicken bones (backs preferred), excess fat removed

2 pounds (910 g) chicken wings

1 pound (455 g) chicken feet

Kosher salt

Preheat the oven to 375°F (190°C).

Lay the bones out on a sheet tray or in a baking dish and lay the wings out separately on a second sheet tray or baking dish. They can be slightly crowded, but keep things in one even layer. Place both trays in the oven and roast until golden brown, 20 to 30 minutes for the wings and 35 to 45 minutes for the bones. Remove the bones and wings from the oven as they are done roasting and carefully set aside to cool slightly. Some of the worst burns come from splattering hot fats in the kitchen, so be careful here; no need to rush!

Once they're at a manageable temperature, transfer the bones and wings to a tall stockpot. You can scrape some of the brown bits off the sheet trays they were roasted on and add those to the pot, too, but pour off the fat before doing so; too much rendered fat in your stock can make it greasy. Add the feet and then add 4 quarts (4 L) water.

Bring the water to a simmer over medium heat, then reduce the heat to maintain a nice low, even bubble. Cook the stock for 2 hours, using a ladle or a large spoon every now and then to skim off any impurities that float to the surface. Once the meat on the bones looks cooked and the stock has a light and roasted flavor, remove from the heat.

Using tongs, carefully remove and discard as many bones as you can. Don't stress about getting all of them; removing them just makes the stock easier to pour and eliminates unwanted splashing when you're straining the stock.

Strain the stock through a fine-mesh sieve into a tall, heatproof storage container; discard any remaining bones. Season the stock lightly with salt and put it in the fridge, uncovered, to cool.

Transfer the cooled stock to airtight containers and store in the fridge for a week or so or in the freezer for up to a month or two.

savory fish stock

MAKES 12 CUPS (3 L)

This is probably the most versatile fish stock we use. Less intense than its darker, more roasted counterpart, the white soy lends a beautiful richness to the stock. Hondashi is another kitchen cheat: a soup base laced with katsuobushi (also called bonito flakes, made from smoked skipjack tuna), MSG, and seaweed. It's incredibly fragrant and imparts the ideal smokiness to the broth.

Katsuobushi flakes would also work in a pinch. After the stock cooks for an hour, turn off the heat and add a handful of flakes. Steep for 5 minutes, then proceed with straining the stock.

- 5 pounds (2.2 kg) bones from white-fleshed fish (cod, halibut, fluke, snapper, etc.), blood, gills, and impurities removed, rinsed in cold water
- 2 tablespoons plus 2¼ teaspoons Hondashi granules
- 1 tablespoon white soy sauce

Preheat the oven to 350°F (175°C).

Lay the bones out on sheet trays or in baking dishes and roast until lightly golden brown, about 30 minutes. Remove from the oven and transfer the bones to a tall stockpot (you may need to use a metal spatula to scrape them off if they stick to the trays). Add 1 cup (240 ml) water to each tray and use the same spatula to scrape off as many stuck-on bits of roasted fish as you can and add to the pot.

Add enough cold water to the pot to cover the bones three-quarters of the way. Bring to a simmer over medium heat, then reduce the heat to keep gentle bubbles on the surface. Cook the stock for an hour, skim often using a ladle or large spoon to remove impurities that rise to the surface, then remove from the heat.

Strain the stock through a fine-mesh sieve into a large bowl or heatproof dish and add the Hondashi and soy sauce while it's still hot. Taste and adjust with more soy, if need be. It should be nicely seasoned, but not salty by any means. Strain a second time and place in the fridge, uncovered, to cool.

Transfer the cooled stock to airtight containers and store in the fridge for up to 1 week or in the freezer for up to 2 months.

KNOWING WHEN TO CALL IT

One thing we never see in cookbooks—or, more specifically, wine books—is mention of the fact that drinking wine is going to get you drunk. Notes of fresh cut grass? Hints of stone fruit and herbes de Provence? That stuff is everywhere! But there seems to be very little discussion about the side effects of consuming all of this fermented fruit. So here it is, folks: Wine gets you drunk and, depending on where you are in life, that's either a good thing or a bad one. We have many friends who have embraced sobriety after a lifetime of excess, and we're proud of them and love them just as much as our inebriated sisters and brothers. We've also had plenty of moments surrounded by wines that we want to taste and wished that they didn't have any alcohol in them so that we could keep opening bottles, but that's just not the way it works. Knowing when to call it a night is in itself an art form, and perhaps one we haven't mastered quite yet. But we're working on it.

YOU DON'T HAVE TO
GO HOME
BUT YOU
CAN'T STAY HERE

ACKNOWLEDGMENTS

THE FOUR HORSEMEN

To our staff, past and present: Your incredibly hard work has made The Four Horsemen what it is and continues to become. You have our deepest and most sincere thanks.

To our guests: Whether you've stopped in once or eat here every week, thank you for making it possible for us to do what we like to do. It's a pleasure to look after you.

Thank you to our food suppliers, wine importers, distributors, sales reps, farmers, brewers, artists, ceramicists, couriers, accountants, bookkeepers, investors, lawyers, PR consultants, food safety consultants, HR consultants, insurance brokers, builders, landlords, architects, expediters, project managers, plumbers, electricians, handy-people, carpenters, steel fabricators, Nightmoves sisters and brothers, and the many friends and peers who have guided us along the way.

Clearly, it takes more people than you might imagine to keep a thirty-eight-seat restaurant running. More than we could possibly list. We're only going to make an exception for those who were essential to the making of this book, and our families.

Randy would like to thank Katy and Andy; Justin would like to thank Stacy and Felix; and Christina and James would like to thank Haldor and Soffy.

The four of us would like to thank Laura Dozier, Deb Wood, and the entire team at Abrams; Michael Lassins, for keeping the lights on; Jay Strell, for working to keep us in the mix; Michael Vadino, for never saying no; and Steve Nebesney, for working on projects no one will ever know about.

Thank you to Mike Paré for creating our visual language, and to Gabe Ulla for working on this book with us for longer than anyone ever thought possible.

Finally, to Nick and Amanda: "thank you" doesn't even begin to cover it, but thank you nonetheless.

NICK CURTOLA

First and foremost, I'd like to thank my wife, Sara, and my daughter, Lillie. You're a true force, Sara. Thank you for pushing me and for inspiring me on so many levels. Lillie, I hope you eat some of the stuff in this book one day! That buttered noodle phase is sure to end soon . . . right??

My parents, who have supported me since day one. Choosing the path of a cook in the early 2000s wasn't glamorous by any means, but you were always so proud and that meant the world to me.

Christina, James, Randy, and Justin, for giving me a chance and for helping steer this ship. You all bring so much to the table and have been incredibly generous with your time and advice.

Gabe Ulla, for letting me marinate on this for what seems like forever and for being so patient and supportive. You believed in me from the beginning and motivated me to do this thing in the first place. Thank you.

David Malosh, thank you for capturing everything so beautifully and for letting me cover everything with grated cheese.

Chantal, my first hire and one of the kindest souls I've ever worked with. None of what we built would have been possible without you. You're a constant inspiration and my rock.

Ben Zook, the GOAT. I love working with you each and every day. You've taught me so much over the years, and I look forward to working with you for many more. I couldn't imagine a better partner in crime.

Amanda McMillan, thank you for your unwavering kindness and for all the hard work you've put into our restaurant. I've loved watching this place grow with you and couldn't have done it with anyone else. I'm so proud of what we've built.

Dylan Takao, the true representation of grace under fire. Thank you for all that you bring through the door here each and every day. Your energy and passion are contagious. A cook's cook.

A huge thank you to my BOH and FOH team both past and present. Special thanks to Zach, Max, and Finn for measuring out everything in here! I've truly had the pleasure of working with some of the greatest staff over the years. Their passion and dedication have been my motivation. Too many to name, but they're all so special in their own way and have each left a mark on The Four Horsemen.

Billy, I love you and miss working with you and just being around you. Thank you for helping me find my voice and for having faith in me in the beginning. You pushed me to be better every day.

Marco, thank you for being a leader and for always going above and beyond the call of duty. Your laugh warms our hearts.

Michael Lassins, we all know this place would fall apart at the seams without you. Love you, man.

Sarah Smith, Rica Allannic—and Laura Dozier, Deb Wood, and the team at Abrams—for walking me through this crazy process and for being in my corner every step of the way.

Jenn de la Vega, for testing all these recipes and for all of the great feedback along the way.

To friends, acquaintances, and peers who have inspired me over the years and are due many thanks. Among them: Alice Waters, Russell Moore, Paul Bertolli, Margot and Fergus Henderson, Rose Gray and Ruth Rogers, Sam Clark, Russell Norman, David Tanis, Nigel Slater, Judy Rodgers, Christian Puglisi, Bo Bech, Phil Krajeck, James Lowe, Alain Passard, Victor Arguinzoniz, Iñaki Aizpitarte, John Adler, Danny Amend, Chris Austin, Stephen Harris, and Fulvio Siccardi. Thank you all for keeping the flame alive.

INDEX

Editor: Laura Dozier
Designer: Deb Wood
Design Manager: Heesang Lee
Managing Editors: Mike Richards and Annalea Manalili
Production Manager: Sarah Masterson Hally

Library of Congress Control Number: 2023932509
ISBN: 978-1-4197-6017-4
eISBN: 979-8-88707-203-6

Additional restaurant photography by Giada Paoloni, Brian Graf, Ruvan Wijesooriya, and Damien Lafargue. Endpaper collage design by Mike Vadino. Image of the *Be Kind* print courtesy Rob Reynolds.

Printed and bound in China
10 9 8 7 6 5 4 3 2

ABRAMS The Art of Books
195 Broadway, New York, NY 10007
abramsbooks.com

THE FOUR HORSEMEN
HORSEMEN
THE FOUR HORSEMEN
EXIT